Dear Shannon,

"The Way to begin is to begin."
—Eleanor Roosevelt.

Mick, May 2024.

Praise for *From Ideas to Impact*

"In these challenging times when politicians are failing to provide leadership, when multilateral peace and security institutions are wrecked from within, *From Ideas to Impact* is timely and offers pathways to solutions, solidarity, and partnership from ground up, from periphery to center."

—Jose Ramos-Horta
President of Timor Leste and
Nobel Peace Prize Laureate

"Mick Sheldrick was with us at the beginning as we shaped the Bridgetown Initiative. In the face of unprecedented challenges, his book bridges idealism with essential pragmatism and outlines how everyone can participate urgently in the crucial task of acting today to save tomorrow. A must-read for those ready to turn solidarity into impactful action."

—Mia Mottley
Prime Minister of Barbados and Co-Chair
of the United Nations Sustainable Development Goals Advocates

"Democracy requires committed citizens who take action and work for what they believe in . . . . Mick has made an impact on many lives through his work combating climate change, giving more children access to education and achieving the end of extreme poverty. He has also inspired thousands of others to drive the change they seek."

—Erna Solberg
former Prime Minister of Norway (2013–2021)

"I know Mick Sheldrick well as we are both board members of the Ban Ki-moon Centre, and I admire his manifold activities in the field of sustainable development, education, and information. In addition, he is an excellent organizer. In a world testing the resilience of institutions like the United Nations, Mick Sheldrick masterfully unveils their enduring impact on our daily lives notwithstanding geopolitical tensions. With flair, he distills compelling insights, guiding readers to unearth common ground in our turbulent era. This is a book for the times: sharp and incisive."

—Dr. Heinz Fischer
former President of Austria (2004–2016)

"Get ready for a must-read! Michael Sheldrick shares the story of the inspiring South African advocates who fearlessly catapulted period poverty and girls' education to the political stratosphere. This timely book serves up practical lessons for anyone seeking to make a real difference."

—Phumzile Mlambo-Ngcuka
former Deputy President of South Africa and former head of UN Women

"Drawing lessons from our work together with former UN Secretary-General Ban Ki-moon, this book offers actionable steps to make a difference and drive social impact. It brings the sustainable development objectives at the heart of the global community where each citizen has a role to play for the planet, prosperity, and people."

—Jean Todt and Michelle Yeoh
UN Special Envoy for Road Safety, and Oscar-winning actress and UN Development Programme Goodwill Ambassador

"This book postulates bringing civility back to society through consistent, ethical action, and by appealing to our shared hopes over fears, thereby, equipping policy entrepreneurs to overcome division and create a more just world for all."

—Tony Tersigni
EdD, FACHE, Executive Chair of Ascension Capital

"To create the world we owe future generations, we need to think differently and act now. And yet most people, including leaders, succumb to the prevailing sense of powerlessness and apathy. Mick's book *From Ideas to Impact* is a clarion call to action. He provides an easy-to-read, inspiring guide on how we can all lead change, and accelerate progress to a greener, more equitable future."

—Simon Mulcahy
President, TIME

"Behind the glitz of their concerts and festivals, Mick Sheldrick and the Global Citizen community have built an impressive campaigning model based on popular engagement, strategic storytelling, and coalition building. Aspiring changemakers the world over have much learn from their example."

—Mark Malloch-Brown
President of the Open Society Foundation and
former Deputy Secretary-General of the UN

"Michael Sheldrick brings a new take to the struggle to move beyond no longer competitive fossil fuels and onto cheaper, cleaner renewables from the outlier in the 'Anglo-Saxon' world. But his scope is far broader—how do you make progressive policy in only partially progressive societies, where private individualism still has a deep hold? And his argument should remind us all that we need to keep tethered in the unique past that shapes every policy struggle worth fighting."

—Carl Pope
senior climate advisor to former New York City
Mayor Michael Bloomberg and co-author of
New York Times *bestseller* Climate of Hope

"Michael leads by example, inspiring everyone he meets including prime ministers, presidents, philanthropists, and rock stars, with his clear goals and strength of purpose. And in the book, Michael insists that what he has done others can do. . . . At a time of global polycrisis, Michael gives us more than reasons to be hopeful; he actually tells us how to go about effecting meaningful change in our world."

—Melissa Parke
former Minister, Australian Government and Executive Director,
International Campaign to Abolish Nuclear Weapons

"In his new book *From Ideas to Impact: A Playbook for Influencing and Implementing Change in a Divided World*, Michael Sheldrick provides an inspiring road map for global citizens seeking to make an impact. Michael's book gives hope to those who are frustrated with the growing challenges faced by social entrepreneurs, urging them to master the art of policy entrepreneurship. *From Ideas to Impact* is a valuable guide for those ready to bridge the gap between great ideas and policy impact, inspiring action for a better collective future."

—Aigboje Aig-Imoukhuede
Nigerian investor and philanthropist

"In a world facing immense challenges, it can feel impossible to affect policy but Michael breaks things down, gives compelling examples, and empowers us all to do what we can in our own spheres of influence. He should know, he's been doing it for over 15 years as a co-founder of Global Citizen."

—Dr. Márcia Balisciano
Director of Benjamin Franklin House
and Chief Sustainability Officer, RELX

"Michael Sheldrick challenges us to go beyond the rhetoric of empty promises and the ubiquitous calls to action. *From Ideas to Impact* is a must-read for current and aspiring development leaders and practitioners."

—Glenn Denning
Professor of Professional Practice at Columbia
University's School of International and Public Affairs and
author of Universal Food Security

"It is very rare you come across a book, which has all the hallmarks of becoming the standard reference for its industry, in this case civil society organizations. Mick Sheldrick, cofounder of Global Citizen, interlaces global climate politics, organizational playbook ingenuity, and personal 'war story' observations in a writing style as if you were in the room. A book to cherish and an act hard to follow."

—Frank Van Gansbeke
executive scholar in residence at Middlebury College

"Coming up with ideas is easy but making an impactful difference is hard. In *From Ideas to Impact*, Mick Sheldrick not only provides a road map for the journey to transformational change but the book also serves as an instruction manual for making it happen. As co-founder of Global Citizen for over a decade, Mick has catalyzed civic actions and policy advocacy to bring about collective impact. In these pages he shares inspirational stories and provides examples of how to accelerate global social impact by driving systemic policy changes. I'm a better leader because of Mick's wisdom. This book allows Mick's wisdom to be shared with the world. Read. Learn. Act!"

—C.D. Glin
President, PepsiCo Foundation and
Global Head of Social Impact, PepsiCo Inc.

"Real power comes from movement building that gets citizens involved in diverse forms of personal action at massive societal scales. We grow bold leaders and lasting action from the roots. No organization has done this better than Global Citizen, and Mick Sheldrick's *From Ideas to Impact* shares the secret sauce behind these efforts and insightful curation of other changemaking we all can learn from."

—Jad Daley
President and CEO of American Forests

"Michael Sheldrick charts a course through some of the most challenging issues of our time... He illuminates successful efforts in translating seemingly abstract concepts, such as 'just transition,' into impactful policy changes that enhance people's lives and help advance social justice."

—Gilbert F. Houngbo
Director-General of the International Labour Organization

"*From Ideas to Impact* outlines practical steps to influence policy, emphasizing that impactful leaders are cultivated, trained, equipped, and empowered. Philanthropies can support policy entrepreneurs if they are willing to rewrite their playbook and embrace a new era of effective, sustainable change."

—Dan Pallotta
entrepreneur and author of Uncharitable:
How Restraints on Nonprofits Undermine Their Potential

"This very timely book has practical advice for those who are distressed about the way the world is going and want to know how to help do something about it. This book reflects knowledge and understanding of working through extraordinary achievements in international conflicts, and is a must-read."

—Dr Sue Boyd AM
former Australian diplomat

"A world in which yesterday's playbook of big-tent consensus building no longer works. Thankfully, Michael draws on his deep experience and that of others to lay out how to make positive change happen. This kind of thinking is needed more than ever."

—David McNair
Executive Director at ONE.org,
co-founded by Bono

"Parts of the world are literally on fire, while the news media reports on political and economic elites generating more problems than solutions.... *From Ideas to Impact* describes what has worked, what has not, and why in order to get past the cynicism that could otherwise prove ruinous. As a leading global changemaker himself, Sheldrick is exactly the right messenger for this crucial message."

—Evan Lieberman
Total Professor of Political Science and Contemporary
Africa and Director of the Center for International Studies at the MIT

"This inspiring book by Mick Sheldrick reminds us not only to have faith in the power of idealism and collaboration but also provides a super useful toolbox for civil societies across the world to achieve game-changing results in their work even as the odds are stacked against them."

—Dino Patti Djalal
*former Ambassador of Indonesia to the US and
founder of the Foreign Policy Community of Indonesia*

"A highly readable and accessible study of the role of advocacy in bringing about fundamental change in our societies and achieving global public goods. Strategic thinkers, policymakers, activists. and philanthropists will all benefit from this lucid and practical guide to an increasingly important dimension of today's world."

—David Donoghue
*former Permanent Representative of Ireland to the
UN and Co-Facilitator of SDG 2030 Agenda*

FROM IDeas TO IMPACT

FOREWORD BY **IDRIS** AND **SABRINA ELBA**

MICHAEL SHELDRICK

FROM

IDeas

TO

IMPACT

A PLAYBOOK FOR INFLUENCING AND IMPLEMENTING **CHANGE** IN A **DIVIDED WORLD**

WILEY

Published by John Wiley & Sons, Inc., Hoboken, New Jersey.
Published simultaneously in Canada.

For general information on our other products and services or for technical support, please contact our Customer Care Department within the United States at (800) 762-2974, outside the United States at (317) 572-3993 or fax (317) 572-4002.

Wiley also publishes its books in a variety of electronic formats. Some content that appears in print may not be available in electronic formats. For more information about Wiley products, visit our web site at www.wiley.com.

Library of Congress Cataloging-in-Publication Data is Available:

ISBN 9781394202348 (Cloth)
ISBN 9781394202393 (ePub)
ISBN 9781394202409 (ePDF)

Cover Design and Image: Wiley

SKY10069053_030824

For my daughter, Miki Grace Yun Sheldrick, whose generation our actions will shape.

And to Grandma Joyce Grace, who has always advised to focus on the present, and not to worry about things we cannot change. Thank you, Grandma.

Contents

Foreword

We have known Mick for more than four years now, and to say he's had an impact on our lives is an understatement. We met on a visit to Sierra Leone with the International Fund for Agricultural Development (IFAD), looking at the effects of Ebola on rural people and farmers. We instantly hit it off. We remember thinking despite how intense, emotional, and humid the visit was, Mick always had a smile and a sense of hope. A kind of glass-half-full guy. We welcomed this, but it shouldn't be any surprise that an Aussie, a Brit, and a Canadian are getting along.

When writing this foreword, we thought about how we would introduce Mick to one of our close friends. As Sabrina puts it: "Mick, over the years, has taught me almost everything I know about advocacy. I sometimes wondered if he would become impatient with all my questions and curiosity over the years, but he's never given me the inclination that he might. Instead, he's always there for you, sharing the wealth of knowledge he has accumulated throughout his career without any second thought. He's as generous with his mind as he is with his heart, always doing the good work, making personal sacrifices with the support of his beautiful wife Wendy (Xinyi). One of the biggest lessons Mick taught me about advocacy is just showing up is half the work, and this stuck with me because Mick, of course, always shows up."

Mick gets it—policy isn't just a set of distant rules and regulations; it's about changing lives. In Sierra Leone, we felt this truth deeply. We met an incredible woman named Isatu, who was raising four children while trying to keep the family farm going. When Ebola struck, she shared a heartbreaking story—her husband and everyone else left as markets closed, and the country became isolated.

In that crisis, IFAD stood by Isatu's side—the one organization that remained when all else crumbled. IFAD became her last hope, ensuring her children could still attend school.

This encounter fueled our determination to help IFAD in any way possible. But the need is overwhelming, and we realized that relying solely on charitable donations wouldn't be enough to tackle the immense challenges at hand.

Through Mick, the Global Citizen team, and IFAD, we have seen the power of influencing big policy change up close. Imagine this: it's January 2021, and we are all on a Zoom call with French President Emmanuel Macron amid the chaos of the COVID-19 pandemic—a situation eerily reminiscent of the challenges those farmers in Sierra Leone faced during their Ebola outbreak. Markets had shut down, leaving many poor farmers and communities isolated. In the midst of this call, something extraordinary unfolded. President Emmanuel Macron's commitment would change lives. He pledged to increase France's support for IFAD by tens of millions of euros. This wasn't just an impromptu promise; it was the result of persistent advocacy, a blend of behind-the-scenes efforts, public pressure, and citizen action—a true testament to the power of making our voices heard. But we didn't stop there.

Fast-forward two years to the 2023 Global Citizen Festival in New York, and Macron stepped up his support even more. He pledged a groundbreaking $150 million—the largest ever—to IFAD. This historic investment is set to help empower 100 million farmers in some of the world's poorest rural communities.

In the end, effective policy is all about making things better at their core. It's about justice, meeting basic needs, and being there when disaster strikes. Good policy guarantees there is always

someone ready to stay behind and help. If you want to make a difference, advocating for these meaningful policies is one of the most
powerful ways to help.

In this book, Mick lays out a guide, encouraging everyday heroes
with bright ideas to drive the change they seek. The world is evolving, driven by science, technology, and communal wisdom. Today,
even if we don't always realize it, more of us can contribute to addressing our most pressing challenges than ever before. We don't have to
stay on the sidelines; we can influence decisions at the highest levels
of power. This book unveils eight powerful ways to do just that.

Mick argues that a better world is possible, but it requires action
from both citizens and leaders. "We" are our last best hope.

Yes, the world is in chaos, and we can't ignore it. As we write this,
122 million more people are struggling to find food than in 2019 [1].
One in ten people goes to bed not knowing where their next meal
will come from. Dire predictions about the consequences of runaway
climate change confront us daily. The reverberations of past injustices
and traumas give rise to fresh conflicts. History casts its long shadow
over our current moment.

But in a world that sometimes feels adrift, we find in Mick's
teachings a lighthouse. The fight for progress is ours to lead, and now,
more than ever, we have the power to act. What can be done, must be
done. By embracing the wisdom in these pages, we can rekindle trust
in our institutions and offer a beacon of hope to those searching for
it. Because, in the end, the most potent antidote to disillusionment is
not just to dream of action but to live it.

Idris Elba
Actor, Artist, and Philanthropist

Sabrina Dhowre Elba
Advocate, Entrepreneur, and Philanthropist

Prologue

"It's a dangerous business, Frodo, going out your door. You step onto the road, and if you don't keep your feet, there's no knowing where you might be swept off to."
—Gandalf the Wizard, J.R.R. Tolkien, *The Lord of the Rings*

Have you ever wondered how to bring about meaningful change in today's divided world, especially when tempting alternatives for validation exist? In today's social media–driven era, seeking affirmation from like-minded individuals through quick posts is easy. It is easier to opt for simplistic, ideologically pure solutions than it is to embrace practical but imperfect ideas when facing complex problems. And it can feel more satisfying to our moral consciousness to reject compromise outright than to find common ground. However, this pursuit of the instant dopamine boost that comes from feeling "right, righteous, certain, and safe" hinders meaningful change. It may even cause more significant harm in the long run [1].

Consider these scenarios:

- Tragic events spark social media solidarity, only to return to business as usual after the fact, even among those who criticize others who didn't post in solidarity.
- Advocates of genetically-enriched Golden Rice face criticism for promoting genetic engineering despite its potential to

address vitamin deficiencies in regions plagued by malnutrition. This is so even as many of the foods we consume are genetically modified [2].

- Affluent nations renege on climate aid promises while emerging economies respond with, "F★★★ you, I won't take any action to reduce our emissions then".[1] The impasse, if unbroken, dooms us all to collective environmental catastrophe.
- Politicians in wealthy nations call for a universal end to fossil fuel production [3]. Meanwhile, poorer countries question how to prosper if their natural resources are not exploited further, having never had the same opportunity to grow rich from such output [4].
- Coal workers share concerns about climate change, yet they also worry about their families and livelihoods, feeling demonized and alienated [5].

Despite our divisions, however, there is hope. Worldwide, people from all walks of life demonstrate that systemic change is achievable and flourishing through united voices, cooperation, and solidarity—often hidden from view but undeniably present. Deforestation in the Amazon has fallen to its lowest levels in years [6]. For the first time, women are represented in every single parliament worldwide [7]. More than a century of research has finally culminated in the world's first malaria vaccine [8].

Numerous studies indicate a shared belief in the power of working together to address our challenges [9–10]. A significant global population supports bold policy changes for the benefit of our planet and its inhabitants [11].

The challenge lies in the sense of powerlessness that is prevalent among too many everyday citizens and even our leaders [12]. When people lack agency they become susceptible to distractions to fill the void, such as policing one another's social media posts. But it doesn't have to be this way.

---

[1] Based on a conversation with an ambassador of a wealthy nation at the UN.

In this book, I will demonstrate how we can unite relevant stake-holders, bridge differences, and contribute to implementing the policies needed to address our shared challenges together. By the time you finish reading, you will be able to identify *how* you can contribute uniquely to the policy process and understand how to transform well-meaning intentions into positive impact.

With more of us ready and able to support policy change, we have the potential to craft fresh impact narratives that can inspire broader change far beyond our initial contributions. After all, a single compelling story of change can ignite countless other tales of success, nurturing even greater hope. It all starts with us. As Eleanor Roosevelt once wisely advised, "The way to begin is to begin." So let's get started.

Introduction: Harbingers of Hope

In 1750, Benjamin Franklin wrote to a colleague, asserting, "Nothing is of more importance for the public weal, than to form and train up youth in wisdom and virtue."[1] He underscored that leaders possessing these qualities were more vital to a nation's strength than wealth or arms, which could lead to ruin when managed by ignorance and wickedness. He concluded by recognizing the transformative impact a wise leader could wield, even in some cases single-handedly saving entire cities from destruction.

Fast-forward to today, and we find ourselves in dire need of such wisdom and virtue, particularly regarding effective policy implementation. We grapple with widespread misinformation online, unfulfilled political promises, corporate interests conflicting with the public good, and policies that often seem to deviate from their intended impact. Agreed on in 2015, the Sustainable Development Goals (SDGs)—the United Nations (UN) 17-point plan to end extreme poverty, mitigate inequality, and address climate change by 2030—have only achieved 12% of their targets [1]. Trust and solidarity have reached alarming lows when we need them more than ever to address shared challenges such as climate change, political conflicts, and economic disparities.

---

[1] From Benjamin Franklin to Samuel Johnson, August 23, 1750. The National Historical Publications and Records Commission.

The heartening news, however, is that despite the negative head-lines often prevalent in the media, studies also reveal that a significant number of people worldwide consistently express a desire for global solidarity, identify as global citizens, and still believe in the potential of our institutions to address pressing global issues [2-4]. They believe this even as a vast gulf exists between what they hope for and the present reality—as we face a crisis of implementation.

So long as there are individuals willing to work together to find solutions, we have yet to reach a point of no return. However, I don't need to remind you of this. If you have chosen to read this book, it is likely because you may already believe in an idea or potential solution to one of our many shared challenges. Perhaps you are searching for guidance on how to implement it.

This book does not give guidance on all possible ways to create change. Many other resources focus on topics such as managing phil-anthropic programs, improving individual giving, and changing lousy consumption habits—all of which I support.[2] However, my specific focus here is on how to create *policy* change. Why? Because tackling the systemic challenges we face requires systemic solutions. The COVID-19 pandemic made this abundantly clear concerning action on climate change. Our collective emissions temporarily decreased by 4.6% in 2020 with the restricted mobility that came during global lockdowns [5]. This is far from the 50% reduction in our collective carbon footprint that we must achieve by 2030 to avoid catastrophic climate change. One-off changes in individual behaviors simply aren't sustainable in and of themselves.[3] To affect our environment mean-ingfully, we must implement policies that significantly reduce carbon emissions from energy, transportation, and manufacturing. This is no easy feat, but engaging in the policymaking process is worth it if

---

[2] One example of something we can all do is have conversations on climate change with our networks. See Hayhoe 2020.

[3] Research suggests that individual and family-level actions could contribute to 14% of the emissions reductions needed to achieve net zero by 2050, while collective action has the potential to account for up to 64% of the required reductions. See Bhowmik et al. 2020; Chater and Loewenstein 2023; Maslin 2021.

there's a chance of creating the scale of change we desperately need. In short, focus on policy change if you truly want to change the world. This playbook is designed to help dramatically increase your odds of success.

By "policy," I mean a specific course of action or set of rules, guidelines, standards, or principles formulated by a government, organization, or institution like the UN. Policies can address a wide range of issues, including hunger, poverty, food waste, gender equity, conflict, environmental concerns, and the promotion of equitable access to resources such as water. They can serve as incentives, such as research and development subsidies, or punitive measures, such as regulations to combat corporate greenwashing.

And when I refer to "policy implementation," I mean putting these policies into action, from enacting laws to negotiating international agreements to allocating a state's resources. In other words, this is about transforming a policy idea or proposal into an impact that improves people's lives.

This book does not comprehensively list every policy idea and prescription for addressing our significant challenges. Many great minds in academia and think tanks have already generated such proposals [6]. The real question I grapple with is *how* to turn such ideas into a reality—a question easier asked than answered.

Steve Jobs once observed: "There's a tremendous amount of craftsmanship in between a great idea and a great product." The same concept applies to policy implementation—a complex process fraught with obstacles. Nevertheless, with the turbulent weather of today's challenges, we desperately need more individuals equipped with the know-how to navigate and land the plane. We need policy entrepreneurs [7-8].⁴

This book is designed as a practical guide for tackling shared challenges and driving policy change. Many of us may perceive international and national arenas as distant and challenging to

_____

⁴ Political scientist John Kingdon is largely credited as one of the first to coin the term "policy entrepreneur."

engage with. However, my experiences and observations of policy entrepreneurship in action have allowed me to witness firsthand the impact individuals can make.

The first part of this book provides actionable takeaways—a playbook for action drawn from the experiences of a diverse group of effective policy entrepreneurs. This includes presidents, prime ministers, cultural icons, corporate executives, and philanthropic leaders through to union representatives, musicians, grassroots advocates, and everyday citizens who have successfully implemented positive impacts in their communities.

Many of the principles of policy entrepreneurship outlined in this book align with leadership styles that people generally prefer and trust, such as the Visionary, the Diplomat, and the Implementer [9–10].[5] Such trust is crucial because policy implementation requires consensus building. The Visionary can rally people around clear and transformative goals. The Diplomat excels at building strong relationships and fostering collaboration among allies and stakeholders, even those they may disagree with. The Diplomat is also an open-minded innovator who excels at finding creative solutions and leveraging diverse networks of partners. The Implementer ensures our ideas translate into tangible, powerful outcomes—changes we can touch, feel, and see, ultimately transforming lives.

The second part of this book delves into four stories that illustrate the principles and steps of policy entrepreneurship in action:

1. **Individual activism:** We delve into how grassroots activists in South Africa leveraged the power of partnership to persuade their government to deliver on its promises to end "period poverty" and keep millions of girls in school.

---

[5] These leadership styles were inspired by those developed by Martijn Lambert at Glocalities. The Diplomat is a fusion of Lambert's Connector and Networker styles. This simplified approach aligns with other descriptions of policy entrepreneurs in the field. Additionally, I introduced a fourth style, the Implementer, emphasizing accountability and follow-through as crucial for influential policy change. See Glocalities. 2022 and Kalil, T. 2017.

2. **Community engagement:** We examine how a small coal town in Western Australia successfully met the moment to safeguard their community while ending its dependence on coal.
3. **National leadership:** We explore how the pragmatic leader of one of the world's smallest nations, Barbados, ignited a movement to bring about change for vulnerable communities on the frontlines of climate change.
4. **Global solidarity:** Finally, we investigate how the UN has navigated its limitations to foster collective action. Beyond the negative headlines, the UN's endurance offers insights for enforcing accountability with limited formal powers.

These case studies inspire hope by showcasing how real transformations take place. The power of sharing such stories should not be underestimated. Sharing good news can reinforce existing attitudes toward solidarity and trust in institutions as drivers of change, inspiring a favorable cycle of ongoing positive impact.

Most importantly, these examples illustrate the playbook outlined in Part 1. They provide valuable takeaways for other individuals, communities, and nations with similar issues and looking for innovative methods to disrupt the policymaking process.

The need to master the art of bold policy entrepreneurship and implementation is particularly pressing as the world stands at a turning point. I am writing this book during a period of heightened frustration and division. Analysts and future forecasters predict that our current challenges will only intensify in the coming decade [11]. Economic downturns, escalating international tensions, and the potential for future conflicts all loom on the horizon. Additionally, the algorithms of social media platforms may exacerbate our existing divisions and weaken our institutions further.

The consequences of failure are high. Many of us still maintain a favorable view of democratic and international institutions and believe that change is attainable [12]. This presents an opportunity to rebuild trust and social cohesion by meeting people's expectations through effective local and global policies. But this window will not remain open indefinitely [13]. When change is perceived as lacking, disillusionment can lead people to turn to alternative, albeit illusory, solutions grounded in populism and authoritarianism [14]. History offers a stark reminder of the dangers of demagoguery when fueled by disappointment [15]. As former UK prime ministerial advisor Michael Barber [16] put it, "Beliefs follow behavior."

However, history is also filled with numerous examples of transformative leadership during times of deep division. These instances exemplify the art of effective policy entrepreneurship. Inspired by Nelson Mandela's unwavering commitment to reconciliation after 27 years of imprisonment, a series of international and domestic policies were enacted to dismantle apartheid. This ultimately paved the way for greater racial equality, reconciliation, and the establishment of democracy in South Africa. Franklin D. Roosevelt's New Deal policies, including social welfare programs and job creation initiatives, gave hope and jobs to millions during the Great Depression. His approach unified a fractured nation through persistence, pragmatism, and savviness. Ellen Johnson Sirleaf made history by becoming Africa's first elected female head of state after her nation of Liberia had been ravaged by years of civil conflict. She implemented various policies and initiatives to rebuild her nation, earning her the Nobel Peace Prize in 2011.

At their core, these leaders all shared at least one area of focus in common: *how* to improve people's lives. In doing so, they exhibited courage, reached out to their opponents, made compromises, and did not get distracted by the need for a dopamine high—that desire to feel "right, righteous, certain, and safe" [17]. As Canada's prime minister, Justin Trudeau, noted in an address to university students, a critical difference between Abraham Lincoln and his Confederate counterpart, Jefferson Davis, was that Davis preferred to win debates, while Lincoln aimed to win the war. In conclusion, Trudeau posed the students this question: Do you want to win an argument or change the world? [18]

If you are like me, you already know the answer to this question. But the question that then follows is *how* to change our world. That's the purpose of this book.

1 | An Eight-Step Playbook to Master Policy Entrepreneurship

"The road to peace is never easy, and it is sometimes dangerous . . . the world desperately needs people who will have
the wisdom and the courage to travel that road and to insist
that their governments make no detour around it."
    —Dr. HV Evatt, Australian foreign minister (1941–49)
    and president of the UN General Assembly (1948–49) [1]

In a world divided, how do we sow the seeds of change? Setting
audacious goals that ignite a bias for action—how do we master this art?

How do we influence those wielding the power to usher in
change? How do we transform the negative perception of policies
into palatable narratives?

Crafting narratives that build trust and inspire impact—what's the secret behind these stories? How do we unify people to confront the colossal shared challenges of our era?

Forging lasting partnerships that leverage our collective strengths instead of fostering competition—what's the key to successful collaboration? How do we ensure accountability for those making grand promises—assuring words translate into action?

A skilled policy entrepreneur addresses these questions to navigate through our implementation crisis, and this part of the book will equip you with the critical approaches to do just that.

You would not be wrong to describe a policy entrepreneur as a "lobbyist for good."[1] They aim to influence specific legislation, budgetary processes, and policies by engaging those in power—in government, business, and philanthropy. However, policy entrepreneurs also understand the power of direct advocacy when combined with other unconventional methods. They leverage partnerships and deploy disruptive approaches to create a favorable environment for their policy ideas to be adopted and fully implemented, improving people's lives. Above all, they are "doers" able to seize opportunities and accomplish things in a chaotic world [2].

Policy entrepreneurs often invest their own resources, such as money, relationships, reputation, technical expertise, time, or energy [3]. But they do not let a lack of resources hinder them [4].[2] They, in fact, excel at persuading those with resources to contribute. Policy entrepreneurs may function daily as professional lobbyists hired to support a noble cause.[3] They may also be in a position of power themselves. Yet, frequently, they operate just as much

---

[1] For more on the rise of the Lobbying for Good Movement, see Alemanno 2023.
[2] Kalil notes that there are limits to what even presidents have the formal authority to achieve. See Kalil 2017.
[3] Lobbying has a shady connotation. Less than a third of US-based nonprofits reported engaging in activities between 2018 and 2023. Yet, lobbying tools themselves can and should be used for good including by both businesses and nonprofits. For a discussion on how lobbying can be reclaimed as a force for good, see Alemanno 2023.

outside traditional political or institutional structures, giving voice to underrepresented interests. They effectively exert influence on others beyond their formal authority or job description [5]. Their payoff lies in the uptake of creative solutions that disrupt the status quo [6]. Such results benefit society at large, not just a select few [7].

In the following chapters of this book, I delineate three leadership approaches that in my opinion constitute policy entrepreneurship: visionaries, diplomats, and implementers—all vital for fostering cooperation, building bridges, and propelling policy implementation past stagnation, conflict, and polarization. A good policy entrepreneur combines these approaches harmoniously to transform an idea into tangible impact.

This section illustrates eight steps that constitute these approaches and collectively form part of the policy entrepreneur's tool kit. It could also be titled "Eight Steps for Getting Stuff Done." Drawing insights from remarkable policy entrepreneurs who have shaped local, national and global agendas, it is divided into three chapters:

- The Visionary: Setting the Foundation for Change
- The Diplomat: Catalyzing Impact through Pragmatism
- The Implementer: Enforcing Accountability and Follow-Through

As you will discover, each of us harbors the potential to ignite change in a world on fire. The power to influence, the capacity for inspiration, and the potential for solidarity reside within every individual.

1 | The Visionary: Setting the Foundation for Change

"Plans are useless, but planning is indispensable."
—Dwight D. Eisenhower

Step 1: Know Your Policy Goal

"Ignoranti quem portum petat, nullus suus ventus est.
If a man does not know to what port he is steering, no wind favors him.
—Seneca. Epistolae, LXXI., 3".

A clear, well-defined policy goal is the linchpin that turns intentions into transformative impact. Successful policy entrepreneurs excel at generating and identifying such goals, actively seeking ideas from diverse sources, including other nonprofits, foundations, and like-minded citizens [1]. In the following pages, we will explore how to identify actionable policy goals to tackle our most pressing challenges.

Why a Policy Goal Matters

Defining a clear policy goal is the first step to setting the agenda. Many well-intentioned initiatives are launched to address significant problems. An oversight of many is the absence of a clear solution. Without this, such efforts tend to waste resources and only raise awareness about the issue, achieving minimal real-world impact. Focusing excessively on problems also reinforces feelings of powerlessness and despair, leaving people vulnerable to populists who offer false promises of security.

In contrast, initiatives guided by a clear vision of how the world would change if specific solutions are adopted have the power to inspire. They offer hope for an alternative world and provide a sense of direction and purpose in our otherwise chaotic and ever-changing reality. When people are concerned that problems are worsening, a clear goal shows them how they can be fixed, reinforcing the belief that we can shape a better world.

Defining a Clear Policy Goal

1. **Identify the challenge:** Start by clearly defining the issue you want to address, whether it is deforestation, ocean plastic pollution, hunger, poverty, or international peace.
2. **Research and collaborate:** Identifying effective systemic policy solutions can be complex. In-depth analysis, collaboration, and consensus-building with partners and colleagues is fundamental. You should leverage data and evidence from trusted sources and organizations to formulate your goals. Many of them have worked hard to figure out solutions for our most pressing challenges. There is no need to reinvent the wheel.

Take the challenge of world hunger, for example. Drawing on the collective input of a diverse coalition, the SDG2 Advocacy Hub has produced a menu of actionable policy ideas to bolster food production and tackle malnutrition [2]. One of their ideas is the "Beans Is How" campaign, which sets out to double global bean consumption by 2028 through specific policies such as requiring beans to be included in school meals. Not only does it promise to nourish lives, but it also does so in a planet-friendly and sustainable manner.

A policy goal is more likely to become a reality if it follows the SMART criteria: specific, measurable, achievable, relevant, and time-bound.[1]

(a) **Specific**

An actionable policy goal is explicit about the world we want to create. It leaves no room for confusion. It states the what, who, where, when, and why of change.

For instance, Fraidy Reiss cofounded the NGO Unchained At Last after being forced into marriage at 19 in New York City's ultra-Orthodox Jewish community. Realizing that rescuing underage girls from forced marriages wasn't enough, Fraidy focused on changing state-based laws that permit child marriage. Collaborating with other NGOs, they have successfully revised laws in at least 10 US states that once allowed child marriage. They aim to end child marriage across all 50 states by 2030.

(b) **Measurable**

Setting goals means creating specific criteria to measure progress and impact. This demonstrates success and keeps partners engaged, which is critical for future achievements.

In early 2023, Craig Cohon, a Canadian businessman and accidental ultra-endurance athlete, planned to launch his Walk It Back campaign—an extraordinary six-month journey by foot from London to Istanbul to "walk back" his lifetime carbon footprint. To put his money where his mouth was, Craig invested a significant part of his pension fund toward supporting the development of carbon removal

---

[1] Its criteria are commonly attributed to Peter Drucker's Manage-ment by Objectives concept. The first known use of the term occurs in Doran 1981.

technologies. He also aimed to catalyze conversations with city mayors he met about the policies needed to remove carbon from the atmosphere at scale.

A significant barrier for partners and cities to initially support the campaign, however, was the inability to quantify its impact. Through detailed calculations of every aspect of his life, Craig identified his lifetime carbon footprint as 8,147 tons—equivalent to the annual energy use of more than 1,000 average US households. Removing this equivalent through policy change became the campaign's initial goal.

Since its start, the "Walk It Back" campaign has engaged 19 city leaders, resulting in policies that will remove 100,000 tons of carbon—over 10 times Craig's lifetime carbon footprint. For example, the city of Deventer in the Netherlands agreed to make all its new government buildings with concrete from sequestered carbon dioxide. With the completion of his walk, Craig continues to leverage his growing network of cities to advocate for policies that could remove an additional 1 million tons, equivalent to the annual emissions of over 215,000 passenger vehicles.

(c) **Achievable**

An achievable goal prioritizes objectives based on available resources and does not try to do so much that it becomes unwieldy. Focusing on a few areas over many can increase the likelihood of delivering real-world impact.

For example, the UN's 17 SDGs have 169 targets. Very few have been implemented since they were agreed to in 2015. Critics argue (not without controversy) that a more achievable approach might have focused the world's attention on a few key priorities, such as reducing child mortality. Ultimately, it often pays not to let the perfect be the enemy of the good.

Breaking down ambitious, daunting goals into manageable, incremental milestones can be helpful. Take Fossil Fuel Non-Proliferation Treaty (FFNPT) as an example, which seeks to accelerate the shift to clean energy by getting countries to agree to a comprehensive phase-out of fossil fuel production [3]. Immediate adoption by major fossil fuel–producing countries, such as those in the Gulf and the US, was and is an unlikely prospect for now. However, that does not mean the effort has no merit. Indeed, the FFNPT effort was launched specifically to bypass the UN Climate Conferences' incapacity to deliver a plan for fossil fuel phase-out because of its need for consensus. The FFNPT, in contrast, relies on generating momentum for a phase-out, even without the participation of the biggest fossil fuel-producing nations.[2] It has steadily done this by securing endorsements from small island nations most affected by the world's ongoing fossil fuel production. The campaign is now gathering backing from additional countries, including fossil fuel producers such as Colombia and Timor Leste to reach a tipping point. The idea is that once there's enough support, it will be able to isolate and pressure the remaining holdout countries, broadening the feasibility of a full phase-out.

(d) **Relevance**

It may seem obvious, but a goal must be directly related to the challenge you are addressing. These days, we often hear about the likely impacts of climate change on all areas of life, from how we grow our food to the spread of infectious diseases. However, not all of these impacts will occur immediately. Although extreme weather frequency has increased in recent years, it will be many decades before climate change emerges as a leading driver of mortality compared to other current influences, such as a lack of vaccines [4]. As a result, policies aimed at mitigating climate change, while necessary, are less relevant to improving mortality rates in developing countries between now and 2030,

---

[2] Taking inspiration from the 2017 Treaty on the Prohibition of Nuclear Weapons, the 1997 Anti-Personnel Mine Ban Convention, and the 2008 Convention on Cluster Munitions, this approach involves constructing treaties without the involvement of powerful nations, notably the US. By generating ample momentum, these treaties not only secured passage through the UN General Assembly but also established new diplomatic norms, making defiance challenging even for nations that refused to ratify them. For example, the US never joined the 1997 Anti-Personnel Mine Ban Convention but did eventually agree to their phasedown. See Burke 2022.

as called for by the SDGs.[3] So if your goal is to reduce preventable child deaths by 2030, focus on policies addressing existing health and development disparities, as they will have the most relevant impact. For instance, increased government funding for organizations such as UNICEF and Gavi, the Vaccine Alliance, can facilitate the rapid procurement and deployment of new vaccines against malaria—one of the leading causes of child deaths worldwide [5].

(e) **Time–Bound**

Setting a timeframe or deadline creates urgency and accountability. It is also necessary to avoid exacerbating problems. During the COVID-19 pandemic, lockdowns had to be implemented rapidly to effectively contain the disease's spread. Suppose we also do not enforce the policies needed to halve our collective global emissions by 2030. In that case, we risk losing the opportunity to keep temperature rises below 1.5 degrees Celsius, which most experts agree is needed to avoid catastrophic climate change.

In some instances, policy implementation involves a long and arduous process. Where the outcome is potentially years away from being won, identify what is achievable in the short-term to advance the issue and build momentum. Setting specific short-term objectives prevents the effort from feeling futile and keeps supporters engaged. This is particularly important in negotiating peace agreements. For instance, accomplishing short-term, time-bound goals such as prisoner swaps or access to aid can help build confidence in the long-term peace process.

★★★★★★★

---

[3] The SDGs health aims include, by 2030, ending pre-ventable deaths of newborns and children under 5 years of age, with all countries aiming to reduce neonatal mortality to at least as low as 12 per 1,000 live births and under-5 mortality to at least as low as 25 per 1,000 live births; and by 2030, reducing the global maternal mortality ratio to less than 70 per 100,000 live births.

The Power of Bold Goals

"Whatever you can do, or dream you can, begin it. Boldness
has genius, power and magic in it."
—Johann Wolfgang von Goethe, German
polymath and writer [6]

Bold and SMART policy goals serve as magnets for raising
resources and rallying supporters. Arrey Obenson, former secretary-
general of Junior Chamber International, highlights how these
goals can compensate for other deficiencies, such as lack of experience, expertise, and access. As he notes, "Others perceive your imagination, believe in it, and join in its achievement" [7]. This holds
particularly true for, as Benson puts it, "naively audacious" goals. In
a world facing numerous crises, this type of audacity aligns with
the craving, especially among young people, for a clear sense of
purpose [8].

I experienced the power of "naive audacity" during Global
Citizen's inaugural policy campaign, "The End of Polio," in 2011.

Our policy goal was to secure an additional A\$50 million from
the Australian government for global polio eradication efforts.[4] Polio,
a debilitating and ancient disease, had already been reduced by 99.9%,
thanks mainly to the leadership of Rotary International in decades
past. However, the eradication program risked being undermined by
a persistent funding gap, and some governments, including Australia,
had stopped funding entirely.

We deliberately focused on polio eradication instead of a broader
goal like ending poverty because the latter seemed too overwhelming for citizens to grasp. We could demonstrate however that the
broader fight against poverty was achievable by showing progress

---

[4] Polio eradication efforts are led globally by the Global Polio Eradication Initiative,
which consists of Rotary International, UNICEF, the World Health Organization,
the US Centers for Disease Control and Prevention, and supported by organizations such as the Bill & Melinda Gates Foundation.

against a specific disease. As for the A\$50 million target, it was not based on any sophisticated analysis. On the back of a napkin, our cofounder Simon Moss and I doubled Australia's previous contributions to a clean A\$50 million. Our next challenge involved convincing the Australian government, led by Prime Minister Julia Gillard.

Without a clear starting point, in March 2011, we drafted a letter to Prime Minister Gillard outlining our request. Though we didn't expect an immediate response—if any—we found the exercise helpful in articulating the arguments supporting our goal. One crucial argument was that the forthcoming Commonwealth leaders' summit was taking place in my hometown of Perth, Western Australia, in late 2011. This summit, we argued, presented a unique opportunity for Australia to renew its funding for polio eradication, particularly considering that, at the time, three out of the four polio-endemic countries were Commonwealth members.[5]

Surprisingly, our letter reached Melissa Parke. A former UN human rights lawyer who was also a local member of parliament in Perth at the time, She agreed to deliver it to the prime minister's office on our behalf. She was sensitive to the possibility that the forthcoming Commonwealth summit, without a clear goal, risked being dismissed as an expensive talkfest by ordinary citizens. Our policy goal could potentially infuse it with a meaningful purpose that was easy to grasp. It could offer a win–win solution.

A few weeks later, we were given an extraordinary opportunity— a 10-minute meeting with the prime minister herself. Looking back, I believe our policy goal's simplicity and clarity are what attracted her initial interest. Following her advice to keep things concise (she mentioned she was already on her third shot of Red Bull for the night), we presented our arguments. After hearing us out, she expressed interest in supporting us. Still, there was a catch: politicians ultimately

---

[5] The Commonwealth of Nations is largely made up of former British colonies (though it has added countries outside of this shared heritage in recent years such as Rwanda). It meets every two years for a Heads of Government Meeting.

require public support to allocate what is ultimately taxpayers' money. Ahead of the summit, she wanted us to demonstrate public backing for the government to announce new funding for polio eradication. She needed a mandate.

In the moment and eager to maintain the prime minister's interest, we proposed a concert to bring people together the night before the summit. Intrigued, she felt this might demonstrate a sufficient level of public support. Upon leaving the meeting, we were thrilled by the apparent agreement and, at the same time, wary of the upcoming challenge: How would we produce a concert and campaign, bringing together thousands of people in just a matter of months? Note I had not organized anything remotely at that scale before. Although my fellow cofounders had some event experiences, they were not in Perth but in London and New York at the time, planning the expansion of Global Citizen internationally.

Nonetheless, our clear policy goal and tacit agreement with the prime minister attracted valuable connections. This compensated for our lack of experience. One particular moment stands out: I received a call from Lindsay Hadley, an American producer, while sitting on a university park bench (at that time, I was still finishing my law degree). An email we had sent out seeking support for a concert had reached her. Despite recognizing our group's inexperience and limited resources, the clarity of our goal and the clear path to secure significant new funding to combat polio resonated with her. It is not every day, after all, that people get to say they helped to make polio just the second human disease in history to be eradicated. Inspired, she chose to support us, turning down other job opportunities.

With Lindsay's support and the efforts of Hugh Evans, Global Citizen's CEO and cofounder, we were able to make additional connections. The late Sumner Redstone of Viacom agreed to support the concert financially. Momentum began to build when Grammy Award–winning artist John Legend agreed to fly to Perth to headline it.

Through these connections, we were also connected with Ryan Gall, a Californian filmmaker and social impact strategist who introduced us to an innovative concept of "gamifying" advocacy. Ryan's novel approach involved offering concert tickets as rewards in exchange for taking action, such as signing our petition calling on Commonwealth leaders to support polio eradication. By incorporating this method into our plans, our campaign attracted 25,000 petition signatures from people hoping to gain one of the 5,000 free tickets we had. We then presented this petition to the prime minister's office, fulfilling her request to mobilize public support.

On the eve of the summit, The End of Polio Concert garnered significant media coverage. It made a strong public call for the Australian government to deliver new funding for polio eradication. The following day, at the summit, Prime Minister Gillard committed A$50 million and urged other leaders to support the cause, resulting in A$118 million in new funding for polio eradication.

Leveraging the momentum from the campaign, we were able to advance our broader goal of ending extreme poverty. Just nine months later, in September 2012, at Ryan's behest, the inaugural Global Citizen Festival occurred on New York's iconic Central Park's Great Lawn. Since then, over US$43.6 billion has been distributed in response to Global Citizen campaigns, affecting nearly 1.3 billion lives with the support of many incredible partners. As for polio, it is now at historic lows, with only two countries remaining endemic and just six cases being reported in 2021. Since 2011, the Australian government has continued to support financially every year.

Ultimately, our campaign's success for polio eradication began with a "naively audacious" yet SMART policy goal that united a diverse coalition, including government officials, musicians, nonprofits, student volunteers, and everyday citizens. This led to unexpected encounters and responses, and helped us overcome our own limited experience and connections.

Step 2: Know Which Stakeholders Matter and How to Appeal to Them

"One thought experiment that I used to pose to the members of my team is to imagine that they had 15 minutes with the president. If he thought that they had a compelling idea with strong evidence to support it and a solid implementation strategy, he was willing to pick up the phone and call anyone" [9].
—Thomas Kalil, former advisor in the Clinton and Obama
White Houses

Identifying Relevant Stakeholders

To influence change effectively, you must identify the key individuals or groups with the authority to implement your policy goals. This groundwork is essential for targeting your efforts and understanding who you must build relationships with, whether at a local, state, federal, or international level. Relevant stakeholders can range from city council members to influential global figures. Still, the real challenge lies in gaining access to and persuading these decision-makers.

Accessing top decision-makers, especially high-profile government leaders, can be formidable. If direct contact proves challenging, consider reaching out to influential individuals within their network. These figures could be advisors, donors, colleagues, peers, or even members of the public who can help convey your message effectively.

Never underestimate the importance of advisors, particularly in the busy schedule of a top public official. Being friendly and building relationships with key staffers is always a valuable strategy. Even if you're familiar with the official in question, their staff will likely play a crucial role in helping them fulfill any promises they make. They are generally critical in deciding which briefs their superiors read, which policy proposals reach them, the messages they deliver in speeches, and even how they schedule their time. Try moving past the formal stage so you can reach them quickly if needed. I always try to get on text message and Whatsapp terms with leaders or their advisors as soon as possible. This helps prevent you from being stuck in the lobby when you urgently need their support. Find ways to also show appreciation for their help, such as recognizing their contributions in front of their manager. Even symbolic gestures will likely be remembered.

Outreach can also extend to those directly benefiting from your proposed policy change. You can garner support through their representatives, such as trade unions or special interest groups, who can advocate for your cause.

Additionally, consider the value of engaging with individuals who may not be in power but are likely to assume influential roles. These individuals are often more accessible and open to collaboration. For instance, former US Secretary of State Henry Kissinger reportedly made it a practice to meet with government officials *and* opposition parties during his visits to foreign countries. This approach can prove strategic, as opposition parties will likely remember these interactions when they eventually come to power.

Being Targeted

Whether your advocacy efforts are directed toward a head of state, a local legislative representative, or a school board member, it is crucial to be clear *who* your target is. This clarity informs the subsequent steps discussed in this chapter. Your goal should be to ensure that your advocacy tactics are centered on reaching and persuading the specific individual(s) necessary to achieve your objectives. To maintain this focus, it's beneficial to continually ask yourself, "How will this tactic effectively reach and persuade the individual(s) I need to engage to accomplish my goal?"

As a follow-up to the previous step, let's consider a real-world example from 2015 when Commonwealth leaders including the late Queen planned to gather in Malta. The Commonwealth had long supported eradicating polio, but there was a challenge. Malta, the summit host, wasn't a significantly wealthy nation or affected country. So why would its then-prime minister, Joseph Muscat, care about ending polio? The only way to find out was to target and try to reach him directly. Those involved in the polio eradication movement, from Rotarians to everyday citizen advocates, utilized various strategies, such as tagging his accounts on social media (what I referred to as "Twit-Plomacy" before Twitter was rebranded as X!) and writing emails to his public address. They even published open letters in the country's leading daily newspaper. The targeted nature of the campaign got Muscat's attention, and he responded, "I've received your emails, tweets, and letters; what about a phone call?" Once he understood how close the world was to eradicating polio, he seized the opportunity to make it a significant focus of his summit, exclaiming, "I feel like this is one of the few things that might make a difference." True to his word, Muscat secured an agreement from over 50 presidents and prime ministers to renew their funding and support [10]. It pays to be targeted and directly ask for help when possible.

Additionally, make it as easy as possible for your targets to be able to help you. Handle any necessary groundwork to save them time and enhance follow-through. Show them the value add of working with you. This proactive approach may contribute to their willingness to collaborate in the future. In Muscat's case, aware of his limited staff already dealing with logistics for over 50 leaders, I drafted much of the invitations, articles, and speeches myself. Given my relationships and expertise in polio eradication, this approach proved more efficient for all involved. During the summit, I even assumed a pseudo-Maltese diplomat role, liaising directly with other government delegations in hotel lobbies to ensure their attendance at Muscat's polio-focused press conference. Chaotic summit experiences have taught me never to assume anything, even when delegates express support verbally. Leveraging our successful partnership, Malta emerged as a key ally in pushing the British government to prioritize polio in the subsequent Commonwealth leaders' gathering a few years later [11].

Leveraging Effective Messengers

Legitimacy and credibility are key when considering who will be the most persuasive messengers for relaying your policy ask to the target decision-maker. This could be you or another intermediary [12]. Research by psychologist Geoffrey Cohen has shown that people are more receptive to ideas from like-minded individuals. Unsurprisingly, Democratic voters offer more support for Republican ideas when they believe those ideas are coming from fellow Democrats, and the same holds vice versa [13].

As a specific example, in 2020 Global Citizen aimed to persuade the Trump administration to support a campaign for equitable access to COVID-19 resources in developing countries during the pandemic. Recognizing the then Boris Johnson–led UK Government's relatively close ties with the Trump administration, Global Citizen leveraged the British ambassador's connections to secure a significant commitment of more than US\$500 million. A message from the British government resonated far more powerfully than if it had solely come from Global Citizen or the World Health Organization, especially given the Trump administration's decision to withdraw the US from the latter.

Lastly, it's crucial not to overlook the importance of your messenger's ability to connect with others [14]. Effective messengers must cultivate authentic relationships and be likable. This greatly influences whether people respond to them, engage in meetings, return their calls, or simply want to grab a coffee. While this may seem self-evident, it's worth emphasizing, particularly in our polarized era where too many conversations start with critiques rather than constructive dialogue. Relationships matter.

The Power of Strategic Framing

Not all stakeholders will initially support your policy goal, especially if they perceive it as conflicting with their constituents' interests. Others may need to discern its benefits to the people they represent. Remember, people and countries are rarely solely motivated by altruism.[6] To gain their support, you must answer a fundamental question for each stakeholder: "What's in it for them or those they represent?" [15] For instance, fiscally conservative governments may be more receptive to arguments for increased foreign aid emphasizing a national interest benefit, such as addressing the root cause of illegal migration.[7] Similarly, leaders of emerging economies such as Brazil, Kenya, and South Africa where youth unemployment is a critical issue, may be more receptive to climate initiatives that deliver jobs for their citizens [16]. When your target stakeholders see a win–win proposition in your policy goal, this can motivate substantial and powerful action.

Think creatively about how you frame propositions and test your assumptions. For instance, we are often led to believe that it is hard to win people over on policies with a short-term cost but a long-term benefit. Studies have shown, however, that strategic framing *can* be effective in certain circumstances by appealing to interests beyond the present. For example, one study involving 59,440 participants across 63 countries asked participants to write a letter to be read by a future child in 2055 describing their personal actions to address climate change. On average, the studies found that those who wrote these letters were more likely to support ambitious climate change mitigation policies—including in the US [17]. Conversely, the same study found that asking people to share doom and gloom messaging on climate change led to a decline in support for such policies.

---

[6] While there is evidence of some decisions being made essentially for moral reasons, including on child labor, landmines, the "blood" diamond trade, small arms, and sweatshops, the research suggests that this is done only when it is convenient or relatively costless for governments to do so, or if values are effectively tapped into. See Busby 2007.

[7] For example, Italy's right-wing coalition government led by Prime Minister Giorgia Meloni favors this frame. However, it is questionable whether foreign aid does in practice result in reduced migration (as opposed to other more concrete outcomes such as on health and education). See Käppeli, Jennison, and Fattibene 2022.

Strategic framing can also drive significant policy implementation by appealing to politicians' political self-interest and personal values. For instance, President George W. Bush increased HIV/AIDS relief funding in Africa following a concerted campaign effort from the faith community, influencers such as Bono, and the NGO he cofounded, the ONE Campaign. This diverse coalition framed the AIDS crisis in Africa as an opportunity for the US to save many lives with relatively little budget while also appealing to the president's Christian values [18]. The collaboration ultimately led to the launch of the President's Emergency Plan for AIDS Relief (PEPFAR) in 2003, alongside the most considerable upsurge in US foreign aid since the Marshall Plan. It's been alleged that Bono's fame, in particular, gave the Bush Administration "some hipness and credibility with liberals" from an unusual ally at a time when the White House was deeply unpopular [19]. For his part, Bono rarely, if ever, criticized the Bush Administration's war in Afghanistan, instead framing development spending as a means to "drain the pool of angry youth who might join militant organizations" [20]. He has since never been shy about praising Bush's commitment—arguably for good reason [21]. Regardless of the Bush Administration's motivations, the undeniable reality remains: PEPFAR has, in two decades, helped save over 25 million lives, reduced AIDS-related deaths and new HIV infections, and contributed to 5.5 million HIV-free births [22].

Reframing issues to align with self-interest can also lead to powerful shifts at the community level. Take the case of sanitation, with nearly 500 million people worldwide still practicing open defecation as of 2020, leading to severe malnutrition, disease, and economic burdens [23]. The problem is that communities that practice open defecation frequently have access to latrines and other sanitary facilities. They just don't use them. Like many issues, this challenge is best addressed locally by community leaders. Motivating them to act relies on first convincing them that it is not only in their interest to do so, but that it is even a problem that needs fixing. This is where "Community-led total sanitation" (CLTS) and the innovative technique of "triggering" come into play [24]. It leverages the emotional impact on the community when they see the direct link between open defecation and the spread of diseases laid out in front of them.

This is how CLTS works: In the middle of the community, local leaders and residents gather around a central meeting point as volunteers draw a chalk map of the village on the ground. A local community health worker brings a bag of sawdust and invites community members to sprinkle it on the map to indicate where they defecate. Soon, parts of the map are covered with piles of sawdust, with a few piles placed inside the village. They see how much human waste has piled up in the village. The health worker then explains how flies transfer germs from human feces to nearby food, making the communities realize they've been effectively consuming each other's waste, resulting in widespread illness and increased health costs. This realization generates pressure on their leaders to act, advocate for funds from the central government to build latrines, and implement policies banning the practice of open defecation.

Figure 1.1 Community in Bihar, India, 2016 implementing CLTS. *Credit:* Jay Gunning.

Such approaches are paying off. In 2014, the global prevalence of open defecation was twice what it is today. Once the world's open defecation capital, India, in particular, has made significant progress by implementing CLTS approaches to change behaviors and offering subsidies for building latrines to meet increased demand. Despite ongoing challenges, and yet to achieve its goal to end open defecation, the UN reports that the practice in India decreased from 41% to 17% in less than a decade [25]. As a result, millions live healthier, more productive lives.

In summing up this step, effective policy entrepreneurs must develop similar skills as business entrepreneurs who create products that meet customer needs. The primary difference here is that those with the power to implement policy remain subject to the whims of their constituencies. In such situations, additional strategies may be required to generate momentum for a specific policy goal and place it firmly on their agenda.

Step 3: Mastering the Art of Timing

"Public officials cannot enact any policy they please like they're ordering dessert from a menu. They have to choose from among policies that are politically acceptable at the time. And we believe the Overton window defines that range of ideas" [26].

—Joseph Lehman, a colleague of Joseph Overton

Understanding the Overton Window

So you have set a clear policy goal and identified the key stakeholders you need to influence. Next, it is crucial to establish a realistic timeline for implementing that goal.

In today's polarized landscape, success often depends on identifying the right moment to advocate for your policy goal and recognizing opportunities to broaden its acceptability—to yank an idea out of the crosshairs of culture wars and partisanship. Understanding the "Overton window" theory can be invaluable.

Named after American policy analyst Joseph Overton, the Overton window defines the entire range of policies generally acceptable to society at a given time. The theory assumes that politicians and those with the power to implement policy more broadly will only support policies within this range. The Overton window is not fixed. The parameters of what society finds acceptable can gradually change as social norms evolve. Conversely, it can rapidly expand or contract in response to a crisis (as many of us witnessed with the quick acceptance of previously unthinkable lockdowns in early 2020 as the COVID-19 pandemic's scale became apparent).

Figure 1.2 Pushing the Overton window.
Credit: Xinyi Chen.

You can generally determine whether a policy is in the Overton window based on available polling to measure society's views. The good news is that abundant polling information exists on various community, national, or global policy issues.

The Open Society Barometer is one such example. It highlights views within and between countries concerning the strategies for effectively addressing global problems. Take climate change as an example. In the 2023 survey conducted across 30 countries, 71% of 36,344 respondents agreed that wealthy nations should take the lead in compensating low-income countries for economic losses caused by climate change [27]. This sentiment was, perhaps unsurprisingly, more prevalent in lower-income countries. Nevertheless, majorities also emerged in the United Arab Emirates, Italy, the United States, and the United Kingdom. This shift in global sentiment may help explain why, after many years of gridlock, countries finally agreed to place "Loss and Damage" caused by climate change on the official agenda of the UN climate talks in late 2022 and even established a loss and damage fund (although, as of the time of writing, it has raised only a fraction of the estimated need).

Regardless of the survey you rely on, it's essential to check the methodology and ensure it's reliable and that the respondent size is broad enough to be credible [28].

Shifting the Overton Window

What should you do if your policy solution falls outside the Overton window? In such cases, policy entrepreneurs, social movements, and think tanks must engage in efforts to convince relevant segments of the public, especially those to whom leaders are accountable, that these policies *should* be within the Overton window. This process can be arduous and time consuming, requiring a long-term commitment to many of the strategies and steps outlined in the next chapter as it relates to leveraging the strengths of allies, nurturing diverse coalitions, and not letting the perfect be the enemy of the good.

Generally, though, the Overton window can be shifted in four practical ways [29]:

(a) **Pushing for Extreme Policy Positions**

Joseph Overton argued that pushing for extreme positions can be effective at changing public opinion and making more moderate policy solutions acceptable [30]. For instance, in the context of climate change, this phenomenon is often referred to as the "McKibben effect," named after environmentalist Bill McKibben, the founder of the advocacy group 350.org [31]. Research indicates that when radical policy proposals such as fossil fuel divestment gain prominence, the public debate transitions from whether action should be taken on climate change to what should be done. This often results in increased support for more moderate solutions such as clean energy subsidies, which seem less radical by comparison. The lasting impact of the McKibben effect is evident in the reshaping of the climate debate in the United States. This is exemplified by the enactment of the Inflation Reduction Act after years of policy failures, which currently represents the most substantial climate change legislation ever approved in US history. Notably, American politicians from both sides of the aisle now openly express support for clean energy, and some Republicans even favor carbon tariffs.[8] This level of support would have been unthinkable a decade ago.

It is worth noting that pushing for extreme positions can be risky, as it may negatively affect public perceptions of a broader movement, leading to the discrediting of even more moderate policies by association [32]. At the time of writing, for example, it remains to be seen whether the Just Stop Oil group in the UK will bolster or alienate public support for ending oil extraction in the North Sea by pursuing disruptive tactics such as blocking traffic for everyday citizens [33]. In other cases, advocates for more extreme positions can undermine support for more moderate policy solutions if they publicly attack the latter for not being pure enough. This is why it's crucial to seek allies and approaches, however extreme, that can enhance rather than undermine the collective

---

[8] The 116th Congress, with the House of Representatives controlled by Democrats and the Senate and the Presidency by Republicans, approved a notable $35 billion investment in clean energy R&D. See Cassidy 2023; Kaplan and Grandoni 2020.

bargaining power of policies within a larger coalition. These strategies should also avoid putting vulnerable segments of the population at risk of further marginalization—a topic we'll explore further in the next chapter.

(b) **The Foot in the Door Technique**

The "Foot in the Door Technique" is often used in sales to convince a person to agree to a large request by first obtaining their agreement on a more minor, manageable request [34]. Similarly, in policy advocacy, it can be practical to advocate for more minor, incremental shifts in policy before aiming for more significant changes.

Such gateway policies serve as specific measures or initiatives that act as stepping stones toward more comprehensive policy reforms in a particular area. They are crucial for initiating reform or progress, eventually leading to substantial changes in the policy landscape through increased political and public support for a specific policy direction.

For example, the conservative Canadian government led by former Prime Minister Stephen Harper (2006–2015) significantly increased funding for child, maternal, and newborn health in developing countries [35]. Harper noted that public support for foreign aid is generally low when framed broadly. However, it increases significantly when specific examples are provided of how aid dollars improve people's lives, disproving the prevalent notion that foreign aid does not work. The positive results of the Harper government's efforts to save the lives of mothers and children thus gave the government the runway to make more profound and more influential changes on international development in Canada, including creating a new Ministry of International Development within the Department of Global Affairs, and establishing Canada's first Development Finance Institution [36].

(c) **Pulling Policy "Ropes" Sideways**

The economist Brian Caplan suggests that in policy implementation, most people focus on one or two so-called tug-o-war "ropes," and they interpret peoples' partisan positions based on where they fall along these ropes [37–39]. Examples of today's policy ropes include, among others, advocating for more robust climate change mitigation measures for businesses versus opposing regulations to protect businesses, advocating for increased corporate taxes versus reduced taxes, and supporting a universal versus private health care system.

In times of hyper-polarization, individuals in positions of influence are under tremendous pressure to emphasize their loyalty to a particular side of these ropes to fit in and be identified with one specific partisan group. Demonstrating support for the other side of the rope leads to cries of betrayal and harsh political consequences. How do you break out from such gridlock? Caplan asserts you can avoid triggering the partisan games that polarize ideas and drag them into culture wars by pulling the ropes "sideways" along unconventional dimensions. These ropes are less likely to be salient in the media and therefore subject to less polarization. The more media prominence given to a particular rope, the more chance you have of getting caught between partisan struggles. Conversely, supporting less common dimensions, even of the same polarized issue, is less likely to be seen as a victory for the other side and, therefore, encounter less resistance [40].

One classic example of pulling the ropes sideways is how the British abolitionist movement, after years of setbacks, accelerated the timeframe within which it was possible to outlaw the Transatlantic Slave Trade. Contrary to popular belief, this support was not entirely based on the moral strength of abolitionist arguments alone; in fact, the trade continued to expand notwithstanding the apparent strength of the abolitionist campaign. As Britain went to war with Napoleonic France (1804–1815), abolitionists were accused of sedition for appearing to undermine the British economy at a time of national emergency. However, the initial legislative steps to undermine the slave trade began with seemingly innocuous laws that, on their surface, supported Britain's war efforts against France. These measures "questioned the wisdom of supplying enslaved Africans to Britain's enemies," especially France and Spain [41]. The first significant anti-slave action was thus a ban on British slave traders operating in the waters of foreign powers. After this action, momentum soon shifted, and a blanket ban on the trade as a whole followed. It took far longer, in some cases decades, before the timing was ripe in other countries to make similar progress against slavery.

More recently, the swiftness with which marriage equality became acceptable to the mainstream in many Western countries can be seen as an example of pulling the ropes sideways. The marriage equality movement shifted its approach from framing the issue along a civil rights dimension to a less divisive one focused on love, commitment, and family values [42]. This change was accompanied by arguments rooted in freedom and the idea that you should treat others as you would want to be treated. This led to a rapid increase in public support. Marriage equality in the US progressed from no state allowing same-sex marriage to nationwide legality within just over a decade [43]. Ultimately, a few pioneer states paved the way, and a pivotal 2015 court decision triggered a wave of state-level actions, culminating in a change to federal law [44]. This brings us to the last way to shift the Overton window.

(d) **Responding to a Crisis or Triggering Event**

In times of crisis, the Overton window of acceptable policies can suddenly burst open. As Lenin famously stated, there are "decades where nothing happens; weeks where decades happen." Recent years have shown us how crises have a unique power to expand the range of policy options, rendering previously unthinkable ideas politically viable.

At the beginning of the 1980s, racial apartheid seemed deeply entrenched in South African society. While international and domestic pressure had been increasing, what truly shifted the situation, though, was the fall of communism in the Soviet Union and the removal of the excuse that Nelson Mandela's African National Congress were Soviet-sponsored terrorists [45]. This change allowed those in the apartheid government who supported reconciliation to win the argument for releasing Nelson Mandela and commencing the dismantling of apartheid. As FW de Klerk, the then president, stated, "I would not have been able to do that . . . if the Berlin Wall did not come down. I was helped by the fact that the threat of expansionist USSR communism fell away, and when we saw that window of opportunity, it helped us to jump through it by accelerating the process" [46].

Sometimes, a triggering event, organized in response to a natural or manufactured crisis, can help challenge societal attitudes toward a particular policy approach. Speeches have traditionally played a significant role in this regard. Martin Luther King Jr.'s iconic "I Have a Dream" speech in 1963 is widely credited with influencing the successful passage of the Civil Rights Act in 1964 and the Voting Rights Act in 1965. King delivered the speech during the march on Washington, responding to widespread racism in the US. Similarly, John F. Kennedy's bold challenge to land a man on the moon captured the public's imagination, and increased Congressional spending for NASA. His 1962 speech aimed, in part, to galvanize Americans in response to increased tensions with the Soviet Union.

Popular culture and entertainment can also change the Overton window. Despite criticisms for being paternalistic, the Live Aid concerts of 1985 influenced an entire generation of Britons to think globally and consider their country's responsibility in eradicating hunger and poverty.[9] As the "Live Aid Generation" assumed positions of power, Britain emerged as one of the world's most generous nations regarding foreign aid spending.[10] For the politicians who supported this commitment, it wasn't just political but personal. For example, former Prime Minister David Cameron faced calls to cut Britain's foreign aid budget in the wake of the 2008 global financial crisis. He cited watching Live Aid on his 18th birthday as a critical factor in his decision not to balance Britain's books on the back of the world's poorest [47]. Regrettably, the combined economic impact of Brexit and the post-pandemic economic slowdown narrowed the Overton window once more. In 2021, the UK government made a controversial decision to cut Britain's aid budget significantly. This move seemed unthinkable a few years earlier but was done with little public outcry.

★★★★★★★

We will return to the concept of the Overton window in the final chapter, where I identify several contemporary opportunities for bold policy implementation where common ground might be found.

In the end, though, one of the most effective ways to persuade people about the merits of your idea is to craft compelling narratives. Even if your policy goal falls within the Overton window and aligns with the interests of those with the power to implement it, the key challenge is getting it on their agenda, particularly if it's a

---

[9] The Live Aid Concerts were organized in response to the Ethiopia Famine of the mid-1980s.

[10] Among the wealthy G7 nations, Britain was, up until 2021, the sole country to fulfill its commitment of allocating 0.7% of its gross national income to development assistance. This level of spending was even enshrined into law due to strong political support.

neglected issue. This is where the power of storytelling and narrative building becomes indispensable.

Step 4: Mastering the Art of Storytelling

"Humans think in stories, and we try to make sense of the world by telling stories."
—Yuval Noah Harari, historian, philosopher and author

Harnassing storytelling can help build trust and rapport. This is an essential precondition for establishing any common ground, whether with affected communities, the public, or the influential individuals holding the power to make a difference. It is an even more critical skill to have at the ready at times of great division, intolerance, and crises like the present.[11] Without open dialogue, our empathy weakens and our fear of the unfamiliar strengthens. Over time, this leads to anxiety and exclusion. A well-told story, however, can plant the seeds of connection and partnership where nothing else resonates. It gives us an excuse to talk—and to keep talking—where there is no other basis for dialogue.

Storytelling also helps us cut through the noise. As political strategist David McKinnon notes, a simple story can help people make sense of our complicated, information-overloaded reality [48]. According to McKinnon, most, if not all, presidential elections have been won based on who has the most powerful story, not who has the best policy or even ideology [49].

And yet . . . countless leaders, from heads of state to charity leaders to peace negotiators, have missed vital opportunities to move policy forward because they did not understand the power of storytelling. Instead of focusing on building a genuine connection,

---

[11] In the US alone, Americans valuing tolerance toward others has declined. In 2019, 80% of Americans viewed tolerance as necessary, but by 2023, this number has dropped to 58%, a worrisome trend. See Zitner 2023.

they perhaps launched into a deluge of statistics or a string of talking points. Maybe they did not notice the skeptical, glazed-over look of the person opposite them, wondering, "Why should I listen to what *you* have to say on this issue? What gives you the right to lecture me?" Answering such questions can often be the difference between the person you are speaking to walking out and forgetting about your policy goal versus becoming a committed champion. Storytelling is one of the best, most effective ways to achieve the latter.

In "Step 1: Know Your Policy Goal," I outlined how Prime Minister Gillard was responsive to our polio campaign. Yes, it was partly because our policy goal was relevant to her interest in needing a purpose for a summit she was hosting, but that only explained half of it. When she announced A\$50 million for polio eradication, I asked why she had followed through. Her advisors told me it was because she liked the stories we had shared: stories of heroic Rotarians who had raised millions of dollars worldwide, and especially the stories of resilient polio survivors who had overcome so much personal pain and still found ways to give back. It was a reminder that we're not moved by facts or statistics but by stories of humanity. In other words, people move people.

How do you tell a memorable story? When I reflect on the most powerful stories shared with me, what stands out the most is the *why* and the *how* rather than the *who*, *what*, or *when*. Regarding *why*, sharing your motivation for promoting a specific policy allows people to respect where you're coming from, even if they disagree with your ideas. It's what helps establish credibility. Understanding why is often the first step to mutual understanding and, even if begrudgingly, respect. It humanizes your intentions and demonstrates sincerity in your efforts. It fosters open dialogue and can be a starting point for finding common ground or areas of compromise. This approach works both ways. It's always worth asking the person speaking why they believe in a particular policy position. Such *active listening* might tell you something about their values and worldview that you can relate to [50]. Finding common ground or shared values helps create a stronger foundation for constructive dialogue. It makes it easier to address policy disagreements.

In terms of *how*, people want stories that demonstrate practical solutions and a way of making sense of the chaos. They want direction in a rudderless world. Solution-oriented narratives can give a sense of purpose to those open to new ideas and approaches, whether in power or not. Even if they disagree with your proposals, good conversations focused on solutions help us refine our ideas and make better, more substantial arguments. This clarity gives us greater confidence in our ideas. It lets us understand different viewpoints without getting defensive, creating an atmosphere more conducive to finding common ground. In summary, such stories "help us develop the essential skill of *negotiation*: learning to manage ego, bridge differences, and reconcile challenges" [51].

While a few of us are born storytellers, it's better to spend some time preparing your story before essential meetings with key stakeholders. Here are a few practical tips to help you craft compelling narratives:

Identify your core narrative: Start by identifying the central message you want to convey with your story. What's the key takeaway you want your audience to remember?

Avoid the common mistake of excessively focusing on the problem. Communications strategist Thomas Coombs's approach of hope-based communications suggests that when we center our narrative on the problem, we reinforce it in the minds of our audience, which contributes to their overall sense of powerlessness and cynicism [52]. This makes people susceptible to other simplistic populist narratives based on fear and security.

Bring it back to the power of *how*. Ground your narrative in solutions. As Coombs notes, "People want to be part of something successful" [53]. Focus on how the stakeholder you're speaking to can contribute to implementing the solution: how they can help build the world as it should be, not how it is. Let that be your takeaway.

For example, consider the story shared by Brianna Fruean, a young climate advocate from the small Pacific Island nation of Samoa. With her country at the frontlines of the climate crisis, Brianna has every right to talk about the existential threat her people face through no fault of their own. Yet, as much as Samoa is a victim, she uses her platform as a recipient of various international prizes to also talk about *how* her people are rising to withstand the crisis. "I bring with me the voices of a Pacific that refuses to give up . . . we can teach you how to fight back like us" [54]. In practical detail, for instance, she talks about how Samoan villages have learned to quickly rebuild after severe winds. Rather than leaving her audiences disillusioned, she leaves them with a clear message about how we can all do something: "We are not drowning; we are fighting. Now the world needs to hear us and follow our lead" [55].

Finally, "Narratives must be continually rewritten, updated, and revised" to remain influential [56]. Similarly, assessing who is best positioned to convey these narratives is essential, ensuring the widest possible pathway to garner support (see "Step 2: Leveraging Effective Messengers").

Ground your story in shared values: Ensure your narrative connects to how your audience views the world and how its implementation is consistent with that view. Connect it also to a value that cuts across ideological divides. Some conservative lawmakers, for instance, shifted their stance on marriage equality after learning about the impact of discrimination on mental health and suicide rates in LGBTQ+ communities.[12] This change aligned with their overall value for life.

---

[12] I once met a legislator who told me he was persuaded to support marriage equality after meeting with the mothers of those in the LGBTQ+ community who had committed suicide.

Demonstrate the possibility of change: If we want people to be part of the solution, show them stories of others contributing to it. This is especially effective if you can showcase how people overcame similar difficulties or tensions your audience might share.

For example, in recent years, business leaders have been increasingly pressured to introduce policies that significantly cut their emissions. Even those willing to do so have been held back by practical questions on implementing them. Perhaps unhelpfully, too much of the campaigning toward them solely focuses on *what* they should be doing, not *how*. To help motivate such leaders, the band Coldplay agreed to share their sustainability story with a group of business leaders convened by Global Citizen.

In 2019, in a BBC interview, Coldplay frontman Chris Martin said the band would not go on tour again until they could do so in a way that was "as environmentally beneficial as possible". One of Martin's major stipulations was that they should cut the tour's carbon emissions by more than 50%. Their manager, Phil Harvey, shared concerns about how they could achieve this. Given the absence of a blueprint for sustainable touring on this scale, he realized they would have to develop it themselves. Just four years later, the band announced one of the world's most eco-friendly tours, incorporating a range of innovations. These new measures include powering the entire show with a rechargeable electric battery from repurposed BMW car batteries. The show battery is partly charged using biodiesel generators that run on recycled cooking oil, solar, and wind power, and partly charged by the audience's kinetic energy via specially designed power bikes and kinetic dance floors. Additionally, the band offers discount merchandise to those who use sustainable travel options to attend the show. By sharing these stories with business leaders grappling with the same challenge, the band moved the dialogue from whether a business should reduce its emissions to the most practical way to achieve it. After all, if one of the biggest bands in the world can do it, so can others.

Demonstrate momentum: Provide evidence through your story that momentum is building behind your proposed solution. List who else is already on board with the proposed policy. Everyone wants to be part of a train going in the right direction. But highlight *why* your audience's involvement is equally and uniquely critical, allowing them to be a hero in the story and supercharge existing momentum.

Idris and Sabrina Elba, UN ambassadors for the International Fund for Agricultural Development (IFAD), embarked on a journey to Sierra Leone in December 2019 to witness IFAD's remarkable work firsthand. They saw how financial assistance, seed access, and equipment could empower struggling farmers to bounce back after a crisis.

But they also saw how they could help far more people by encouraging governments to contribute as much as US$2 billion in total to help up to 100 million farmers. This was far more significant than any charitable donations they could make themselves.

After this eye-opening experience, the Elbas took their mission to the world stage, touring the capital cities of major wealthy economies. In these meetings, they passionately advocated for increased support for IFAD. They highlighted the growing list of countries already stepping up to help but tailored their message to explain why the support of each particular country was crucial.

In some cases, they emphasized that certain nations served as role models for others. In others, they pointed out that a lack of support would send a discouraging signal to potential contributors. They also underlined how specific countries' dedication such as Canada to empowering female farmers would lead to IFAD also making this a priority.

During a Zoom meeting amid the pandemic, their efforts paid off when President Macron announced a 50% increase in France's commitment to IFAD. This success story demonstrates the power of showcasing momentum and how your audience's involvement can have a significant impact.

Show, don't just tell: Don't assume your listener will automatically agree that something is important. Humanizing your story is the best way to demonstrate why they should care. Try to focus on stories about individuals. People respond less to abstract ideals or statistics, no matter how horrific. Telling personal stories is also an effective way to circumvent division.

As the Israel-Hamas conflict kicked off in October 2023, many people became hyper-concerned about inadvertently choosing the wrong words or even how to have a conversation about the divisive conflict. A woman at a conference I attended cut through this by telling a story about a scholar she had supported. He had left the Gaza strip some years prior to pursue a research opportunity, knowing he could never return. The lady giving the talk rang the man a few days after the conflict broke out to see how he was getting on. He was distraught, as his family and kids remained in Gaza. Trying to distract the man from his pain, the speaker told us how she shifted the conversation toward the fact that he had become a US citizen. "Suddenly, it dawned on me," she recounted, "I said to him, you can vote in the next US election." The man responded that he had never voted before as he was too young when the last elections took place in Gaza back in 2005, in which Hamas was elected. Many in the audience were surprised. In telling such a personal story, the woman simply made the point not to condemn all of the Palestinians and hold them responsible for the horrific actions of Hamas. After all, they haven't had a chance to vote out their leaders for 18 years.

Authenticity matters: People can often tell when someone is genuinely enthusiastic about a cause. However, being authentic also means not forcing your passion or coming across as insincere, which can have the opposite effect. Your story should also be truthful and supported by credible evidence. Exaggerated or implausible claims can undermine your credibility and the impact of your narrative. It's best to let the merits of your story speak for themselves. This means being up front about what hasn't worked and how failings have been overcome.

The polio eradication program is a case in point. It has set multiple deadlines for eradicating polio, beginning in 2000. Each deadline has been missed. Yet, it has managed to maintain the support of donors and Rotarians, mostly everyday citizens, for decades because it has been up front about its failings and how it has addressed them. Indeed, it has a special independent monitoring board devoted to this purpose. Being open about our learnings can sometimes disarm critics, inviting them to be part of the solution.

2 | The Diplomat: Catalyzing Impact through Pragmatism

"People don't want to talk about trade-offs, don't want to talk about power, don't want to talk about sacrifices, don't want to talk about difficult choices between lesser evils. If you are not prepared to get into that conversation, you can feel good about yourself and very pious, and feel that the whole world is refusing to listen to your great prophetic vision but you are unlikely to change anyone's life. You have this delight of purity without impact" [1].
　　—Rory Stewart, co-host, *The Rest is Politics* podcast

Have you ever engaged in discussions with people holding radically opposing views, knowing that finding common ground is more valuable than being right? Did you consider compromising because you needed their support to move an idea forward? Perhaps you kept the conversation going, hoping to open their minds just a little bit to a broader perspective?

The reality is that significant policy breakthroughs often result from pragmatic, cooperative, or centrist approaches. These methods involve finding common ground, building consensus, and discerning when and where to advocate for "extreme" positions to propel change forward (see "Pushing for Extreme Policy Positions" in Step 3). They require compromises with people we do not always agree with or like. While they may not offer the immediate satisfaction of the dopamine high from winning an argument, they prioritize creating real-world impact over being "right." This chapter delves into how to blend pragmatism and idealism effectively, avoid common pitfalls, and harness the power of a broad and influential coalition of supporters.

Step 5: Embrace Pragmatic Idealism

"I have come to believe that as well-intentioned as they are, impractical idealists are dangerous and destructive, whereas practical idealists make the world a better place. To be practical one needs to be a realist—to know where people's interests lie."
—Ray Dalio, investor and author, *Principles* [2]

In policy entrepreneurship, achieving progress requires a delicate balance of idealism and pragmatism. This means accepting that generally not all objectives can be realized simultaneously and that concessions are essential. Most successful policy breakthroughs are marked by no one party getting everything they want. This approach can be demanding, especially in our polarized world, where advocating for compromise may put us at odds with our tribal loyalties. Yet, the courage to accept imperfect settlements is what allows us to move agendas forward.

Advancing policy change requires a cohesive relationship between means (policy tools and levers) and ends (policy goals) [3]. Pragmatic idealism acknowledges compromised means are often necessary to achieve desired ends. Pure pragmatism—where ends justify any means—is, of course, vacuous. For example, a politician advocating for curbing overpopulation by sterilizing half the population may aim to protect Earth's life-supporting systems: biodiversity, a stable climate, and enough arable land. But the politician's means are so reprehensible that they will unlikely gain any support from a reasoned populace.[1]

Pure idealism, on the other hand, would leave us forever searching for the perfect means to achieve our ends. This is so, even when those means aren't immediately available. Pragmatic idealism, however, accepts a degree of comfort around using less-than-ideal means. It strives for real-world progress toward implementing goals in the here and now.

In the early 21st century, politicians in the United States, including Barack Obama, initially supported civil union legislation while opposing full marriage equality. This compromise garnered support from the LGBTQ+ community, who recognized that achieving some progress was better than none and could pave the way for further change. Their foresight proved accurate as progress was made despite the compromised means. Civil unions represented an improvement over the existing status quo, although they still recognized LGBTQ+ couples as less equal than heterosexual couples. While civil unions did not offer the same social recognition as marriage, they did grant similar legal rights and benefits.

Another powerful example of embracing compromised means to advance progress is the Belfast/Good Friday Peace Agreement in Northern Ireland.

The Good Friday Agreement: Lessons from the Irish Peace Process

The Good Friday Peace Agreement, now over 25 years old, is a testament to the power of pragmatic compromise. Each party achieved something, but not everything they desired. Yet the overall outcome was worth it, even as tensions continue to exist to this day [4].[2]

---

[1] This is not a hypothetical scenario. A senior politician once told me, "I know that too many children die in developing countries. But we also have too many people on the planet."

[2] Note President Biden's visit for the 25th anniversary was overshadowed by a reported bomb plot. Northern Ireland's elected assembly is vacant, and armed protesters firebombed a police truck in Derry/Londonderry before Biden's visit. See Blair, T. 2023.

Although we might now perceive relative peace in Ireland as a natural progression, those who remember the "Troubles" recall the turmoil, violence, and bleak prospects for peace. The Good Friday Agreement, signed on April 10, 1998, marked the end of three decades of sectarian violence in which 3,600 people (mostly civilians) died.

The peace negotiations that led up to the Good Friday Agreement succeeded where others failed after several mutual and hard-fought concessions on both sides. Irish Republicans seeking a united island of Ireland agreed to respect Northern Ireland's status as part of the United Kingdom. At the same time, so-called Unionists agreed to respect Northern Ireland's possible reunification with the Republic of Ireland in the future should a majority of the population of Northern Ireland agree. By far, though, the most difficult concessions involved the giving up of arms by paramilitary organizations and controversial prisoner releases. Individuals convicted of horrific and violent crimes were released on both sides. At times, this threatened to undermine peace negotiations altogether.

While leaders from Ireland, the US, and the UK all played their part, the success of the Northern Irish peace process largely depended on the courage of leaders from both sides. They were willing to compromise in the face of deep criticism and public cries of "betrayal" within their communities. As BBC Ireland correspondent Mark Devenport notes, "[Moderate nationalist leader John] Hume faced an awful lot of criticism for talking to [the more radical republican politician Gerry] Adams, particularly from people in the unionist community who thought he was engaging with people beyond the pale, while Adams was seen to be backing down from a maximalist position, which would have opened him up to accusations of betrayal." Adams was a leading member of Sinn Féin, the political wing of the Provincial Irish Republican Army (IRA) that had been designated a terrorist organization by both the British and Irish governments. As Devenport further noted, "The risks were real and personal" [5].

On Good Friday, April 10, 1998, the Good Friday Agreement faced a critical moment when unionsts threatened to abandon the process over the timeline for the IRA's decommissioning of arms. David Trimble, a unionist leader, displayed remarkable courage by resisting calls from his side to walk away. His pivotal decision at this "fork in the word" juncture had a "touch of the miraculous about it" [6]. Indeed, Trimble's own political support collapsed in subsequent years. Ultimately, the success of the peace process relied on former enemies putting aside their past grievances. Though it was futile to try and fully rectify past injuries to one another, they overall recognized the net benefit of working together toward a better future.

Still evolving, the Northern Irish peace process story offers valuable lessons for those aspiring to be pragmatic idealists. For those interested in delving deeper into the talks that ended the Troubles, I recommend reading *One Good Day*, an insightful insider account by former Irish diplomat David Donoghue [7].

In 2023, as we marked the 25th anniversary of the Good Friday Agreement, former British Prime Minister Tony Blair emphasized its profound and far-reaching impact. It has significantly improved the lives of many, whether they fully grasp its importance or not. As Blair aptly put it, "What matters is that it was done" [8].

★★★★★★★

In pursuing pragmatic idealism, centrism, or cooperation—whatever label you choose—there are several tips and pitfalls to watch out for.

Avoid the Purity Test

In today's polarized world, there's immense pressure to demonstrate unwavering loyalty to our tribe's beliefs and principles. This can lead to a "purity test," where we judge everything, from policies we support to who we partner with, based on how well they align with our moral code. If they fall short of this test, even by a little, we are told to say no or risk being accused of betraying the tribe. The psychologist Adam Grant calls this test by another name: the "binary bias," where we collapse shades-of-gray spectrums into black-and-white categories [9]. While our values are crucial, rigid adherence can lead to both self-righteousness and intolerance, preventing us from deciding necessary trade-offs and, thus, can be overall detrimental to progress. As a colleague of mine put it, "Obtuse idealism is just as bad as any other form of despotism or dictatorship in that for it to prevail, dissonant voices need to be silenced."

Look no further than His Holiness Pope Francis himself for an example of avoiding the purity test to seek common ground. During the COVID-19 pandemic, he brought leaders of different faiths together to pray despite condemnation from ultra-conservative Catholic groups for fasting with "infidels" [10]. In response, His Holiness effectively told them that if they thought they were all praying to a different God, they had completely missed the point.

In another example, during the 2023 Dubai UN climate conference, Pope Francis urged political leaders to resist subjecting each other to a purity test. Instead, he encouraged them to embrace a "good politics" transcending division. He stated, "History will be grateful to you . . . as will the societies in which you live, which are sadly divided into 'fan bases' between prophets of doom and indifferent bystanders, radical environmentalists, and climate change deniers" [11]. He concluded by sharing a story about his favorite saint, Francis of Assisi, who preached forgiveness and understanding to settle a conflict between a local bishop and civil authorities.

Engage with Everyone

In Netflix's *The Diplomat* series, the fictional US diplomat, Hal Wyler, gives an unconventional speech that challenges the notion that talking to your enemies legitimizes them. He emphasizes the importance of engaging with everyone, including dictators, war criminals, and even terrorists. Failure may happen, he admits, but it's a necessary part of the process. "Brush yourself off. And fail again. Because maybe . . . Maybe" [12].

Wyler's advice is essential, as many successful real-life diplomats and politicians will tell you. The former executive director of the UN's World Food Programme (WFP), David Beasley, was also a bit of a maverick. A past governor of South Carolina, Beasley, would hop on a plane at a moment's notice to meet the leaders of wealthy nations if he heard they had even an ounce of concern about their work. "Let's go and talk to them," he would say. He regularly pounded the floors of Congress, meeting with holdout Republican senators and explaining why it was in the US interest to eradicate hunger and make the world more stable. The results spoke for themselves. When he arrived in 2017, the WFP's annual budget was $6 billion. By the time he left, he had more than doubled this to $14 billion, including record contributions from the US—from both the Trump and Biden administrations. Sadly, the organization is missing Beasley today. Since his departure and energetic approach to engaging everyone, the annual funds raised are back to around $6 billion. Meanwhile, the world is hungrier than ever, with almost 800 million people facing chronic hunger worldwide [13].

A symptom of today's division at all levels is that we are pressured not to talk to those on the other side. The world is poorer for it, and we must resist this trend if we're serious about making a real difference that improves lives. Those sincere about change do not have the luxury of hitting the pause button on such engagement.

Adhere to the "Do No Harm" Principle

After the negative consequences of the Iraq invasion, one of Barack Obama's organizing principles for his approach to foreign policy was "Don't Do Stupid Shit" [14]. Its application did not always lead to satisfying outcomes, as in the Obama administration's controversial approach not to intervene in the Syrian civil war in fear of creating a larger conflict. However, it arguably avoided further unintentional catastrophe.

Recognizing the complexities of supporting morally right causes is essential. Failing to do so can lead to counterproductive outcomes, regardless of the strong desire to show solidarity through words or deeds.

In January 2021, the Australian ambassador to Ghana attended a fundraiser at an LGBTQ+ rights community center. This well-intentioned act led to a severe anti-LGBTQ+ backlash over perceived meddling by outsiders. Shortly after, the ambassador left the country and the center was closed down after being raided by police. The incident also galvanized local members of the parliament to support a bill to criminalize LGBTQ+ rights and advocacy [15]. While it is unclear whether the center could have continued its work discreetly if not for the ambassador's visit, this example underscores the need to be mindful of the potential consequences of well-intentioned actions. Some local LGBTQ+ groups have quietly urged Western diplomats and NGOs to refrain from public statements, as they fear these actions might fuel further backlash towards them.

For those of us who support LGBTQ+ rights, this situation can be intensely frustrating. Some of us might pursue engagement behind closed doors, believing that some form of engagement is better than none. Conversely, some might feel a strong moral conflict and opt for non-engagement. This reflects the broader challenge of working with those whose moral code differs from ours, raising questions about how to proceed.

This is where the Do No Harm principle offers guidance. It encourages us to assess whether our public expressions of solidarity will shift the Overton window (thereby advancing favorable policies) or merely harm the people we aim to help. Having the wisdom to know when to compromise and when not to compromise to achieve your goal is fundamentally important. Seeking input from the affected communities is crucial in this regard, as they are often the best judges of the most effective course of action. And, of course, the Do No Harm principle also applies to you. In extending an olive branch to those you disagree with, be sure not to put yourself directly in harm's way.

Leverage Existing (Imperfect) Institutions

We can apply the idea of pragmatic idealism to leveraging institutions. These include existing political, legal, diplomatic, and economic systems. We may see them as flawed or even as the cause of problems we are trying to solve. Many people blame capitalism for environmental degradation. They say its focus on economic growth at all costs is a key cause. A pure idealist might choose not to work within this system. Instead, they might call for revolution or regime change. Or they may choose not to engage at all, unwilling to dirty their hands through impure means. They retreat to the safe confines of commentary and academia to maintain their purity even as the world burns down around them.

In contrast, a pragmatic idealist seeks "optopia," a term coined by American author Joanna Russ to describe the best outcome we can achieve given the cards we're dealt [16]. It can be contrasted with efforts that aim for utopia, which are often a fruitless hunt at best [17]. Pragmatic idealists recognize that the need for urgent action now. In an era of poly-crisis, there's no time to discard the impure system or build new institutions from scratch. Instead, we must work with and trust the hand— the existing but imperfect institutions—dealt to us. It's beside the point that they may not be the most well-equipped; they are all we have. As Raj Shah of the Rockefeller Foundation has noted, "If we want to have the biggest impact possible, we have to engage our . . . institutions" [18].

Kim Stanley Robinson's [19] fictional but realistic *Ministry for the Future* illustrates this tension. The novel is set in our immediate future. It follows the efforts of an elite team of policy entrepreneurs who confront climate change on behalf of future generations.[3] As the novel progresses, it reveals the ineffectiveness of extreme actions such as eco-terrorism. In contrast, it shows that working within capitalist institutions can produce the optimal solution in the time needed.

Ultimately, the Ministry of the Future persuades central banks to issue "carbon coins" to those with fossil fuel resources.[4] This approach mirrors quantitative easing, a policy that rich nations used to inject money into their economies during the COVID-19 pandemic. The

---

[3] The team's leader is an Irish diplomat based on the real-life Mary Robinson, the former president of Ireland who served as UN High Commissioner for Human Rights and currently serves as Chair of the Elders.

[4] The Carbon Coin concept was first conceived by geohydrologist Delton Chen. See Chen n.d.

innovation involves compensating fossil fuel–producing companies and countries, paying them to leave their fossil assets in the ground. In return, they must redirect resources toward building clean energy infrastructure [20]. This reformed capitalist system essentially bails out institutions responsible for climate change, even the worst offenders of greenwashing. It raises questions about climate justice as it doesn't immediately force them to pay for the damage caused. However, it effectively averts the worst catastrophic impacts of climate change. Robinson acknowledges that this approach is "controversial and expensive," yet he asserts that "weaning [Petro-states] off that dependency is in everyone's interest. It must be done. And what must be done can be done"[5] [21–22]. After all, for many of these states, the income from fossil fuel assets is seen as a potential guarantor of future public welfare.[6] To deprive developing countries of this might constitute another form of injustice.

Robinson is far from a pure pragmatist. His approach advocates for reforming our imperfect capitalist system from within. This vastly differs from today's pure techno-pragmatism, which believes technology and the market alone will be our savior—a notion bordering on far-fetched utopianism. Despite the clear severity of climate change, eye-watering profits continue to surge from ongoing fossil fuel production [23]. This alone underscores the need for public policy incentives and reform, as behavioral change on the necessary scale will not occur without them. Society itself must change the terms of the corporations' engagement with society [24].

---

[5] A 2022 study concluded that the estimated cost of paying off coal companies is $50 billion, with the majority of expenses linked to transitioning to renewables and compensating for the opportunity costs of coal. Ultimately, the findings reveal that an international agreement to phase out coal could result in a net gain of $85 trillion for the world. The study emphasizes that compensating polluting nations to halt pollution results in net benefits to wealthy G7 countries contributing funds to this objective. See Adrian, Bolton, and Kleinnijenhuis 2022.

[6] In recent years, I've engaged in discussions with leaders from developing countries who express concerns that an abrupt phase-out of fossil fuels, without accompanying financial support, could perpetuate existing economic inequities.

In this regard, working within the system does not preclude the future evolution of purer alternatives. As demonstrated, incremental change can expand the Overton window, meaning that policy options can grow over time as they gain momentum. In the previous example, fossil fuel producers are compensated today; tomorrow, they actively contribute to averting a climate disaster and are duly rewarded. This scenario doesn't rule out the potential for such polluters, especially those who knowingly caused harm, to be compelled to pay restitution in the future as the consequences of climate change become increasingly apparent.[7] Society may insist on repayment or seek compensation for climate-related damages, reminiscent of current calls for descendants of British slave-owning estates to return compensation received when slavery was outlawed.[8] In other words, true climate justice, with the ultimate responsibility placed on the polluter to foot the bill, may be deferred but remains achievable in the long term.

However, one must start somewhere. An effective policy entrepreneur strives to do their best with the resources at hand and within the time afforded for action. Despite the abundance of alternative economic theories, such as Kate Raworth's "Doughnut Economics," which aims to transform our global capitalist society into an economy meeting the needs of all citizens without overshooting Earth's ecological boundaries, these changes are rarely achieved overnight, and often rely on compromised means [25]. Indeed, to do otherwise and insist on achieving everything outright might lead to more pain and suffering through prolonged inaction brought about by a lack of consensus.

The Paris Agreement on Climate Change is itself an imperfect means to a noble end. It reflects the reality that we still live in a world where the nation-state remains the principal stakeholder in global relations, with the most powerful unwilling to accept limits on their

---

[7] Even on 1.5 degrees Celsius some impacts of climate change are baked in. See Cuff 2023.

[8] Slave owners were compensated with the equivalent of 308 billion pounds (as of 2018), a debt that British taxpayers only paid off after 182 years. See Cork 2018.

sovereignty. This constraint prevented consensus around a global agreement based on national emission targets. As a compromise, nations committed to limiting global warming to below 2 degrees Celsius by 2100, using pre-industrial emissions as a baseline. The underlying premise was that having any agreement was preferable to none, as it would generate subsequent pressure for increasing ambition over time. Almost a decade later, we find ourselves still in the danger zone of dangerous climate change. However, the world's ambition for climate action has grown significantly. This can be attributed, in part, to the impact of the Paris Agreement despite its shortcomings (see Chapter 7).

Ultimately, policy entrepreneurs prove effective by fully leveraging compromised institutions to achieve the outcomes our shared challenges demand. This path is not for the faint-hearted, but it's needed to navigate the coming decade and ensure a positive and sustainable future for all.

Step 6: Leveraging Your Partners' Strengths

"Alone we can do so little; together we can do so much."
—Helen Keller, author and advocate

Achieving systemic change often requires building support from diverse partners who can complement and mitigate each other's strengths and weaknesses. Effective coalitions thrive when partners are in the right roles, poised to harness their unique strengths for change. Doing this effectively often requires putting our differences aside and recognizing that we are stronger when we work in unison together.

An illustrative example of the importance of collaboration over competition unfolded during the Glasgow UN climate talks in November 2021. One activist lamented on X (formerly Twitter) that thousands of conference attendees were competing for the same media interviews, panel slots, and event space to reach the same audience. Katherine Hayhoe, one of the world's leading climate scientists and author of the fantastic book *Saving Us*, responded to the tweet by highlighting how they could add value by instead focusing on building new platforms that reach audiences beyond the conference [26].

To avoid these pitfalls and cultivate partnerships that complement each other's impact, first identify and honestly communicate your strengths. Ask yourself, "What is my super power?" Then, assess the areas where you require allies. "What can I uniquely bring to the cause, and where do I need support?" Identify like-minded partners to complement your strengths.

Partnerships can help meet various needs:

- **Securing access:** If you lack access to decision-makers, recruit partners with that access (as discussed in "Step 2: Know Which Stakeholders Matter and How to Appeal to Them"). A small number of individuals with the right access and political intelligence, working in close concert, can often achieve more than what mass protests crying outrage do. As the famous quote by Margaret Mead goes, "Never doubt that a small group of thoughtful, committed citizens can change the world. Indeed, it's the only thing that ever has."
- **Credibility and authenticity:** Partners representing affected communities who stand to benefit from the proposed policy solution or those who bring technical expertise and research can add credibility to your argument. They can also help generate SMART policy goals (see "Step 1: Know Your Policy Goal").
- **Funding:** Efforts to influence policymaking can take time and resources. This requires financial support, which is such a vital need that I elaborate further later on how policy efforts can leverage the power of philanthropy to achieve their goals.
- **Electoral power:** Identify groups within your target official's constituency who can support your cause. Research by Harvard political scientist Erica Chenoweth shows that nonviolent protests that involve around 3.5% of the population have never failed to bring about change—this is known as the "3.5% rule" [27].

- **Finding the most appealing messenger:** The choice of the messenger is crucial, (as discussed in "Step 2: Know Which Stakeholders Matter and How to Appeal to Them"). Depending on your target stakeholder, these partners may be larger organizations with big public constituencies or niche representatives of relevant interest groups. Sometimes, more moderate organizations can also act as bridges to connect with a broader range of stakeholders. Often, the pivotal question to consider is: Who possesses the most legitimacy and credibility with the target audience?

- **Offering recognition platforms:** Governments, particularly elected officials, often seek recognition for their stance on an issue. Some partners can fulfill this need by providing highly visible platforms to acknowledge leadership. For example, the polio eradication effort leverages the ability of 46,000 Rotary clubs worldwide to recognize and award individual local government officials for continued support of the program [28].

- **Broadening the acceptability of a policy:** As explained in "Step 3: Mastering the Art of Timing," consider how partnering with organizations that advocate for more extreme positions can make your policy appear more reasonable and socially acceptable by comparison.

Two final but essential pieces of advice regarding maximizing partnerships: First, individual meetings with prospective partners can be more effective in gaining their buy-in than large group meetings. Large forums can quickly become chaotic if individuals use it to challenge the group's fundamental premise. Get your ducks lined up first! Second, prioritize action-oriented partnerships. When you do organize a significant group meeting, ensure each party explicitly outlines their contributions at the outset. This will foster momentum and an action focused culture.

****

Bridging Divides for Climate Action

Building coalitions and networks is a nuanced process with trade-offs and risks. It often requires making concessions to create a broad constituency built on trust. Nonetheless, it's often the most viable path to achieve meaningful change.

Jad Daley, CEO and president of American Forests, has decades of experience building coalitions effectively, generating billions of dollars to protect existing forests and plant more trees. It took a lot of work.

The climate movement encompasses a broad range of perspectives. One common division is between those focusing on protecting nature and those dedicated to reducing emissions from fossil fuels. The latter group often views the former as a distraction or even as an enabler of corporate greenwashing, lacking credibility with the broader climate community.

Around late 2007, as Congress prepared to pass climate legislation for the first time, these divisions intensified, and the lack of trust became a significant obstacle. Jad's response throughout 2008 was to bring together a wide range of stakeholders ("even the super left-leaning ones") from various environmental communities, investing in relationship-building through private meetings and discussions. They agreed to temporarily set aside specific issues to move the climate agenda forward. The result was a broad and trusted coalition committed to the long term.

Although major climate legislation failed to pass in 2010, the diligent and patient coalition-building endured. As Jad emphasized, "The cool part is, we walked up there as the most diverse coalition ever seen in the US [on the climate front]. We presented a plan with agreements on issues people never thought we'd agree on. Even after all these years, that same team is still together."

In the 117th Congress of 2021 and 2022, these partners seized an opportunity they could not afford to miss again to unite behind comprehensive policy change. Tens of billions of dollars for nature-based solutions became part of the successfully passed Inflation Reduction

Act and Bipartisan Infrastructure Law. Today, funding is rapidly pouring in to support reforestation and conservation efforts enabled by these laws.[9] Thanks in part to this effort and the policies they have secured, America's forests are capturing a growing share of US carbon dioxide emissions—now up to nearly 17%, equivalent to the emissions from more than 160 million passenger vehicles [29]. This impact is a testament to what's possible when the collective strengths of a broad coalition are successfully leveraged.

★★★★★★

Leveraging Philanthropic Giving for Policy Entrepreneurship

Philanthropy can serve as a force multiplier of policy change efforts. It can do this by investing in the capacity of partners to deploy one of the most effective approaches available for catalyzing such change: policy entrepreneurship. After all, funding is essential for commissioning research, building strategic relationships, employing advocacy staff to cultivate and maintain connections with key decision-makers, covering travel expenses for meetings with policymakers, organizing events, and communicating policy solutions. Such resources are especially needed since citizen advocates and grassroots movements often find themselves up against highly paid corporate and partisan lobbyists representing influential brands with seemingly limitless budgets in the battle for policymakers' time and attention. These lobbyists can pour substantial resources into shaping policy agendas. They can invest in think tanks, research institutes, marketing, and $10,000-a-head tickets to attend dinners with influential politicians. Meanwhile, outdated models of philanthropic giving struggle to view supporting policy entrepreneurship as a legitimate use of their funding. Risk aversion and long drawn-out grant application processes starve the

---

[9] For an example see US Forest Service 2023.

advocacy sector. Given this, the question is how to persuade philanthropists and foundations to invest in your policy effort.

First and foremost, avoid seeking support for policy advocacy within the traditional framework of how foundations historically grant funds. The impact of policy change cannot be defined in a neat, linear fashion in the way programs such as soup kitchens or building schools can be. Moreover, policy advocacy activities are typically categorized in conventional terms as overhead expenses, a category that philanthropy has traditionally been reluctant to fund. An entire organization's budget that only conducts policy advocacy might be considered overhead. Dan Pallotta has addressed the harm caused by overreliance on the "overhead myth" in his book *Uncharitable* [30]. He explains why the myth surrounding overhead is self-defeating: "Everyone wants charities to spend as little as possible on overhead. That's backward. Overhead is what drives growth. If charities can't grow, they can't solve problems. So overhead is a good thing."

To make your pitch for a philanthropic partnership more appealing, shift the focus away from a dialogue about where the money will be allocated. Instead, emphasize the social return on investment it will generate. In policy advocacy, success should not be measured by how philanthropic dollars get spent but by your ability to secure the adoption of essential policy solutions. What truly matters is the human impact these policies can have. Try to get your potential partner to see the power of their contribution in these transformative terms. In essence, make the case to potential philanthropic partners that they can empower your organization with the capacity needed to create sustainable change over the long term. This extends to investing in inclusive platforms to profile systemic policy proposals supported by much of the world's population.[10]

This might sound bold, but consider this example from Global Citizen. In 2020, four foundations collectively donated $3.5 million to a campaign to ensure equitable access to COVID-19 tests, treatments,

---

[10] As an example of public support for such proposals, see Open Society Foundations 2023.

and vaccines worldwide. Thanks to their contributions, the campaign saw $1.5 billion in government grants being disbursed. For every dollar the donors invested, the campaign helped mobilize almost $430 in cash funding directly to partner organizations working to support marginalized communities.

Of course, there is always a risk that policy change efforts will fail. If they were guaranteed to succeed, then there would be no need for them in the first place. However, hesitant partners can be persuaded by previous examples of where big bets on policy change have paid off. As a case in point, in his exceptional book *Universal Food Security,* Glenn Denning outlines how the Ford Foundation and the Rockefeller Foundation both played seminal roles in launching the Green Agricultural Revolution in the 20th century, now credited with helping to save one billion lives from starvation [31]. The foundations funded the early research *and* the advocacy needed to translate research ideas into impact through public policy.

The good news is that there is an estimated $2.4 trillion global philanthropic sector, and foundations are increasingly receptive to this kind of pitch [32]. Many increasingly recognize how, in partnership with civil society organizations, leaders of communities living in vulnerable conditions, and everyday citizens, they can leverage their dollars to have a much more significant impact. As Darren Walker, president of the Ford Foundation, noted, "Philanthropy as a sector has to move from just focusing on generosity and charity to fundamental structural solutions" [33].

As a final point, to establish successful philanthropic partnerships focusing on policy change, strive to formalize partnership agreements that align with the following principles:

1. Emphasize long-term engagement, recognizing that policy change is a time-intensive process that is rarely linear.
2. Prioritize core and flexible funding, as building relationships and maintaining dedicated staff are often crucial to the success of policy change efforts.
3. Ensure the project deliverables are achievable and can be completed within a realistic timeframe where funding is tied

to specific projects (use the SMART formula outlined in "Step 1: Know Your Policy Goal").

4. Align reporting requirements up front to avoid having difficult conversations later. Ensure flexibility is built into the framework (since work focused on policy change often requires agility and adaptability to achieve its main objectives).

5. Align on short- and medium-term outcomes that ladder to the longer-term policy goals and capture the added value of policy entrepreneurship efforts.

6. Take your funders on a journey to see themselves as cocreators of solutions rather than roadblocks to transformational impact.

Finally, as policy entrepreneurs, we share a collective responsibility to champion increased investment in systemic change. The active involvement of nonprofit organizations and citizen advocates is indispensable for achieving inclusive policymaking and addressing the needs of vulnerable populations.

Nonprofits should be able to secure the necessary funds to compete on a level playing field for policymakers' attention. Regrettably, they are not as empowered as they should be. In some countries, there have been commendable efforts to limit the influence of large corporations and powerful actors in policymaking. However, certain measures, such as spending restrictions, have inadvertently hindered nonprofits' policy efforts [34]. Meanwhile, in the US, a potential misinterpretation of nonprofit law paradoxically leads foundations—including those that see "themselves as change agents" preferring systemic change over mere service delivery—to forfeit "one of the most effective" mechanisms available to them for spurring systemic change [35].

By collectively pushing back, we can gradually shift the prevailing norms, regulations, and laws that guide philanthropy toward more significant support for policy change initiatives.[11] Even if a fraction of

---

[11] In 2021, Global Citizen achieved a legal victory against the then-Australian government, securing the ability to receive tax-deductible gifts. Traditionally, organizations primarily focused on advocacy, such as Global Citizen, faced challenges in obtaining this status. See Knaus 2021.

the world's philanthropy is spent differently, it has the potential to catalyze substantial systemic transformations. Nelson Mandela was right when in 2005 he said, "Ending poverty is not an act of charity but an act of justice." If ending poverty is in fact a multi-hundred billion dollar problem, then surely it demands a multi-hundred billion dollar solution. To champion such solutions, we need philanthropy to invest in the capacity of policy entrepreneurship. And to do that, policy entrepreneurs need to first disrupt the existing norms of philanthropic giving.

3

The Implementer: Enforcing Accountability and Follow-Through

"Downtime is not the name of the game."
       —Usher, American artist, songwriter, and advocate

Step 7: Know Your Endgame

"All these things happened, and they were glorious, and they changed the world. Then we fucked up the endgame."[1]
—Charlie Wilson, politician and former US Representative
(1973–1996)

---

[1] Based on a quote from the real Charlie Wilson in Mike Nichols' movie *Charlie Wilson's War.* The movie shows how Charlie Wilson, a Texan member of Congress, convinced the US to give weapons to Afghan fighters during the Soviet-Afghan War. These fighters, called the Mujahideen, kicked the Soviets out, but many of the

Once we have secured a promise to execute a policy, we must ensure it's delivered on. And yet, even presidents and prime ministers of the world's most powerful nations find that their decisions are rarely self-executing [1]. People's lives only change when commitments are properly implemented. During the process of delivery, which can sometimes span extended periods (e.g., addressing climate change over 30 or 40 years), several challenges can disrupt follow-through:

- **Premature celebration:** Movements often celebrate victories too early, losing interest and neglecting the hard work of ensuring policy delivery.
- **Change in leadership:** Those in power who agreed to implement the policy may leave office or retire, and their successors may not honor the commitment.
- **Emerging crises:** New crises can arise, diverting attention and resources from policy implementation.

A clear endgame strategy and a certain level of tenacity are essential to address such challenges [2]. Policy entrepreneurs rely on three main avenues of endgame strategies: legal, non-legal, and long-term sustainability.

Legal Avenues

(a) **Contracts:** The most straightforward way to ensure accountability is through contracts. Legal action can be taken if someone fails to fulfill their promise. Bono once suggested that developing countries hire lawyers and sue wealthy nations for not delivering on aid promises. The only challenge was that such moral contracts were not legally binding, so there was no basis for a legal suit.

---

weapons ended up with the Taliban, which helped Al-Qaeda grow. Charlie Wilson wanted to help regular people in Afghanistan. Still, sadly, the country didn't have much peace after that, especially for women and children.

(b) **Regulation and government rules:** For example, non-compliance with publicly stated corporate climate goals can increasingly result in regulatory consequences for companies that engage in greenwashing activities.

(c) **Creative legal methods:** Other innovative legal methods, such as court actions, can hold responsible parties accountable in courts. A notable example is the *Milieudefensie et al. v. Royal Dutch Shell Plc* case, which ordered a major energy company to cut carbon emissions by 45% by 2030.[2]

Non-legal Avenues

Not all promises can be legally binding or have tangible consequences for nonperformance. In such cases, other incentives or punishments can encourage compliance:

(a) **Public shaming:** When commitments lack legal force, public opinion can drive accountability, especially where a reversal in policy isn't seen as reasonable. Where key stakeholders are repeatedly unresponsive or break promises, consider mobilizing partners and coalitions to publicly call them out (see "Step 6: Leveraging Your Partners' Strengths"). In 2023, environmental advocates took a stand when the Canadian provincial government of Ontario's Premier Doug Ford initially approved development on the Province's previously protected Greenbelt. They applied public pressure through various means, such as letters, petitions, phone calls, op-eds, social media posts, and community discussions. This collective effort resulted in Ford backing down and the ongoing preservation of the ecologically sensitive Greenbelt.

(b) **Monitoring, consultation, and reporting:** We won't make progress unless we can measure our progress. To this end,

---

[2] Shell didn't take this lightly—after losing in the Hague District Court, they removed "Royal Dutch" from their name and moved their headquarters to London.

tracking, monitoring, and publicly reporting progress can motivate those responsible for implementing to stay on track. Consider using a relationship management tool such as Salesforce to track implementation and record follow-up interactions with critical stakeholders. At Global Citizen, we use this to monitor the delivery of over $60 billion in promised support for anti-poverty efforts.[3] This helps institutionalize knowledge so if you step away from the effort, someone else can easily step in and pick up where you left off. The fear of scrutiny through regular reporting of impact (or lack thereof) can compel compliance. This process need not be confrontational. As we'll see in the case studies in subsequent chapters, there are many examples of policy implementers organizing consultations among relevant stakeholders to track delivery and identify gaps that need to be filled. Encourage relevant stakeholders to see you as a helpful partner rather than a nuisance, and give them adequate notice to respond if you publish an adverse report. Remember, you are interested in creating impact, not a gotcha moment!

(c) **Third-party verification:** Independent third parties can verify and authenticate claims. For example, the UN Human Rights system has several so-called special rapporteurs, whose job is to fact-check the claims made by governments and then release their findings publicly. However, such a system requires funding and some level of access to function effectively (see "Step 6: Leveraging Your Partners' Strengths"). The development of digital tokenization and blockchain technologies may also be a powerful way to boost transparency and hold those who make promises accountable, such as ensuring funds go where they were pledged. It would also enable the legitimacy of claims to be verified.

---

[3] My thanks to PriceWaterhouseCoopers, especially Paul Chew and Prashan Nimalan, for helping us build out an accountability framework. See PwC n.d.

(d) **Renegotiation on reasonable terms:** When difficulties arise during policy implementation, consider strategies such as renegotiation, third-party intervention, or postponing the commitment. Trust and open communication are vital in these decisions. Various challenges may hinder implementation, and not all are within the implementing authority's control. For example, the COVID-19 pandemic disrupted many promises governments made worldwide, especially in developing countries.[4] Resources were redirected away from existing priorities to meet the crisis. Without increased levels of aid, it would have been unfair to criticize a government of a poor country for delaying investment in infrastructure [3]. Blame should be tempered with understanding if appropriate, and support should be extended to help those in vulnerable situations to meet their commitments.

Sustaining Policy Implementation for the Long Term

"There has to be an organization calling us all out and asking, are you doing what you said you're going to do? Because, let's be honest, many people make promises just to get elected. And then they never actually deliver" [4].
—Jennifer Jones, president of Rotary International (2022–23)

To effectively hold decision makers accountable, it is helpful to identify other advocates and implementers who share the same passion and commitment. This becomes even more critical when dealing with long-term policy delivery that extends beyond our lifetimes. Developing a succession plan and securing long-term funding and

---

[4] Several countries' commitments we were tracking at Global Citizen fell into this category.

resources for sustaining ongoing advocacy efforts (as discussed in "Step 6: Leveraging Your Partners' Strengths") can be invaluable. Neglecting to do so can seriously jeopardize the long-term prospects of your policy ideas.

In 2007, Australian activists, mostly university students, persuaded the Australian government to double its foreign aid assistance. Over the following years, the aid budget increased to meet this promise. However, complacency, a lack of ongoing advocacy efforts, insufficient investment in campaign capacity, and a change in government in 2013 resulted in a collapse of support and significant cuts to the aid program. Unfortunately, the Australian aid sector still struggles to reorganize itself consistently, conducive to reversing this stance, leaving Australian aid levels significantly below those of similar wealthy nations.

In contrast, in 2014, then–Prime Minister Tony Abbott received three standing ovations from 20,000 Rotarians for pledging A$100 million toward polio eradication. He was even given Rotary's most prestigious award for a world leader. However, in Australia, prime ministers do not have a long life span, and Abbott was replaced a year later. One of the first things the subsequent government did was make cuts, including those affecting polio. This turned out to be a bad idea. 40,000 Australian Rotarians rose up in arms. They wrote, emailed, and called their local officials. It worked. The government brought forward its funding, and since then, governments from both sides of politics have offered bipartisan support to the polio effort.

One practical approach to ensuring the long-term sustainability of change efforts is establishing and securing funds for a dedicated advocacy organization to oversee the work of tracking, evaluating, sustaining public support, and pursuing legal and non-legal avenues to maintain buy-in and ensure full policy implementation. Philanthropist Patrick Grace recounts how his father, businessman J. Peter Grace, recognized this necessity in the 1980s. After producing a report for President Reagan on potential government savings, Grace understood that without an ongoing advocacy organization to engage with members of Congress, none of the 1.6 million page report's recommendations would be implemented. The report would simply gather dust [5]. As a result, Grace joined forces with a journalist, Jack Anderson, and established the Citizens Against Government Waste organization to advocate for the Commission's recommendations. Originally, US$425 billion in government savings were projected. But once the recommendations were implemented, US$1 trillion was saved by 2000. Grace Jr. estimates that US$2.4 trillion has been saved to date.

Investing time and effort into building the foundations necessary for implementing long-term systemic change is difficult because we may not be around to see the total payoff. It also doesn't help satisfy the thirst for that quick dopamine high that comes from channeling our short-term emotions into protests, solidarity social media posting, and other reactionary tactics. And yet, no one lives forever. Sometimes, we must put aside what we want to win today to ask ourselves what we can build that will last forever.

One last benefit of establishing long-lasting advocacy organizations is that they also can help communicate the actual impact being achieved. This is critical for encouraging ongoing buy-in for further policy reform efforts from relevant stakeholders. This brings us to the final step.

Step 8: Communicate Stories of Success

"There is much . . . reason to be hopeful for the future. . . .
We can make a difference because we have made a
difference" [6].
                    —Kathryn Sikkink, author, *Evidence for Hope*

Real stories give us hope [7]. They show us that our actions matter. When you've translated a commitment into tangible impact, share that story with your networks. Inspiring others to believe in the potential for change is crucial for driving progress and countering disillusionment in the state of democracy and global solidarity [8].

Success stories, particularly those achieved through collaboration, can motivate and unite people [9]. This effect is even more profound when shared by individuals we know and trust within our circles.

Here's a personal example: Not long after the success of my first campaign, The End of Polio (discussed in "Step 1: Know Your Policy Goal"), an article profiled the campaign in a local newspaper and drew significant interest. Shortly afterward, I was contacted by a nine-year-old named Josie and her mother, Lorraine. They asked me for help with their campaign to save elephants in Bali, Indonesia to address the issue of illegal hunting. I agreed to meet with them, and together, we brainstormed how they could launch a local petition and collect signatures from her school community. She later presented the petition to her local senator, who agreed to present it to the Australian government. Soon, Josie was sharing her own story on a local radio station about her efforts to make a difference as a primary school student. I often wondered how many other school students listened to her story and felt inspired to take action. People naturally seek and are drawn to relatable, solution-orientated stories.

Here are some important considerations when communicating your story:

1. Be sure to give credit where it's due and thank all the partners who have contributed. This fosters long-term loyalty among your audience. Remember, your future impact increases from stronger relationships when you're willing to defer credit to others and forgo personal glory. Find ways to empower stakeholders who played a key role, making them feel like heroes in your story. This is especially crucial for public officials who value looking good. Remember to extend this recognition to your funders to keep them motivated. They may be more likely to support future initiatives, allowing you to leverage the infrastructure and partnerships you've built for other issues.

2. Sharing lessons learned provides a blueprint for others to follow, offering insights and the means to implement solutions in

their local contexts. Every situation is unique, but there are always valuable takeaways that can be applied. Lessons from seemingly unrelated areas may prove crucial in addressing similar challenges. If your approach succeeds, it could inspire others to adopt and scale your policy goal.

For instance, Sweden's commitment to building a fossil-free steel industry is partly motivated by its potential to set an example for other countries with heavy industrial and manufacturing sectors [10]. It showcases what a successful transition to fossil-free practices can look like, supporting jobs and livelihoods while benefiting the environment.

3. Avoid declaring victory prematurely, even if you aim to maintain supporter motivation. Most people remember the image of George W Bush's "Mission Accomplished" declaration in what turned out to be just the start of America's long and costly involvement in Iraq. While communicating milestones is essential, claiming false victories can lead to misplaced hope and long-lasting disillusionment if performance later ends up lacking. Instead, if implementation is off track, use it as an opportunity to reengage partners in a constructive conversation about how to remedy the situation.

No one can deny that the COVID-19 vaccine rollout was grossly inequitable. Poor nations had to wait while wealthy nations hoarded all the available vaccine supply. Millions died unnecessarily due to the uneven distribution of vaccines in many parts of the world. However, *The-delivery.org* website powerfully showcases what had been achieved through the collaborative efforts of countries and organizations, including the World Health Organization, throughout the 1,221 days of the COVID-19 pandemic to ensure global vaccine accessibility. The account celebrates "the fastest development of vaccines" ever and one of the fastest, most effective, and far-reaching vaccine rollouts in history. Simultaneously, it candidly identifies valuable lessons for the future. After all, 28% of the world's population remained unvaccinated. Transparency around what could be improved is crucial for future fundraising efforts. It allows donors to assess how the impact of their contributions can be maximized while demonstrating how universal vaccine access can be achieved if learnings are properly shared and implemented.

Success Stories
of Policy
Entrepreneurs

In the Annex section of this book, I've summarized the eight steps to become a successful policy entrepreneur. While there's no one-size-fits-all approach, real-life stories demonstrate how each one of us can apply these steps in their own way. In the upcoming four chapters, we'll delve into examples at the grassroots, community, national, and global levels. These show how policy ideas have made a real impact, addressing challenges such as helping small island nations withstand natural disasters, keeping girls in school, transitioning away from coal, and fostering international cooperation.

Each chapter maintains a similar structure. It begins with a story highlighting breakthrough moments where ideas moved from talk to action. It then outlines the challenge faced by the idea in question. The crux of the chapter is then spent dissecting how policy entrepreneurs-visionaries, diplomats, and implementers-successfully achieved their policy goals. While not exhaustive, I have highlighted the most relevant steps in each case.

Above all, these stories testify to the practicality of this playbook. I hope they inspire others to forge a meaningful and lasting impact in their neighborhood, community, or nation.

4

Advancing Access: Equal Education for All

I'm in a car traveling through Gauteng on the outskirts of Johannesburg, South Africa. One of the wealthiest provincial regions on the African Continent, Gauteng is also among the most unequal.

I'm joined in the car by "Jeanne," who works with a multinational consumer goods corporation. Jeanne oversees many of the company's community service commitments—including ending period poverty and keeping girls in school.

"We have a problem with implementation," Jeanne explains as she steers the car through the surrounding townships to a school where her company provides menstrual hygiene education and products in partnership with local NGO Footprints Foundation. "In South Africa, we have all of these wonderful policies and laws that are beautiful on paper, but we struggle to make it a reality."

When Nelson Mandela became South Africa's first post-apartheid president in 1994, he prioritized gender equality and girls' education, Jeanne recounts. The country's new constitution recognized equal education as a fundamental right. However, numerous barriers, including access to period products, still keep far too many girls out of school. This is particularly the case in impoverished South African communities where menstruation remains the subject of taboo, stigma, and shame.

We arrive at the school, and the contrast is starck compared to the modern, pristine buildings in Johannesburg's affluent inner-city Sandton district. The school building is no more than a shack, yet children's laughter emanates from the playground.

The headmaster, Solomon, welcomes us, and we proceed to an assembly area where the school's teenage female students have gathered. As we walk, Solomon shares that most of these girls come from households with monthly incomes of R2,000 (US$130–150) or even less. Many parents work in the informal economy, and many others are unemployed altogether.

Taking our seats in the front row, we observe a passionate menstrual hygiene instructor addressing the girls while handing out free period products. Once the workshop ends, the instructor asks the girls to repeat after her in loud, bold, confident voices, "I am beautiful." They enthusiastically chant in unison, "I AM BEAUTIFUL." For these girls, having access to period products represents a step closer to completing their education and with it a fulfilling life. However, the same cannot be said for all girls nationwide.

Change may be on the horizon, driven by a diverse coalition led by grassroots activists who draw from their lived experiences. The corporate-funded program I observed represents the tip of the iceberg of a much larger movement in South Africa and globally dedicated to empowering girls and protecting their education. Their mission is clear: replicating the program I witnessed in schools everywhere.

★★★★★

Six Weeks Later
December 2018
FNB Stadium, Soweto, Johannesburg

At the 2018 Global Citizen Festival: Mandela 100 ("Mandela 100"), featuring Beyoncé, Jay-Z, Pharrell Williams, Ed Sheeran, and Chris Martin, a 90,000-strong crowd passionately chants, "She Is Equal." The atmosphere sizzles with energy, yet backstage, anxiety and alarm are palpable.

Cyril Ramaphosa, the President of South Africa, is about to arrive on site. However, we've just received an advance copy of his prepared remarks from his chief of staff. A few days earlier, we were assured that he would address a pressing issue that has garnered significant attention: period poverty in schools.

To our surprise, the president's speech lacks any new commitment.

Expectations are high. Many young people in the audience have passionately supported this campaign and will be disappointed at this lackluster response. We relay this back to the president's chief of staff. The response back is not encouraging.

Suddenly, we receive word that the president is heading toward us next to the stage. Before we have a moment to react, he's seated beside us. We can barely hear each other with our headphones on amid the blaring music. It's a surreal moment. We lean in and, shouting to be heard, express our belief that he is about to miss an opportunity to address the countless petitions, emails, and phone calls his government has received.

The president takes a moment to reflect. Then, he grabs his iPad and quickly edits his speech. Shortly after, Oprah (yes, the Oprah!) calls him to the stage.

His voice echoes throughout the stadium as he proclaims: "Nelson Mandela has taught us that it is not the influential, the rich, or the powerful who make history, but those citizens who are determined to make a difference. . . . **We have heard the call of**

the girl child who is deprived of education because she cannot afford sanitary products. . . . We have heard these calls, and together, we will act to create a better life for all of us. . . . Here, in the southernmost tip of Africa, we too have heeded the call of the Global Citizen" [1].

The applause that follows is deafening. However, in a country where grand promises often fall short of action, some in the audience can't help but feel skeptical. After all, seven years earlier, there was hope when former President Jacob Zuma had first highlighted the need to address period poverty in his State of the Nation address. However, this supposedly game-changing speech had yielded little results, leaving campaigners with a sense of disappointment—a sentiment all too familiar to everyday advocates worldwide who tirelessly fight for promises, even those related to fundamental rights and necessities, to be fulfilled.

As the initial excitement following President Ramaphosa's speech begins to subside, pressing questions linger: How exactly does he plan to heed the cries of those in period poverty? How much funding will genuinely be allocated to provide access to period products and education? How many girls will be able to stay in school?

The Challenge: Keeping Girls in School

"Sanitary dignity in South Africa means that every girl, child, and woman in the country can manage their menstruation in a dignified manner. This means that all girls and women, irrespective of socioeconomic status, will have the menstrual information and knowledge; menstrual products; safe, hygiene and private spaces to carry out their menstrual health practices and will be able to walk away from these activities feeling clean and hygienic" [2].
                —Maite Nkoana-Mashabane, Minister of Women,
                Youth and Persons with Disabilities (2019–2023)

In a flourishing society, contributions are valued from everyone, including women and girls, who make up half the population. Realizing this is contingent on ensuring that girls have equal access to quality education. Such access is vital for them to realize their full potential, contribute meaningfully to society, have a say in government, and, particularly in developing countries, play a pivotal role in breaking the cycle of poverty for themselves and their communities.[1]

Sadly, in countries worldwide, regardless of their wealth, size, or status, both boys and girls encounter everyday barriers to education. Girls and individuals who menstruate—referred to as menstruators[2]—face additional obstacles that put them at risk of being left behind simply because of something natural that should never be a hindrance: their periods.

Approximately 1.9 billion people, nearly a quarter of the world's population, have menstrual cycles [3]. To live a fulfilling life, menstruators need to ensure they have safe access to period products.[3] Unfortunately, at least 500 million menstruators globally face period poverty each month, meaning they lack access to period products or facilities to manage their periods properly [4].

Period poverty keeps girls in both developing and wealthier countries out of school when they can't control their periods [5]. Even in the US, the most affluent economy in the world, one in five teen girls miss school because of period poverty [6]. Meanwhile, four in five girls reportedly either cut class time themselves or knew someone else who did because they did not have access to period

---

[1] The World Bank calls investment in girls' education "the highest return on investment available in the developing world." It is also one of the best things we can invest in to mitigate climate change. See Patterson et al. 2021.

[2] Menstruators is an inclusive term for all people that menstruate, which includes cisgender women, transgender men, and non-binary and intersex people.

[3] I have used "safe period products," which encompass a wide range of products including pads, tampons, period underwear, and/or reusable pads/menstrual cups.

products [7]. Across sub-Saharan Africa, one in 10 girls miss school during their menstrual cycle [8]. In Kenya, for example, 95% of girls miss school for one to three days per month due to period poverty. Seventy percent of these report lower grades and over 50% feel they're falling behind in school [9–10].

As well as keeping girls out of school, period poverty can also place them in risky situations, leading to exploitation and human rights abuses. In a study in rural western Kenya, for instance, where many people live on less than a dollar a day, 10% of girls aged 15 or younger said they engaged in prostitution to get period products [11].

Period poverty results from many factors, including

- **Affordability:** In many countries, period products are still costly and taxed heavily. Some governments (including 30 states in the US) classify such products as luxury items; in other words, fancy stuff only rich people buy, rather than everyday essentials. So-called luxury taxes, or tampon taxes, make period products more expensive than regular goods.[4]
- **Social stigma:** Cultural beliefs, taboos, shame, and fear of teasing can exacerbate period poverty, keeping girls out of school [12]. For example, one student in Uganda recounts how a sanitary pad accidentally fell out in front of her classmates at school. She felt terribly ashamed as the other students laughed at her. She didn't go to school for two days because she was worried about how her fellow students would treat her [13].
- **Lack of education:** In South African schools, for instance, formal instruction on managing periods is lacking, especially in rural areas, where girls are less likely to attend regularly. Most learners share that they primarily learn about menstrual hygiene from their mothers. This lack of education has been found to result in many girls experiencing trauma when they menstruate [14].

---

[4] Though the tax on period products is technically a sales tax, the sector refers to it as a luxury tax because it is taxed similarly to nonessential items. See "What Is the Tampon Tax?" n.d.

Fortunately, in recent years, there has been a movement afoot—consisting of activists, companies, and governments—worldwide to end period poverty:

- Many countries have removed taxes on period products, such as Kenya, Nigeria, Malaysia, Lebanon, Tanzania, Ireland, Scotland, Colombia, and Mexico [15].
- More and more companies directly provide period education and products to communities and schools in need. Proctor & Gamble's Always Keeping Girls in School program is a case in point. It alone has donated over 50 million pads to more than one million disadvantaged girls across Africa since 2019 [16].
- A growing number of initiatives focus on challenging stigma and shame and boosting self-confidence through creating opportunities for women-owned businesses. In Uganda, making and selling reusable pads has become a source of income for families as well as addressing period poverty [17].

The following pages delve into the successful efforts of policy entrepreneurs, in this case, activists in South Africa. It explores how they have addressed period poverty through securing government commitments, holding relevant stakeholders accountable for delivering these promises (like that made by President Ramaphosa at Mandela 100), and ultimately improved the lives of millions of girls. Their collective efforts demonstrate potent strategies to ensure that lofty and noble promises are transformed into tangible reality. These insights are undoubtedly transferrable to addressing other equity issues marred by neglect, taboos, or outright discrimination.

Before the start of these efforts in 2018, the situation across South Africa was dire. Studies released up to 2020 showed the following:

- Around 35% of its 22 million women and girls who have their period every month have to choose between a loaf of bread and a period product [18].

- One in seven school-age girls reportedly do not have access to period products while menstruating [19].
- Over four million women and girls in schools, universities, and sports clinics miss approximately five days of education and training a month during their monthly cycles. This amounts to 60 missed school days, because they cannot access or afford period products [20].
- In total, almost 1 in 3 South African girls miss school while on their period [21].
- Only one in three students said they received period products from school [22].

Policy Entrepreneurship in Action: Ending Period Poverty

Know Your Policy Goal

Before President Ramaphosa's promise at the end of 2018, addressing period poverty in South Africa faced several challenges even though the government acknowledged menstrual health as a fundamental human right [23]. These included the absence of a national law to ensure access to affordable period products [24]. Related to this was the need for more funding across the various provincial governments, especially those with many no-fee schools in poorer areas. As a result, activists had a twofold policy goal focused on ensuring the affordability and availability of period products:

1. Removal of sales tax on period products. By the time activist networks began advocating with South Africa's government in 2018, several countries across Africa, such as Kenya and Uganda, and countries globally, such as Canada and Australia, had already eliminated such taxes on period products.

2. Securing government commitment and implementing a nationally funded strategy encompassing the free provision

of period products and education in schools, particularly in poorer provinces. By October 2018, South Africa's menstrual equity advocates sought to persuade the South African government to allocate at least two years of funding to provide free period products to these schools.

Know Which Stakeholders Matter and How to Appeal to Them

"It's important to leave the comfort and the predictability of your office and listen to what broader South Africa is saying. Lest you are trapped in your own dogma" [25].

—Sipiwo Matshoba, Women, Youth &
Persons with Disabilities, South Africa

When addressing period poverty in South Africa, particularly among school-going teenage girls, there are three primary stakeholder groups: community activists, boys, and the government. Let's start with the policy entrepreneur—community activists—at the forefront of change.

Community Activists

Many activists addressing period poverty in South Africa are motivated by their personal experiences. They work to break taboos, advocate for separate boy/girl bathrooms, solicit donations from businesses, and fundraise for the so-called "dignity packs" containing essential hygiene and period products.

Candice Chirwa, in her late 20s, earned the title "minister of menstruation" due to her unwavering dedication as a menstruation activist, speaker, and academic [26]. Chirwa attributes the shame she felt during her first menstruation as her primary motivation to take action. "There was little to no discussion about periods," she tells me. In response, Chirwa founded the nonprofit organization Qrate, which challenges stigma among young people, including boys. Through Qrate, Chirwa today hosts engaging workshops that provide comprehensive menstrual and sex education. Her mission is to replace subjective and restrictive myths with objective and helpful period advice and tips, ensuring that menstruators receive the support they deserve. In her words, it is about eradicating "the fear a young person might feel when they have their first period" [27].

Figure 4.1 Period education class.
Source: Gideon Fakomogbon / BeyGOOD Fellow

The strength of South Africa's menstrual equity movement, exemplified by the likes of Chirwa, lies in the informal yet powerful collaboration among its activists. Bound together by their shared experiences, over the last decade, they have formed networks around the idea that advocating for national policy goals is necessary to achieve systemic change across the country in the long term rather than addressing period poverty school by school. Nokuzola Ndwandwe, a campaigner from Durban living with endometriosis, which causes severe menstrual pain, has played a pivotal role in these policy change efforts, having advocated against tampon taxes since 2014.

Sustaining these networks among themselves and appealing to the broader gender equity and feminist movements to get buy-in has not always been easy. At times, menstrual equity activists face backlash within these broader movements, stemming from differing views, such as the use of the term "menstruator," which some feminist activists feel is dismissive of their lived experiences as women. Nonetheless, alongside these activists, several influential and critical NGOs also added their voices, including Mimi Women, WaterAid, Days for Girls, and many others.

Boys

South Africa, like many countries, grapples with deep-seated gender inequality, biases, and prejudices, underscored by high rates of sexual assault and gender-based violence. One particularly prevalent idea is that menstruation illustrates the inferiority of women and girls as compared to men and boys [28]. To combat stigma and taboo in this context, it is vital to shatter the silence around menstruation and actively involve both genders. This is especially important given that boys, in particular, would eventually grow up and assume leadership roles in government, business, and the community. To this end, from 2018 onward, Chirwa created resources for parents and teachers to educate children about menstruation. She conducted workshops to empower girls to discuss their periods, addressing stigma head-on openly. Boys were encouraged to join these workshops. "We use a role-play where a boy experiences a period for the first time, which captivates their attention and gets them involved," Chirwa explains. The hope is that biases will gradually disappear, and men and boys will become ardent supporters of policy change supporting menstrual equity.

Government

From the outset, it was evident that the South African government, under Ramaphosa's leadership in Pretoria, possessed the power to drive change. Even if provincial governments would eventually be responsible for implementing access to free period products in schools, they still relied on the South African government for funding. Yet, getting traction was difficult; as Chirwa pointed out, "It's often men who are predominantly in decision-making roles, determining priorities."

Despite the efforts of activists in preceding years to challenge stigma and taboos, deep-seated biases and prejudices persisted among the gatekeepers within the government. Many gatekeepers, including advisors, staffers, and cabinet ministers, were not intentionally against the movement's policy goals; their involvement in the anti-apartheid movement had left them with a profound commitment to social justice. Some had even endured imprisonment and torture during the turbulent 1970s and 1980s when clashes between security forces and anti-apartheid activists intensified.

While there were champions of the feminist movement among these veteran activists, such as Phumzile Mlambo-Ngcuka, the former deputy president of South Africa and head of UN Women, the influence of patriarchy ran deep. Even today, it's not uncommon to hear government ministers openly share stories of extramarital affairs with other women on official trips or boast that having a mistress signifies masculinity. This is often met with pride by their male peers while leaving the rest of those in the conversation feeling uncomfortable. These overt expressions of gender bias were not the only challenges faced by activists.

Sometimes, stigma takes a more subtle and subconscious form, often seen in policymakers, predominantly men, who may not consider specific issues essential or worthy of attention, leading to real-life consequences such as underinvestment. In an early conversation about period poverty following my first encounter with the South African movement, I informed a government official about its significance in mobilizing people for action. Their response, asserting that the issue was trivial compared to others and unworthy of focus at a prestigious event such as Mandela 100, highlighted the challenge of prioritizing a neglected issue among those in power. South Africa's activists, already successful in putting forth a clear vision of policy goals, needed allies and supporters who could help them cut through the noise, shape the agenda, and get presidential attention. This would also provide much-needed ammunition for public cover for the many sympathetic supporters, including the then finance minister, who supported tackling the issue.

Leveraging Your Partners' Strengths

South African activists sought Global Citizen's platform as soon as the Mandela 100 Festival was announced in mid-2018. When we were invited by the South African government and the Mandela family to hold an event in honor of Nelson Mandela's centenary, I didn't antici-pate that period poverty would take center stage.

When Global Citizen first unveiled the Mandela 100 Festival campaign, the hashtag #ItsBloodyTime surged in popularity, stand-ing alongside #Beyoncé and #Mandela100 on the trending charts. Recognizing that this campaign needed to be by and for the people, we enthusiastically backed these activists and NGOs such as Mimi Women, ensuring it was indeed a "bloody time" for change.

Shortly after, South African activists, such as Nokuzola Ndwandwe and university students, had a breakthrough in addressing taxes on period products. In October 2018, students rallied and marched under the hashtag #BecauseWeBleed, making it a trend on what was then known as Twitter. By the end of the month, they received an announce-ment from the government that sanitary napkins would be tax-exempt beginning in April 2019.

Building on this success, in the crucial month leading up to Mandela 100 in December 2018, South Africans took nearly 100,000 actions urging the government to fund free sanitary products for schools. These ranged from signing petitions to calling government officials and tweet-ing at the ministers responsible for funding allocation. The goal was to get the president of South Africa himself to respond at the Mandela 100 Festival and commit to providing the funding.

One action-taker was Palesa Mokoenanyane, a 28-year-old from Johannesburg, who was inspired to join the Mandela 100 Festival campaign to address period poverty in South Africa. She had previously used her social media to donate period products to support Lets Pad South Africa, an organization that distributes period products to schools in poorer communities. After hearing about Mandela 100 on a radio show, she registered as an action-taker. Famous names joined alongside citizen action-taking as the campaign peaked in late November 2018, just days from the Mandela 100 Festival. South African TV presenter Bonang Matheba and US TV presenter Gayle King joined Global Citizen in advocating for change. Matheba, a staunch supporter of girls' education, even directly tweeted Ramaphosa, urging him to invest in menstrual health.

Alongside citizen action-taking, by October 2018, activists such as Chirwa and Ndwandwe in the classroom were joining activists in the boardroom to shine a light on the pressing need for girls in school. For example, Procter & Gamble was already providing free Always sanitary pads to 13,000 schoolgirls annually as part of their corporate social responsibility, which included providing funding to advocates working to destigmatize the issue and build support from the government [29].

With all this momentum, we arrived at the country's Parliament a few days before Mandela 100 with a substantial and thickly bound folder filled with nearly 100,000 petition signatures. I can still picture one of the official's stunned expression as we placed the folder before him. One of my colleagues, Dr. Okito Wedi, commented, "This is not from us but from your people, your constituents."

During this meeting, we received assurances that the message had been heard, and that the president himself would address it during his remarks at the festival. True to their word, we managed to secure a somewhat vague promise. In his remarks, the president pledged to keep girls in school and address period poverty. The question remained: How much of this commitment would be delivered, and how many girls would benefit from it? That would have to be sorted out in the aftermath. Still, the president's highly visible pledge provided a tangible commitment to follow up.

In the months following this announcement, the possibility of negative criticism from third parties and continued advocacy from concerned citizen advocates helped ensure government allocated funding to addressing period poverty in schools. As one minister in the South African Cabinet noted in early 2019, as it released its initial budgetary allocation, "Global citizens' campaigning helped us realize that South Africans wanted us to prioritize menstrual health management. In considering the priorities of our 2019 budget, we took this into account and decided to make this commitment" [30].

Ultimately, in 2019, as an initial follow-up to its 2018 announcement, the South African government officially launched the Sanitary Dignity Programme (SDP). This initiative addressed the two policy goals mentioned earlier, making significant progress. In April 2019, the government fulfilled its commitment to eliminate the 15% value-added tax on sanitary pads (although taxes on tampons and other products persisted).

Furthermore, to honor President Ramaphosa's promise at Mandela 100, the government allocated R157 million (over US$11 million) in funding for provincial governments to provide free period products and education in public schools. While this funding alone did not cover all girls in need, it doubled the previous budget. Between 2018 and 2019, Mpumalanga Province in the country's east successfully reached 69,000 students. Nonetheless, this still fell short of the R400 million the government projected was needed to meet intended students [31]. The idea was that the budget would increase annually as part of a phased approach to scale up and eventually benefit, over subsequent years, an estimated 3.8 million menstruators across the country's no-fee schools, farms, and special schools.

Ultimately, South Africa's commitment to menstrual equity activists reinforces two crucial lessons:

Firstly, when you need to captivate political attention, consider tapping into and leveraging existing high-profile platforms instead of starting from scratch (the costs of which might be prohibitive to most community activists). Event organizers may be open to supporting your cause if your intentions are just and your policy goal is clear.

Secondly, meaningful impact requires having the right individuals and organizations in the right positions to leverage their strengths. Sadly, people (and organizations) too often find themselves in roles ill-suited to them. The collaboration outlined earlier demonstrates a combination of unique stakeholders leveraging their strengths— activism, high-profile campaigning, media, social media, and, most importantly, government—to complement one another and achieve a policy win.

Inspired by this example, Global Citizen, along with various partners, including DDB for Good, Plan India, the Miss Universe Organization (including Miss Universe 2021 Harnaaz Sandhu who helped conceive the idea), P&G, and Changing Our World, launched the Global Menstrual Equity Accelerator in September 2022 [32]. This coalition unites diverse partners to address stigma and affordability issues, mobilize resources, advocate for policy change, and provide global education about periods. Its goal is to support over 500 million women and girls globally.

Know Your Endgame

"We are trying to break down the silo mentality [because] when we operate in parallel, and are not in competition with one another, this eventually improves the impact on the ground" [33].
—Thobile Mthiyane, deputy director at the Department of
Water and Sanitation

Since promises to address period poverty were first made in 2011, South Africa's menstrual equity activists have learned a crucial lesson: securing a government commitment is merely the first step. While the path to progress has been anything but linear, much progress has been achieved since the latest promises made in 2018. Those in positions of power have been held accountable through rigorous monitoring, ongoing consultation, and transparent reporting, often further motivated to deliver by the potential for adverse public scrutiny. However, the collaborative synergy between the government, activists, and other vital stakeholders stands out. This partnership has helped to foster trust and a shared commitment to transparency, providing a fertile ground for driving ongoing improvements in the battle against period poverty.

In 2019, the South African government's Department of Women, Youth and Persons with Disabilities (DWYPD) was tasked with coordinating and monitoring the SDP, with implementation occurring at the provincial level. DWYPD's Sipiwo Matshoba oversees the SDP and regularly visits the provinces.

Matshoba led efforts in 2020 to establish the South African Coalition on Menstrual Health Management to foster trust and collaboration by regularly convening quarterly calls with relevant stakeholders [34]. These include international agencies such as the United Nations Population Fund (UNFPA), NGOs such as WaterAid, the Footprints Foundation, and Days for Girls, as well as grassroots activists such as Chirwa. This open-door forum welcomes anyone interested in contributing, and Matshoba provides transparent updates on the SDP's status, encouraging feedback on program delivery. More stakeholders and companies are joining the conversation, and the stigma surrounding menstruation is gradually fading, if not entirely eradicated. Matshoba underscores the vital importance of partnerships and acknowledges the financial challenges of reaching every girl to address period poverty nationwide. He states: "It will be fair and objective to bring in partners that we have worked with because we were very clear about this as a government that this is not something that we can journey alone. Therefore, we need partnerships outside of government as well" [35]. Notably, Matshoba views the participation and questions from advocates not as a nuisance but as valuable input that contributes to improving the SDP's implementation. This constructive approach also reflects the collaborative spirit of the activists and other stakeholders.

A multi-stakeholder coordinated approach paid dividends in reaching girls during recent times of crisis. In 2019, floods in Kwa-Zulu Natal and in 2020, the COVID-19 pandemic disrupted the program, with no products being delivered to any school in any province during the COVID-lockdowns [36]. In Gauteng province, funds initially allocated for the program were redirected to provide essential food parcels. Procter & Gamble, Footprints Foundation, and UNFPA stepped in to offer disposable sanitary pads, and NGOs such as WaterAid and Days for Girls offered educational resources on how to use them [37]. UNFPA also coordinated workshops in select provinces to help address stigma and myths [38].

Of course, the government is a complex machine. Matshoba is not responsible for the SDP's funding resources—politicians and the country's Parliament are. Nevertheless, the information from DWYPD empowers activists and stakeholders to pressure the government to maintain or increase its support. In this effort, consistent and unrelenting calls from supporters played a vital role in ensuring the government does not become complacent. This includes the continued unwavering determination of activists such as Nokuzola Ndwandwe and Candice Chirwa. "We've marched, and we've pushed," as Chirwa put it.

Additionally, these activists have identified and cultivated champions for menstrual equity within the country's Parliament. In 2021, concerns arose about the perceived slow pace of reporting, program delivery, and transparency. In response, concerned parliamentarians inquired about these matters during parliamentary sessions [39]. DWYPD clarified that from 2022 onward, they had delegated substantial responsibility for reporting to provincial departments. They argued that the provincial departments were better equipped to provide funding information for these programs since they received the funds directly. The fact that members of the South African Parliament are now actively probing these issues represents a significant departure from the situation a decade earlier when discussing the topic was more taboo.

Some impressive results have been achieved between 2019 and 2023 thanks to this inclusive monitoring, consultation, and reporting process, as well as ongoing public and political pressure. Firstly, the government's commitment to addressing period poverty has remained steadfast, with subsequent years seeing continued or increased funding notwithstanding crises such as the COVID-19 pandemic:

- In the fiscal year 2020/21, R209 million (US$14 million) was allocated for the free distribution of menstrual hygiene products to impoverished schools, marking a significant 30% increase compared to 2019/20 [40].
- Support has continued to increase year on year. By the 2023/24 financial year, the government was allocating R235 million toward the SDP (although bear in mind that inflation has also increased over this period) [41]. The disbursements to each of the provinces have continued to increase year on year since 2018.

DWYPD has committed to approaching the National Treasury to evaluate the impact of removing sales tax on period products and will conduct a comprehensive evaluation of the SDP's impact between 2024 and 2025. Nonetheless, it is difficult to deny that these policies have already significantly affected girls' lives. By the end of 2021, 2.3 million students had received period products [42]. As of the end of 2023, since the SDP launched in 2019, more than 4.3 million students have been reached [43]. Anecdotal evidence also suggests that period product prices have also shown signs of decreases after making them tax-exempt [44]. Ndwandwe characterizes this as a "monumental victory." Perhaps most significantly, these initiatives promoted self-confidence and challenged taboo. A third-party study showed that the acceptability of sanitary pads went from 3% to 55% after the SDP began and the education workshops began to be rolled out at a greater scale [45].

Nonetheless, while the SDP has already reached its initial target of 3.8 million individuals across all no-fee schools, much work must be done to address period poverty throughout the country. While incrementally increasing its budget, per its decision in 2019 to phase up funding gradually, it still needs to catch up to the R400 million projected need. As of 2023, approximately 7 million girls nationwide still lack access to period products [46].

Notably, several challenges remain. Firstly, ongoing reporting from provincial governments has been mixed in terms of the level of detail on how funds are used. This effort to collate reliable data has been complicated. This is especially the case in those provinces controlled by a political party different from Ramaphosa's African National Congress, which controls the South African government. Moreover, there are some concerns over accountability around the use of funds. In a province where funds allocated for period products were misused, authorities failed to secure any successful prosecutions [47]. Ndwandwe is identifying and bringing other voices into the discussion to ensure the issue stays on the political agenda and drives accountability at the provincial government level, where much of the money is spent (or even misspent). "Provinces do their own thing. There is no structure. There is no accountability. We can't monitor or track what is happening" [48].

Secondly, other concerns and frustrations revolve around the urgency of delivery and inadequate budget allocations, including essential services such as education workshops to teach girls how to manage their periods [49]. Advocates also point out that a significant issue is ensuring menstruators have access to safe spaces and separate bathrooms, which is still a challenge in many schools despite increased efforts since 2019 to address it.

Thirdly, Chirwa contends that the government could do more to explore cost-saving opportunities by promoting reusable over single-use products (which meet menstruators' needs for a more extended period). Challenges also exist in ensuring efficient transportation and delivery of period products to those in need.

Lastly, despite the significant progress made, the emphasis on period product availability still needs to fully address the persistence of taboos in the country, including among school boys. Candice Chirwa sums it up: "It is still unacceptable [in some cases] to talk openly about menstruation, to make it visible. . . . Understand that the silence we continue by not talking openly about our periods has an impact on people who menstruate and go to school and work." In response, in early 2023, Chirwa launched the #PeriodPositiveTour, traveling across the country to promote menstrual education access [50].

Despite these ongoing challenges, the overall picture reflects that South Africa has made considerable strides in addressing period poverty and keeping more girls in school. Unlike previous instances when promises of access to period products were made but not fulfilled, this time, thanks to sustained activism of our policy entrepreneurs, there has been a notable improvement in implementation and follow-through. An additional four million girls have access to period products who otherwise wouldn't have.

Additionally, unlike in the past, the coalition set up by DWYPD provides an open forum to raise many of the challenges outlined openly and transparently, encouraging stakeholders to work through them collaboratively. Overall, this marks a successful ongoing story of implementation worth sharing.

Communicate Stories of Success

"In the years I've advocated with them [South Africa], I feel like of all the countries I've worked in, they really are putting menstrual health at the forefront. I know they have a lot of challenges with funding and other things, but they're doing what they can, and I have been really pleased with the progress that's been made" [51].

—Diana Nelson, Days for Girls

One area of surprise in researching the impact of South Africa's policies on period poverty was the degree to which not everyone, beyond those involved in the coalition, knew about it. As Chirwa noted upon hearing from Matshoba about university programs on menstrual equity, "I applaud the effort that the government and organizations are making. I wish this information were easily accessible as this is indeed good work."

The importance of sharing such stories of successful policy entrepreneurship and implementation should not be understated. Understanding what impact has been achieved is crucial to building trust in institutions and motivating others to get involved if they believe change is possible. It also helps build confidence among potential partners, including those in the private sector who can contribute funding toward the efforts and supplement the shortfall in government funding.

Fortunately, the government's commitment to publish an evaluation of the SDP by the end of 2025 will provide a focal point to communicate the program's positive impact and demonstrate what is possible through partnership, not just to South Africans but globally. UNFPA is also documenting stories and lessons learned [52]. After all, despite being a work in progress, South Africa has been one of the few countries in the world since 2019 to unconditionally commit finances and have a specific policy focused on ending period poverty. This sets a powerful blueprint and example for others to follow.

Already inspired by the progress achieved through their actions and the proof that their advocacy has made a difference, a new generation of activists is building on the efforts of campaigners such as Ndwandwe and Chirwa. They have launched campaigns to remove remaining taxes on all period products and are championing *The Menstrual Health Rights Bill*. Supported by a coalition of 31 organizations and the current speaker of the South African Parliament, who presented their petition in Parliament, this bill aims to establish access to menstrual products as a fundamental human right across the country. Framing it as a health issue, as well as a gender equity challenge, they have the ultimate goal of providing period products for free to society as a whole, along with a nationally funded plan to supply dignity kits for all girls in schools [53]. The journey toward a South Africa free of period poverty continues.

Conclusion

The period poverty movement in South Africa offers valuable lessons, not only for combating period poverty but also for addressing other forms of inequality and injustice, such as child marriage and gender-based violence. Their story illustrates how grassroots activists—the policy entrepreneurs—harnessed their strengths, leveraged networks, and held the government accountable for delivering on promised actions.

Most importantly, this narrative is a powerful example of partnership, collaboration, consultation, and perseverance in turning their vision of an equitable world into reality, thus granting millions of girls the opportunity to stay in school and lead fulfilling lives.

5 | Empowering a Community: Just Transition beyond Coal

June 14, 2022
Collie, Western Australia (WA)

It was an extraordinary moment.

In a room full of workers, anticipation hung in the air. Something unusual was about to happen.

Mark McGowan, Western Australia's premier, renowned for his rock star–like popularity due to successful management of the COVID-19 pandemic, is en route to the small town of Collie in the state's southwest.

With just over 7,500 residents, Collie is a small town located approximately two-and-a-half hours' drive from Perth, WA's capital city. As the state's most crucial coal town, Collie lies just west of its only coalfields. Once labeled a "dirty mining town," Collie's picturesque surroundings are, in fact, recognized as a sacred area by the Noongar people, the First Australians residing in WA's southwest [1]. For a century, its coalfields have powered the energy needs of WA's populous southwestern region, including Perth, home to most of its 2.6 million residents.

Donning a blue worker's jacket for the occasion, McGowan is accompanied by his minister for energy, Bill Johnson, as they prepare to make a significant announcement—one that will change the economy, but perhaps not the character of this little community forever.

Upon arriving, the pair are greeted by Jodie Hanns, the local representative for the Collie-Preston area in the Western Australian Parliament.

Hanns, a former school teacher whose husband works at one of the nearby coal-fired power stations, only won her parliamentary seat the previous year. She easily secured victory in the historic landslide reelection of McGowan's Labor Government, which won an unprecedented 53 out of 59 seats in the state legislature.

Premier McGowan insists on visiting the largest state-owned power plant in town, the Muja Power Station, which is not only the state's oldest but also recognized as one of the highest emitters of air pollution in Australia [2]. He wants to speak directly with the workers, avoiding the risk of intermediaries garbling his message.

The atmosphere is abuzz with speculation as the workers—including Hanns's husband—gather at the Muja Plant. People have been expecting this day for a while, and the whole town is charged with a sense that a significant moment—a day of reckoning, has finally arrived. The main question on most workers' minds is surely: What's in it for them, if anything? Will there be any new jobs or training opportunities? Will they and their families still be able to make ends meet in this cherished town?

Coal is deeply ingrained in Collie's identity. Coal mining and power generation have been the lifeblood of this close-knit community for generations—many in that room are third- or fourth-generation miners themselves. Attend any local barbecue—you won't have to wait long before conversations turn solely to coal mining and power generation. However, with the growing global momentum to address climate change and the surge in renewable energy, with coal power becoming increasingly expensive by comparison, even die-hard coal communities such as Collie can no longer avoid the inevitable.

And then it happens. The premier starts to address the assembled workers. McGowan is known for his directness and candor—it's why the people of WA fell in love with him when he closed the state's borders to the rest of the country during the pandemic. Without beating around the bush, he makes the announcement: the Western Australian government will shut its last coal-fired power plants by 2029.

The room falls silent at first, and then, surprisingly, someone starts to clap. And then, like a ripple effect, others join in until the entire room breaks out in applause.

One voice in the back asks, "Why are you clapping? He's just told us we've lost our jobs."

Another voice responds, "Because he actually bothered to come down here in person to tell us himself. That's a sign of respect for us as workers, and we should show him the same respect."

A year later, Jodie Hanns reflects, "So it was that moment, you know, which to me tells the story of how much work had been done behind the scenes with 'Just Transition.' That's the story."

Figure 5.1   Mark McGowan at a (socially distanced) press conference in 2022 after addressing workers at the Muja Power Station.
Credit: Mark Reed.

★★★★★★

The Challenge: Delivering a Just Transition Out of Coal

"Solar [has] become the king of electricity markets. The old king—coal—is over; now solar is the new king. Not only for climate reasons, but because it is cheap, the cost is coming down" [3].

—Dr. Fatih Birol, Executive Director, International Energy Agency

The end of coal is in sight for the US, Australia, and much of the world. It is no longer a matter of policy choice or a question of if, but when [4–5].[1] The need to avert catastrophic climate change demands it, but it is economics that is writing this obituary [6]. Although some politicians would like to believe the opposite, the cost competitiveness and rapid rise of clean energy alone have ensured that coal-fired electricity generation is in terminal decline in many parts of the world [7]. The only real choice facing coal communities, such as Western Australia's Collie, is whether their transition is just or not. This involves considering how society, more broadly, can support and protect workers and communities affected by the change.

Internationally, the phase-out of coal, while still the world's leading source of electricity generation, is well underway. Although hurdles remain due to conflict and entrenched interests, the trajectory is clear [8]. The US has retired the most coal capacity globally in the past decade. Many more of its power plants are scheduled for closure in the coming years [9–10].[2] Europe has seen several countries achieve

---

[1] Regarding China, despite the construction of new coal-fired power plants, many are anticipated to stay idle, functioning as backups for wind and solar panels—technologies gradually replacing coal for baseload electricity. The Chinese government has implemented a compensation mechanism for plant owners facing losses due to idleness. The impact of this approach on the transition's duration and cost is the subject of debate and may create new winners and losers if mishandled. Chinese authorities will increasingly grapple with how best to implement a just transition from coal in the coming years. See Ambrose 2023; Hove 2023.

[2] However, a few notable exceptions, such as Poland, have set unreasonably lengthy deadlines. See next footnote.

nationwide coal phase-outs.[3] This momentum extends beyond wealthy nations. Climate-vulnerable Bangladesh contributes just 0.46% of global emissions. Yet it has canceled 10 power plant projects worth $12 billion in foreign investments [11–12]. As of April 2023, almost one-third of the world's 2,400 coal-fired power stations have scheduled closure dates. Wealthier nations have set retirement dates for 70% of their power plants [13].

While international efforts to phase out coal are gaining momentum, the assurance of just transitions remains uncertain. History is filled with chaotic, hasty, and clumsy examples where workers and sometimes entire communities have been left behind. Northern England still bears the economic scars of its abrupt and sudden transition from coal in the 1980s [14]. What was once South Africa's largest coal-fired power station closed in October 2022 without giving workers and the surrounding community enough time to adequately prepare [15]. The fear is that this fate may await other coal communities worldwide without proper planning and leadership. For example, in Germany, concerns exist about the current deadline to switch off its remaining power plants by 2038. This target is set eight years after the 2030 deadline recommended for wealthy nations by climate science [16]. There's fear that as the urgency of climate change becomes more evident and external pressure mounts on Germany to expedite its transition, coal-reliant regions may face new abrupt deadlines, causing severe hardship. This would be a catastrophic failure of leadership, and the resulting upheaval risks widening divisions and triggering a public backlash that may delay broader efforts to address climate change [17–18].

The failure of past transitions is perhaps why there is pushback to the phrase "just transition" in different parts of the world amid speculation on whether they are even possible to implement. A former Australian government minister described its use as "highly objectionable," dismissing it as a euphemism for job destruction [19]. Similarly, in Alberta, Canada—a region renowned for its oil export-driven wealth—one politician has described "just transition"

---

[3] Poland has cynically set a phase-out deadline of 2049. See IEA 2021.

as "polarizing" and code for adversely "restructuring society . . . and redistributing wealth" [20]. Sometimes, to be sure, politicians who make such statements may simply be looking to delay the inevitable to protect entrenched interests. In other cases, however, at its core, such distrust and backlash may be less about the term "just transition" itself and more about concern over whether affected workers and communities are being asked to shoulder a disproportionate amount of the transition's costs.

As WA union leader Steve McCartney points out, "The only reason it's not working is because it is not just" [21]. To illustrate the viability of a just transition, let's look at the example of Collie. Being warned from the outset by colleagues in other Australian states that pursuing a just transition from coal was a fool's errand because "it doesn't work and backfires," McCartney was one of the earliest champions of this cause in WA [22].

To begin with, however, his colleagues appeared to be correct. McCartney recounts a story from 2007 when he first spoke to the coal workers in Collie to ask them what they wanted out of a just transition given coal's expected decline. "I was run out of town that day," he says, not before getting abused "for a couple of hours" by 200 or so people. One worker, pointing out that McCartney wasn't from the town and so did not get it, declared, "'The first thing that happens in Collie when a baby boy is born is he gets his mother's tit in his mouth. And the second thing is a piece of f**king coal . . .' that's when I knew I was starting to lose the audience" [23]. They cheered as McCartney retreated from the hall.

Fifteen years later, however, the community applauded the announcement of Collie's just transition and the plant's closure. A lot had changed since that first meeting.

The following pages examine how community leaders, union representatives, employers, and government officials established common ground to implement a just transition in Collie, accepted by the community. This story showcases policy entrepreneurship in action at the community level. Its takeaways are transferable to other coal communities or fossil fuel transitions and to different situations requiring accommodating local interests to achieve a greater societal purpose.

Policy Entrepreneurship in Action: Calling Time on Coal

Know Your Policy Goal

> "The government usually comes into these things with a preconceived idea of how they will save the day. And that's why just transitions don't work ... The community wanted to own the outcome" [24].
>
> —Steve McCartney, WA Union Leader

Originating in the 1980s, a just transition in the context of coal emphasizes three key goals [25–26].

Firstly, clear deadlines are crucial, with sufficient notice given for retiring remaining plants to provide workers and surrounding residents with certainty and ample planning time. Climate science dictates that wealthy states such as WA must phase out their power plants no later than 2030 [27]. WA currently hosts two state-owned coal-fired power stations, along with one privately owned plant, all situated in Collie, collectively accounting for 9.4% of the state's energy consumption.[4]

Secondly, substantial financial investments in clean energy are essential to offset the decline in coal-powered production, prevent power outages, and meet climate emission reduction targets. Climate science advocates for WA to set a target of being powered by 50%

---

[4] The privately owned power plant, Bluewaters, is also in Collie and is expected to close in 2029 following its owners writing it off as a stranded asset. See Australian Broadcasting Corporation 2023; for breakdown of WA's energy mix, see Department of Climate Change, Energy, the Environment and Water n.d.-b.

renewable energy by 2030 to align with its climate change obligations [28]. While more progress is needed, generous subsidies and the widespread installation of rooftop solar panels have already doubled renewable energy generation between 2017 and 2023, constituting nearly one third of WA's total energy production [29].

Lastly, a just transition calls for fair compensation and job opportunities for affected communities [30]. In total, as of 2019, shortly after the just transition process began, Collie's coal industry employed about 500–600 people, accounting for almost a quarter of the town's entire workforce [31]. Collie's power plants are strategically located near coal mines for efficient transportation. Since these mines primarily exist to supply the plants, the fate of these mines and their workers is closely intertwined with that of the power plants: if there are no plants, there are no mines.

To define explicit goals for Western Australia's transition away from coal—particularly fair compensation and job opportunities—McCartney and local leaders, including Collie's member of Parliament Mick Murray, took a proactive approach. It was an unorthodox one, emphasizing the importance of inclusivity. They believed that allowing the government alone to define the goals would jeopardize success. The transition needed to be responsive to the community's needs to secure their trust and endorsement. Thus, the community's ownership in defining outcomes was paramount: "Nothing about Collie's future, without Collie's input" [32]. Extensive involvement from major coal workforce unions, including McCartney's leadership in the Australian Manufacturing Workers Union (AMWU), would help ensure this.[5]

In 2018, following a decisive election victory the previous year, the WA government, led by Premier Mark McGowan, established a multi-stakeholder Just Transition Working Group (JTWG). Tasked with developing a comprehensive transition plan, the JTWG sought input from the workforce and the broader community. Recognizing the importance of community representation, McCartney appointed

---

[5] Other unions, such as the Australian Services Union, were also heavily involved.

Alex Cassie to articulate the workforce's perspectives within the JTWG. Cassie had been working abroad for the Australian diplomatic service. McCartney convinced her to return home and make a difference at the community level to provide the world with an example of a successful just transition.

The unions and the JTWG were acutely aware that addressing the concerns of affected workers and the Collie community necessitated time and thoughtful consideration to determine effective policy goals. They dedicated a year to actively engaging with the workforce and community, ensuring a comprehensive understanding of their needs. They needed to get it right. Otherwise, the process would backfire.

In one early and influential meeting, Cassie recalls one worker's response to their initial plan to ensure the transition delivered jobs: "Alex, we can find a job anywhere; that's not the issue. We want to stay in our homes and be able to do meaningful work close to the places we love" [33]. Transitions in other single industry towns across Australia had resulted in workers taking "fly-in, fly-out" jobs in remote areas, where employees fly in for weeks at a time, work long hours in mines, and then return home—hardly conducive to building a thriving local community. The workers' connection to their home in Collie, however, was more significant than their jobs. In short, the workers wanted a just transition to deliver "an economy that works for us" [34]. Cassie could empathize with this sentiment, having experienced homesickness while working in Mexico as a diplomat. She understood the sacrifices made when leaving home for employment.

Recognizing the importance of preserving the workers' connection to home, the workforce clarified that they were less interested in alternative industries such as tourism, hospitality, and arts and culture, even though these were important for keeping other family members in town. As energy industry professionals with well-paying roles averaging over A$100,000 annually, they sought similar paying jobs that utilized their skills. Eventually, they identified a policy goal that could be the basis of a win–win policy solution for all relevant stakeholders.

While the community shared the desire for the coal industry to continue indefinitely, many also knew that coal was just one successful means of generating power. Recognizing their skills' potential for broader energy needs and Collie's role in a post-coal world, they believed with proactive government leadership, Collie could shape WA's energy future. The construction of additional battery storage was critically important to WA's renewable energy growth. This would store surplus renewable energy during low-wind and -solar periods. The community insisted this facility must be built in Collie with government subsidies. This would incentivize the private sector to invest swiftly in the town in response to government tenders. This would also attract ancillary industries (such as green steel), creating more jobs. Staggering the power plant closure to allow for the construction of batteries *before* the coal industry shuts would ensure a smoother transition for workers and the state's electricity supply. To this end, a transparent and credible timeline was essential.

The community also emphasized the need for investments in skill retraining and incentives to entice other alternative sectors, such as tourism and hospitality, to come to town, providing jobs to keep workers' kids in town—a significant priority for "small towns in Australia, as it keeps the town running" [35].

Aligned with the community's vision for a diversified and sustainable economy, unions, supported by local leaders such as Members of Parliament Murray and later Hanns (who succeeded Murray in 2021), sought these outcomes as part of the just transition. The AMWU and allies framed the overall outcome not just about helping 500 coal workers find jobs, but about "making sure the town survives" [36]. Their premise was simple: good, well-paid jobs will follow if batteries are made in Collie. This would ensure a prosperous future for the town as a whole.

In seeking an economy beneficial to the region, the union and allies aimed to turn Collie into a model of a just transition. This would show how active government participation could create a thriving local community and address the state's broader needs.

Now, they had to convince key stakeholders of this argument's merits.

Know Which Stakeholders Matter and How to Appeal to Them

"Collie's community leaders don't underestimate the challenges but they want firmer leadership and better communication from the State Government about what is often referred to as 'the transition' and less of the negative stereotyping."

—*The West Australian Newspaper*, March 2019

Carl Pope, the former chairman and executive director of the US-based Sierra Club, who is now focused on retiring the US' remaining 200 power plants, underscores the importance of securing the buy-in of three critical stakeholders for a successful just transition: the public at large, plant and mine owners, and communities dependent on coal.[6]

The Public

By 2018, the Australian public supported phasing out coal by 2030 and transitioning to cleaner energy sources. Polls consistently showed this support, provided the transitions were government-supported and implemented orderly to ensure a reliable electricity supply [37–39]. This stemmed from the growing awareness that the cost competitiveness of clean energy sources would, at the very least, not cost taxpayers more than they were already paying in power bills. It might even save them money in the long run as coal power became more expensive. The community's proposed solution of building battery storage *before* switching off Collie's power plants thus aligned with the public's conditions for continued support.

---

[6] Pope successfully opposed over 125 proposed new coal-fired power plants. In recent years, Pope has been a key figure in Mike Bloomberg's $500 million initiative to end US reliance on coal and gas power. See Pope 2023.

Growing concerns over coal's contribution to climate change, fueled by environmental organizations such as the Conservation Council of Western Australia (CCWA), further influenced public opinion [40].

Plant Owners (WA Government)

In general, working for a powerful union such as the AMWU, Cassie had relatively easy access to the *most* influential figures in the WA government which owned most of WA's power plants. As a funny side note, the unionists quickly dismissed the notion that they could jump on a plane to meet Elon Musk to convince him to donate a battery facility for Collie! Nonetheless, the advantage of union involvement is the collective strength it provides. Politicians were aware that in speaking with Cassie, they were addressing hundreds of employees whose support they needed if they wanted to avoid backlash and negative publicity from any announcement to shut down Collie's power plants. Even this leverage, however, had its limits. As Cassie notes, "[this] power will get you into the room, but it's up to you to work with the people in there" [41–42]. Leveraging the power of strategic framing was critical.

The WA government needed little convincing when it came to setting a timeline for shutting down the plants. If anything, they wanted to move faster. The surge in renewable energy, supplying up to 81% of WA's daytime energy requirements even before large-scale battery storage solutions were introduced, was a key source of motivation [43].[7] As renewable energy increasingly met a significant portion of WA's daytime power needs at a lower cost, expenses related to frequent power plant shutdowns and restarts soared to accommodate fluctuations in wind and solar generation. Each plant start-up and shutdown incurred a cost to taxpayers, ranging from A$50,000 to A$150,000. By 2022, these operations were occurring more frequently, and forecasts

---

[7] In usual times WA's access to natural gas accounts for over 50% of WA's electricity generation.

indicated dire consequences if the power plants were to continue operating over the next decade [44]. It was estimated that household electricity costs would rise from their current average rate of about A$1,800 per year to more than A$3,000 per year [45].

Nonetheless, while the WA government recognized the benefits of rapidly increasing its investments in electricity storage solutions to make WA's clean energy transition more viable, the pivotal question remained: What incentive would prompt them to bring this investment to Collie?

The union's central argument was Collie's status as home to one of the state's largest energy workforces, boasting hundreds of experienced professionals. Moreover, the existing transmission lines from Collie's power plants could efficiently transmit energy from new batteries to the broader grid, saving the state significant costs in building such infrastructure and training workers elsewhere.

To convey this message, Cassie and her partners meticulously mapped out key decision-makers, including politicians and critical officials at Synergy, the state-owned utility that operated the power plants, and public servants responsible for implementing retraining programs. They made it a point to talk to anyone potentially relevant and who they could reach about the proposed benefits of investing in Collie's future. At one point, she reached out to Synergy's chairman via LinkedIn to request a conversation about the workers' concerns. He agreed to speak. Cassie would later reflect, "That's often how it happens"—a collaborative, nonaggressive approach yields positive results [46].

Mine Owners (Private Investors)

Griffin Coal, a major mine operator supplying a significant portion of the power plants' coal, required no additional incentive to close its mine.[8] The mines' business model had long been distressed. Griffin Coal had sparked the state's lengthiest-ever coal-related industrial relations dispute by removing workers' additional pay benefits in a

---

[8] The other major mine operator in the region is the Chinese-owned Premier Coal.

cost-cutting move. This led to the intervention of the WA government, which at the time of writing had already provided A$23.2 million in taxpayer subsidies to resolve the dispute and sustain the company [47]. It has committed to underwrite support until 2026 if need be to ensure a steady supply of coal to meet the state's energy needs. Ultimately, Griffin Coal would end up filing for bankruptcy. The fear of additional sunk costs in taxpayer money has further intensified the WA government's urgency to expedite its transition from coal.

Figure 5.2 AMWU members at Griffin mine in Collie during their pay dispute in 2018.
Credit: AMWU WA Branch, https://www.search.org.au/collie_just_transition_plan.

Community

"I'd love us to be known as more than a coal mining town . . . We are very proud of our roots, there's nothing wrong with that. But that's not all we are" [48].

—Sarah Stanley, local Collie community leader

From the outset, McCartney believed that the Collie workforce and broader community could be convinced to support the just transition. The community initially supported the proposed policy goals, especially concerning battery storage. However, sustaining their endorsement and support would rely on ongoing engagement. As Murray noted in reflection, the people of Collie would "reluctantly understand that they had to change; they just needed to know what was going to happen so they had sufficient time to plan their lives" [49].

Endless speculation about when the power plants would close meant many workers initially did not trust the government's words. Their anger was justified by the fact uncertainty had resulted in reduced house prices and investment in local businesses, hindering residents' and coal workers' ability to plan their lives [50]. Older workers held on to their jobs, possibly delaying retirement for redundancy payouts. Those in mid-career, however, were uncertain whether to leave town to find another job or stay. These life-changing decisions were difficult without a transparent and credible end date.

Even as recently as 2019, Premier McGowan contributed to this uncertainty by suggesting that coal-fired power would persist "for some time to come." One of the mines' private operators said they were contracted to provide coal to the state for up to 30 years. This was well past the 2030 deadline for advanced economies such as WA to wean themselves off coal power. The local town council also advocated retaining coal-fired power generation in WA until at least 2040 [51]. Given all this confusion and uncertainty, it was perhaps no surprise that, at first, "no one simply thought it [the plants' closure] was going to happen" [52].

The union's role as a trusted messenger was essential to restore community confidence. Several community meetings were held at the outset to get the community on board with the transition. The first two or three were simply for people "to vent all their anger" and move beyond the "initial frustration" they had to transition [53]. But rather than "run away," union leaders "kept having that discussion about what to do when coal ends" [54]. Eventually, their engagement turned more proactive to focus on securing the best outcome.

Once people were willing to give the process a chance, the AMWU, Murray, and later Hanns provided ongoing updates to inform the community about the progress, potential impacts, and associated benefits of any proposed agreement. Crucially, they never let the government take over the JTWG process. They "were sitting around our table, which made things a lot easier" [55]. Its workload included intense working groups and consultations and focusing on listening to workers' ideas and feedback. This also helped ensure no sudden surprises appeared in the media that might lead to a loss of trust. After all, many workers were "highly knowledgeable about power generation and engaged in the discussions about new technologies with the interest of professionals" [56]. To quote Cassie, "They can 'smell a rotten fish' if it is not legitimate. They want and deserve details" [57]. Such constant engagement also changed much of the dialogue's tone from where it had been.

Through engaging in the process, the workforce could also see how they could make an active difference in outcomes, reinforcing their confidence in the process. One key victory, for instance, was getting power plant and mine operators to respond early on to concerns about what would happen to contractors in the coal industry who did not have permanent jobs. The workers, both permanent and temporary alike, had agreed to stand together and oppose any just transition process that did not include a road map for all their colleagues [58]. Ultimately, power plant and mine operators agreed that any just transition should cover both the coal industry's permanent staff and contractors. Approximately one third of the workforce fell into the latter category. These victories demonstrated that engaging in the process through the unions yielded significant benefits.

Embrace Pragmatic Idealism

"When I walked out of the room [after the first conversation], everyone just got out of my way because they didn't want to be the one standing next to me . . . sure enough, five or six years later, the government's talking about shutting down the coal mines. I look like Nostradamus" [59].

—Steve McCartney, WA Union Leader

Local representatives, unions, and the community showed pragmatic idealism in embracing the just transition process. This involved their willingness to engage with those they didn't always agree with and to accept compromise. In their ideal world, the workforce would "rather be doing coal mining for the rest of [their] lives" [60]. However, the end of coal was the only certain outcome. In the end, the community reached a compromise. They decided to actively engage to save the town they loved rather than resist the march of history, even if it meant accepting the end of their beloved jobs.

Murray himself took time to adopt this view, given his two-decade career in the coal industry before entering parliament. In 2002, he famously confronted the state's then-premier with a wheel-barrow of coal, emphasizing the importance of Collie's coal industry to ongoing reliable electricity supply. In 2005, he threatened to resign from the Labor Party the last time they were in government, during which they considered supporting a gas-powered station instead of a new coal one. After all, around 200 years' worth of coal were left in the mines near Collie. Any other alternative just did not seem to make sense.

However, even before the cost competitiveness of natural gas and clean energy began to challenge coal's dominance, Murray had his "come to Jesus" moment about the inevitability of coal's decline; he could see where the global debate on climate change was all headed. Painful memories of the abrupt closure of Collie's underground mines in the 1990s, leaving 300 workers suddenly unemployed, also factored into his U-turn.

As the community came around to support the need for a just transition, many demonstrated a newfound willingness to engage with new stakeholders. They did not allow their natural biases and assumptions to blind them. In the past, environmentalists had a strained relationship with the coal community. Their tendency to stage protests, such as tying themselves in front of power plants, didn't endear them to the workers. However, the union recognized that many young people in the climate and environmental move-ments had valuable ideas about where the transition should lead. They brought these activists to engage with community representatives about green energy and the future opportunities it presented. "That was the first time the workforce listened to an environmentalist" [61]. This marked a significant departure from previous encounters when such activists had been met with resistance and even run out of town.

As for the environmentalists, they, too, developed a newfound appreciation for what the workforce wanted. Jayde Rowland of the CCWA acknowledges that the environmental movement has been "pretty bad at times" in advocating for a just transition due to a lack of complete understanding of workers' needs [62]. For instance, environmentalists had already (perhaps unintentionally) made dismissive remarks such as suggesting a closed coal mine could be converted into a "BMX track" or another community project. They might suggest that coal workers could become gardeners or café baristas in such endeavors, even though "that's not a just transition going from a A$120K a year job to a A$30K a year job" [63]. Despite some lingering distrust toward climate activists, as acknowledged by McCartney, both the environmental movement and workers came to recognize their shared common cause: holding governments accountable for the delivery of clean energy and battery storage, and ensuring a just transition that creates ongoing, high-paying jobs in Collie matching the workers' skill sets while addressing climate change.

The unions also advocated for a policy compromise among the workforce, the government, and the mine operators. This agreement allowed mine workers to learn new skills while keeping their current jobs, with retraining funded by the government. It provided a pathway for workers to prepare for future opportunities and new industries while ensuring they stayed in their existing jobs to keep the mines running in the interim. This approach would minimize worker hardship while preventing premature disruptions in the coal industry.

Ultimately, the community's pragmatic approach to drive and own the just transition, rather than wait for events to unfold, paid off. In June 2022, the WA government finally announced the closure of Collie's two state-owned power plants, setting a firm deadline of no later than 2029; this clear timeframe gave the workforce several years advance notice to plan their personal lives [64].

To address the community's specific needs, the government also committed A\$500 million for power plant decommissioning and post-shutdown employment support. Notably, a substantial portion of this funding, A\$200 million, was allocated to the Collie Industrial Transition Fund. This fund was purposefully designed to attract major projects and new industries to the town, focusing on battery construction, advanced manufacturing (i.e., wind turbines, green steel), and workforce transition initiatives. This funding was in addition to a previously announced A\$100 million, which mostly went toward boosting tourism and community development. It brought the total to more than A\$600 million.

The community's overwhelmingly positive response to the premier's announcement marked a significant turnaround from previous years. It was the culmination of extensive efforts involving government, community, employers, and union leadership. It also underscored a fundamental shift in perspective—the pragmatism to acknowledge the inevitability that future generations in the community would not follow in the footsteps of coal workers. This acknowledgment, while difficult, paved the way for proactively engaging with relevant stakeholders to secure an alternative and no less idealistic future for the town.

Know Your Endgame

"People that think Collie is going to be finished within a couple of years are far off their mark, well and truly off the mark. I do see Collie has a future and a good one" [65].
—Mick Murray, Collie's former member of Parliament

Cassie described McGowan's announcement as a "day I'll always remember." She also acknowledged it was a "promising but abstract" commitment. Like any promise of support, the success of Collie's just transition would be contingent upon continued follow-through and accountability.

Given the length of time involved, the success of any just transition is dependent on the depth of its governing and implementation framework; it is much bigger than any single individual. Leadership changes are inevitable. Following the June 2022 announcement, key figures, including Cassie and Premier McGowan, have since resigned and been replaced by others; Murray had already passed the baton to Hanns in 2021 as the local member of Parliament.

The transition has also not been problem-free. Following the June 2022 announcement, the government had to defer some planned plant shutdowns by up to six months, prompting concerns about the just transition's credibility. Critics, including opposition parties, question whether the WA government is "running out of runway" to meet its 2029 target.[9] They express concerns about potential bottlenecks that could impede the continued surge in renewable energy. They question whether the state will have enough new energy sources coming online in time to compensate for the closure of plants and meet the rising energy demand, especially with more households adopting electric cars. These setbacks are part of a broader construction bottleneck that has resulted in delays in all industries, not just energy.

Nonetheless, under pressure from environmental groups such as the CCWA and unions, the WA government, led by McGowan's successor Premier Roger Cook, has reassured relevant stakeholders that they remain on track to close the remaining power plants by 2029 [66]. At the end of 2022, the government also introduced interim targets to reduce its greenhouse gas emissions by 80% below 2020 levels by 2030 [67].[10] New climate change legislation and investment was subsequently approved at the end of 2023. These policies will in

---

[9] Under pressure from environmental groups and unions, the WA government has reassured the public that they are on track to close the remaining stations by 2030.
[10] Note the government does have interim emissions reduction targets of 80% below 2020 levels. See Government of Western Australia 2023.

the government's own words help "accelerate" WA's transition to "becoming a renewable energy powerhouse" [68–69].

Overall, despite the potential for further delays, as far as Collie is concerned, the transition appears to be on track. Some skepticism and anxiety did arise in early 2023 about whether the WA government would follow through on its commitments to build new battery storage facilities in Collie. Murray pointed to announcements that seemed supportive of this but lacked clarity. Referring to a May 2023 announcement of A\$2.8 billion for constructing an energy storage battery in Collie and another industrial hub in Perth, Murray expressed concerns: "Not all those billions announced are coming here" [70]. "You have to make sure it's real" [71].

Fortunately, unions and local leaders, such as Hanns, remain actively engaged, monitoring and tracking these commitments and collaborating closely with the government to ensure accountability. As a former teacher at the local school that oversaw the school's vocational educational program, Hanns is particularly passionate about ensuring the state delivers on its promise to provide skills retraining and job opportunities. Accordingly, Hanns has ensured that the WA government has established a monitoring unit to oversee the transition's successful implementation. This sustained pressure is delivering results. In June 2023, the WA government announced an A\$1 billion contract to construct battery energy storage systems, one of the world's largest, to be operational in Collie by the end of 2024 [72]. This alone will create 500 construction jobs. A week after this announcement, Hanns and the WA government unveiled plans for a new A\$6.3 million training center to diversify the local economy and create new jobs for workers affected by the transition. Investors in other industries have also begun to move into town, such as green steel smelters, hiring a few dozen people here and there and piloting projects before hopefully scaling them further.

Collie appears to have new energy as investment dollars flow. Buildings have been improved on the main street, resulting in recognition and heritage awards in 2022 as old hotels and pubs reopen their doors to a significant surge in tourists. New adventure sports companies have been set up since the June 2022 announcement, and new venues and infrastructure, including mountain bike trails, have been completed with government investment. Hanns jokes that she thought she "knew everyone," but on Sundays, she can walk down the street and "know not one person" as tourists flock to town [73].

People have also bought houses, with retirees attracted to Collie's beautiful scenery and affordable housing prices. Murray jokes that the bowling club has "never been busier . . . [it has gone from] being defunct to about fifty or sixty members" [74].

Where necessary, sustained advocacy, monitoring, consulting, reporting, and public shaming might be required at certain junctures to keep the transition on track, maintain community confidence, and hold everyone to their word. For now, the local community appears to be broadly supportive, even as they are somewhat apprehensive about what the future might bring. "They're optimistic. They're impatient but optimistic," says McCartney [75]. When reacting to news of potential delays, a local coal miner, Shannon Boston, aptly stated "[At the least] we're not kept in the dark." That alone is an improvement on what existed before the just transition process began.

Conclusion

> "The ability of the Premier to come to town without being
> run out on a rail was the culmination of years of work from his
> public servants, us, locals and others. His announcement and the
> response—a day I'll always remember—was not a starting point
> in the transition but a marker of a success" [76].
> —Alex Cassie, former trade union organizer

I'm reminded of the words of the eminent Australian historian Peter FitzSimons, explaining why WA stories often remain unknown. Introducing his epic account of the improbable *Catalpa Rescue*, one of history's most remarkable prison breaks, FitzSimons writes about a peculiar unspoken pact Western Australians share with one another: "Don't Tell Any Bastard East of Kalgoorlie" [77]. (Kalgoorlie is a prominent gold mining town in the heart of WA's outback, where vast desert stretches for miles east until you reach major Australian cities like Melbourne and Sydney; Perth lies miles to the west).

As a proud Western Australian, some might accuse me of breaking this pact to share Collie's example of a just transition with the rest of the world. If that is the case, I offer no apologies.

In many parts of the world, just transitions face backlash. Sometimes, it's due to entrenched interests or fundamental disagreements about the necessity of transitioning to clean energy. However, more often than not, it's because of poor implementation. To reiterate McCartney's words, "It doesn't work because it's not just." Instead of fostering collaboration, finding common ground, and embracing what is both inevitable and possible, division and complacency take hold. Many simply do not begin early enough. Most critically, transitions often fail to genuinely involve affected communities and give them a meaningful role in the process. The government tries to own it instead.

For example, consider Australia's automotive manufacturing industry collapse. Its transition failed because the government focused solely on providing education for workers who lost their jobs in shuttered manufacturing plants in regional towns [78]. Unfortunately, there was insufficient effort to cultivate new industries to offset manufacturing job losses in these towns. As a result, communities suffered, and people had to move away to find new jobs.

Collie's experience highlights the pivotal role of unions representing affected workers and the local community in implementing a just transition. From the beginning, they demonstrated the foresight to be candid with workers about their "dying jobs" [79]. Moreover, these unions worked hard to maintain the community's trust through regular community meetings, ensuring they could proactively advocate for their interests to shape a truly just transition. Most of all, they ensured the outcomes were community-owned. As a result, when the announcement of the timeline for retiring Collie's power plants eventually came, it was seen as a positive step forward in a plan the community already felt part of.

Conversely, had government officials or even environmentalists led the effort, it's possible that most of the workforce "would have shut down the conversation before negotiations even began" [80].

Ultimately, the community widely welcomed the announcement. This was a testament to the pragmatism of those involved. They embraced the process early on and drove long consultations and preparation. This ensured a smoother and more successful transition. It prevented an abrupt end that could have left behind workers and those economically dependent on an outdated industry.

Whether they fully comprehend it or not, coal communities worldwide are in a race against time as pressure grows on the world's remaining 2,400 coal-fired power stations to shut their doors [81]. Global coal consumption is reaching a plateau—if it has not already.[11] The forces sealing coal's fate are twofold. First, there's the greater availability of cheaper energy sources. In 2014, renewable energy was cheaper than new coal-fired power stations in just 1% of the world; today, they are the cheapest form of new generation in countries covering more than 70% of the global economy [82–83]. Second, there's a growing public sentiment for governments to follow through on climate change commitments. These forces will only continue to increase with time.

This does not mean just transitions will be easy to achieve. In major Asian economies, retiring recently constructed power plants poses a significant public policy dilemma [84]. However, one clear takeaway for potentially affected communities in these countries is that it is never too early to begin planning to avoid abrupt and negative transitions.

Cassie diligently maintained a diary while negotiating Collie's just transition. In one of her initial entries, she expressed a hopeful aspiration: that Collie's success would redefine the concept of a just transition. Today, Collie's experience should serve as a beacon of hope

---

[11] Some reports suggest coal consumption already peaked in 2023. See IEA 2023.

to communities facing similar transitions worldwide. It demonstrates that the noble ideals behind the theory of just transition, combined with the right collaborative spirit, can be transformed into powerful change. It is a formidable example of community-led policy entrepreneurship, showcasing that a sustainable future can be achieved while safeguarding people's livelihoods, homes, and identities.

6 | Building Bridges: Small and Mighty in a Warming World

Barbados is a small country; its population, just under 300,000, is comparable to that of Newark, New Jersey. If you lined up US cities in terms of economic output, you'd have to go far down the list—all the way to Gettysburg in Pennsylvania—to find one that matched the Barbadian economy's modest size. The difference, of course, is that a federal safety net ultimately backs any American city, while Barbadians must fend for themselves in a warming world.

Nevertheless, Barbados is more than prepared to tackle this challenge. Throughout its history, the country has earned a reputation for "punching above its weight."[1].

On the one hand, it boasts a high standard of living for its citizens, often referred to as the "Barbados model," serving as a developmental example for other small island states with limited natural resources [2]. On the other hand, owing to its historical role in the insidious slave-driven sugar plantation economy, Barbados was once a vital and strategic colony in the British Empire. At one stage, it was even described as the "Jewel of the empire" [3]. All this to say, Barbados, as both a colony and a nation, has consistently had a significance that belies its size, both for better and worse. What's more, it has always exuded a sense of confidence. Its first female Prime Minister is a direct product of this heritage and history and is actively building on this legacy.

Mia Amor Mottley was first elected prime minister after sweeping all thirty legislative seats in the 2018 elections, an unprecedented feat she repeated in 2022. She led Barbados to becoming a republic and breaking its last ties with the British monarchy in 2021. In 2022, Mottley became the second Barbadian to grace the cover of TIME magazine as one of its 100 Most Influential People, after Rihanna.

However, it is for Mottley's tireless advocacy on climate justice that she has become most well known.

★★★★★★★

June 22, 2023
Paris, France

Mottley was preparing to address a massive crowd of 20,000 people on Paris's historic Champs-Élysées, the large public greenspace in front of the Eiffel Tower. The Global Citizen event, *Power Our Planet*, was set to feature world-renowned artists such as Billie Eilish, Lenny Kravitz, Jon Batiste and H.E.R. who had rallied their fans behind Mottley's call for action.

Just before taking the podium, Mottley took a moment to find a private area behind the stage to record a quick video message back home—an update about an approaching hurricane that posed a potential threat to her Caribbean nation [4].

This was not the first time Mottley had to warn her citizens about the dangers of an impending hurricane, and it wouldn't be the last. Earlier in the day, Mottley had contemplated leaving the summit for home altogether but ultimately chose to stay. After all, her purpose in Paris was to fight for the financial resources to help nations like hers prepare for and recover from such natural disasters. It was a cause she had been dedicated to for years. Fortunately, this time, the hurricane was projected just to miss Barbados.

With the message recorded, Mottley walked out in front of the awaiting crowd to jointly announce a win from the summit. Standing alongside her was the new president of the World Bank Group ("World Bank") and former Mastercard CEO Ajay Banga. Together, they announced that the World Bank, one of the largest sources of funding for developing countries, was committing to offer so-called Natural Disaster Clauses ("Pause Clauses") in their loan agreements with climate-vulnerable countries such as Barbados [5].

Pause Clauses were "one of the greatest policy innovations of 2023" [6]. And they are a big deal for countries on the frontlines of the climate crisis, such as Barbados. In practical terms, Pause Clauses empower governments to temporarily halt their debt payments during a natural disaster, allowing them to focus on recovery efforts, and bounce back from such devastating events. This frees up precious money that can be spent on everything from fixing homes, roads and schools that sustained damage, to keeping hospitals running, providing food, and getting everything back to normal. There is a good chance these clauses will have to be relied on in the next few years as countries experience more frequent and harsher extreme weather events: hurricanes, cyclones, wildfires, floods and droughts.

On that summer evening in Paris, however, in front of 20,000 chanting activists, Mottley was savoring a win. The global community had finally begun to respond to her agenda even as just months prior, it had been dismissed and ridiculed by some.

"Today is a good day," Mottley had told a reporter just before addressing the crowd, "in that we have had almost everybody accept the validity of natural disaster clauses" [7].

Embracing Banga on stage, Mottley had reminded the audience, to huge applause, that "we must act today to save the planet for tomorrow," the event's tagline that she herself came up with [8]. In response, Banga said, to equal cheers, "That was made possible because of you. Because of your voice and what you have said."

★★★★★★★★

The Challenge:
Who Should Pay For The Climate Crisis?

"Things will have to change if they are to stay the same."
—Tancredi (as said *The Leopard*, by Tomasi di Lampedusa)

The world is today 1.2 degrees Celsius warmer on average than it was before the Industrial Revolution [9]. The impact can be seen all around us, from record-breaking wildfires in North America to deadly floods in Europe. Such events, collectively, have cost the global economy an estimated $4 trillion in damages over the past 50 years [10].

The brunt of this impact is felt disproportionately by the world's poorest and smallest countries, which have contributed the least to climate change [11]. The same disaster hitting Tokyo versus Haiti results in a dramatically different scale of damage. Climate-related loss and damage occurs at a rate three to four times higher in the Global South—including Africa, Latin America and the Caribbean, Asia and the Pacific—than in other regions [12]. In some cases, natural disasters can wipe out entire economies in just a matter of hours, as it did when Hurricane Maria hit Dominica in 2017 [13].

Yet, these frontline nations have also shown remarkable resourcefulness in their responses. For instance, Fijian farmers protect their fruit seedlings from hurricanes by storing them in inexpensive shipping containers [14]. Governments across sub-Saharan Africa have introduced innovative crop varieties better equipped to endure extended periods of drought and minimal rainfall [15]. And leaders in the low-lying Pacific atoll nation of Kiribati are devising plans to build infrastructure to be able to withstand flooding from rising sea levels [16].

These affected nations understand how to adapt to climate change; their struggle lies in accessing the money to implement these solutions at the scale needed. In this, they face the added challenge of being burdened by heavy debt repayments, diverting much of their revenue away from investing in essential needs such as schools, hospitals and homes better able to withstand natural disasters [17]. In 2017, Barbados, with the third-highest debt per capita globally, spent 55% of its GDP on debt payments [18].

High debt levels of climate-vulnerable nations have often resulted from borrowing funds for recovery and rebuilding following natural disasters. Caribbean nations, including Barbados, Jamaica, and Trinidad and Tobago, have frequently seen their debt levels increase despite running large budget surpluses due to unforeseen disasters [19–20]. To be clear, debt itself is not necessarily wrong per se. Having access to loans after a disaster is essential to funding recovery efforts. But those loans often come with a hefty cost, borne by people who did not contribute to the cause of the tragedy they're affected by [21]. Put differently, Barbadian interest payments—funded by taxes that could go to education or health care—are band-aids covering wounds that are anything but self-inflicted. Unfortunately, this story spans much of the Global South—from the Pacific to sub-Saharan Africa.

After enduring numerous climate-fueled disasters, many countries now face limited capacity to respond effectively to future crises, lacking the funds needed for resilient infrastructure investments [22]. Instead, any available money is directed toward servicing debt payments. As one colleague aptly noted, a country can spend two years preparing a proposal for a $2 million grant when they are hemorrhaging 10 times that amount in monthly interest payments [23]. Alas, this is the unfortunate reality for many nations, caught in a vicious cycle, struggling to cover the costs of loss and damage caused by others [24].

In pure climate justice terms, the primary responsibility for meeting these costs would rest with the industrialized nations that have historically emitted most greenhouse gas emissions. However, waiting for action based on morality alone rarely renders results. A landmark decision to launch a long-awaited loss and damage fund is a case in point [25]. While a hard-won victory that marks an important step forward, the fund will still depend largely on voluntary donations, as wealthy nations refuse to acknowledge liability and compensation. Unfortunately, the initial contributions of $700 million to the fund represent just 0.2% of the estimated $400 billion in losses developing countries are likely to face annually [26]. Like all forms of progress, climate justice requires astute, unwavering, and strategic policy entrepreneurship.

Fortunately, just as vulnerable communities possess answers for adapting to climate change, they also have identified solutions for paying for them. Mia Mottley's so-called "Bridgetown Initiative" ("Bridgetown")—named after the capital of Barbados—is one such example. In the following pages, we explore how Mottley's efforts to implement the Bridgetown solutions exhibit many of the steps of our playbook. Ultimately, while there is much more to be achieved, we witness how Mottley has started to succeed in changing the rules of the global financial system to better serve the needs of countries like hers.

Policy Entrepreneurship in Action: Securing Climate Justice

Know Your Policy Goal

"Many of the things that I've put before us today don't require money, but they require a commitment, and they require political will. And with the power of the pen, **we can impose natural disaster and pandemic clauses** in our debt" [27].

—Prime Minister Mottley of Barbados addressing the
UN General Assembly, September 2022

Mottley is not the first leader from a climate-vulnerable country to speak about the challenges of climate change, and she will not be the last. Bridgetown's resonance, however, comes from the fact it offers truly implementable and well-defined policy solutions to the question of how to pay for the climate crisis. This is demonstrated by its coverage in mainstream media, including top-tier publications such as the *New York Times* [28].

To construct this plan before its launch in 2022, Mottley sought and convened experts with a deep understanding of economics and banking. Avinash Persaud, Mottley's special climate envoy, is one of its most pivotal authors. Persaud, a London-based banker of Caribbean Indian descent, had been providing economic and financial counsel to Mottley since 2007 [29].

Transforming the global financial system is a gradual process. For instance, the World Bank, was established in 1944 when the latest medical innovation was the icepick lobotomy (literally an ice pick through the eye socket to cure madness) [30]. It takes time to reform the way it provides funds. That's why focusing on what is winnable is key, as Mottley astutely pointed out during an address at the United Nations: "Simplicity gets us to the end. We must strategically choose what we can win rather than attempting to do it all." Part of Bridgetown's collective success reflects this discipline to avoid the temptation to back a grab bag of every conceivable policy idea—a trap many campaigns often fall into.

One example of the simple solutions Mottley has successfully implemented domestically is Pause Clauses. They automatically suspend debt repayments for up to two years when an independent agency declares that a natural disaster has surpassed a specific impact threshold (i.e., wiping off more than 5% of annual GDP). This frees up substantial funds for disaster relief and recovery precisely when countries need it most, negating the necessity to raise their debt levels even higher [31]. While Pause Clauses alone are not a silver bullet, no other instrument (i.e., insurance or aid policies) comes close to freeing up such high levels of funding—including concessional financing likely to be made available from bodies such as the World Bank [32]. For example, incorporating Pause Clauses into all of Barbados's loan agreements would allow it to access up to approximately $700 million, equating to almost 15% of its entire economic output, by temporarily deferring loan repayments [33]. As Mottley stated, "There is no country, no company . . . that will give us the equivalent of [this] should a disaster happen" [34].

Ultimately, Pause Clauses are an emergency lever that frees up more funds for recovery when it is urgently needed. And because governments now know they have a source of funds when disaster strikes, these clauses can help them make more prudent budgeting decisions and be better prepared to tackle climate change's worst consequences in the years to come.

Mottley and Persaud became acquainted with Pause Clauses through their Caribbean neighbor, Grenada, which, as part of its debt restructuring in 2015, negotiated the world's first loan agreements featuring these clauses, allowing for debt repayment suspension for up to one year [35]. Upon being elected in 2018 and aware of the financial vulnerability to natural disasters, Mottley successfully negotiated some of her country's new debt agreements to include Pause Clauses after the International Monetary Fund (IMF), in a somewhat unorthodox move for them, sending a solid message to creditors that Barbados's bonds were sound [36]. However, this was just the beginning.

Mottley, Persaud, and various civil society organizations understood that private financiers, motivated primarily by returns and reluctant to change, wouldn't be the primary driver of future lending to meet the resilient infrastructure needs of climate-vulnerable countries. The burden would largely fall on increased lending from institutions such as the World Bank and wealthy governments, including the US.

Therefore, in mid-2022, as part of Mottley's Bridgetown Initiative, they set a clear goal: persuade the World Bank and major economies, including the US Treasury, to offer Pause Clauses in their existing and future lending. This would help normalize and scale their use and make it less foreign for the private sector, which currently owns about three-quarters of all developing country debt, to also adopt them without charging a premium [37]. Bridgetown also aimed to expand the application of Pause Clauses to cover a broader range of crises, including pandemics, considering the impact of COVID-19 on many Global South economies.[1]

Mastering the Art of Timing

"The momentum is building for serious reforms to a global financial architecture designed without the developing world in mind. . . . This is the time to extinguish the fire before it burns down our homes. The moment for action is now" [38].

—President Akufo-Addo of Ghana and
Prime Minister Mottley of Barbados

A hallmark of a capable policy entrepreneur lies in their ability to accurately grasp the prevailing zeitgeist, gauge public sentiment, and understand broader societal shifts and transformations. In this regard, Bridgetown, in many ways, leverages the recent convergence in discussions of racial discrimination, legacies of slavery, and their inter-section with the climate justice movement. It is an idea whose time has come.

This yearning for change—and justice specifically—was espe-cially evident in the wake of the global revaluation of history trig-gered by George Floyd's murder in May 2020, which accelerated Barbados's reckoning with its colonial past [39]. Alex Downes, who would later serve as Mottley's press secretary, led the successful cam-paign to relocate a statue of British naval hero Horatio Nelson from Bridgetown's National Heroes Square to the Barbados Museum. The figure was a magnet for controversy due to Nelson's defense of the

---

[1] If all developing countries had incorporated these clauses into their loans during the pandemic, it would have unlocked one trillion dollars in freed-up funding, which they could have allocated to various critical needs, ranging from health care to employment protection schemes. See Bolton et al. 2020.

transatlantic slave trade, which formed the foundation of Barbados's plantation economy [40]. As Downes explained to me on one of several trips to Barbados, "What was important was the way we went about it. We didn't want to give our detractors an excuse to paint us as vandals. We did it through peaceful and lawful means".

Having spearheaded the effort to sever Barbados's last ties with the British monarchy, Mottley fearlessly and unapologetically links her advocacy for climate justice with this broader awareness of racial injustice. She frequently cites Barbados's historic role as a significant colonial asset in the slavery-based agricultural system. She argues that this system contributed significantly to the wealth and industrialization of the former colonial powers—which, in turn, contributed to the emissions causing the climate-related loss and damage we see today [41]. "We financed the Industrial Revolution with our blood, sweat, and tears. Now, are we to pay for its greenhouse gases? That's fundamentally unfair" [42].

Couching policy proposals in such fiery rhetoric might have been counterproductive a decade ago, potentially alienating international institutions and their Global North constituents. Today, however it resonates with citizens worldwide who are impatient for action as the threats of climate change, evident through more frequent wildfires, flooding, and hurricanes, underscore the urgency of global solutions that address the needs of all countries [43]. This concern has translated into strong public support for the type of international solidarity championed by Bridgetown. As seen in Chapter 2, most countries from the Global North and South believe wealthy nations should compensate climate-vulnerable countries for climate change costs. Additionally, 84% of people polled in the top 21 global economies agree that rich nations should assist countries struggling with debt by renegotiating repayment terms [44]. Populations everywhere seem to recognize that climate change will impact all countries in one form or another [45]. They understand the frontline of the climate crisis "will come to you if it has not already. We live worlds apart but also on top of each other" [46]. The imperative is clear to overwhelming majorities in public opinion: all countries must collaborate, or we all suffer the consequences.

Amid this strong public sentiment, institutions such as the World Bank face mounting pressure to do more, making them more receptive to ideas such as Bridgetown than they might have otherwise been. In the fall of 2022, for instance, the World Bank faced substantial criticism, primarily due to its perceived sluggishness in responding to the current global climate crisis and the specific needs of the Global South. This situation escalated dramatically when former US Vice President Al Gore publicly accused David Malpass, then-president of the World Bank, of being a climate denier [47]. Malpass's refusal to refute Gore's assertion led to a PR crisis and eventually his resignation, fueled by a significant civil society uproar. In early 2023, US Treasury Secretary Janet Yellen nominated Ajay Banga to succeed Malpass. In his first global listening tour, Banga made it clear that a top priority was to respond better to the demands of the Global South, which he understood was increasingly eager for change [48]. On the lookout for possible solutions and an early win, and given the momentum behind Bridgetown already, Banga pledged to consider its proposals [49]. He would, ultimately, commit to offering Pause Clauses in new loans for 12 pilot countries just days into his new role.

Leaders from the Global South have also been increasingly vocal in their criticism of perceived Western hypocrisy [50]. From their perspective, despite being major carbon emitters, Western nations still need to fulfill climate financing promises [51]. They also attack the West for advocating global solidarity during the pandemic while practicing vaccine nationalism [52]. The West's swift response to Russia's invasion of Ukraine, directing significant aid to the latter while offering limited support for the Global South's long-standing challenges, further increased their frustration [53].

In response, at least some Western leaders have begun to realize that they must make visible efforts to regain the Global South's trust and be more sensitive to addressing their needs [54]. Showing support for Bridgetown, including its ideas for reform of the World

Bank, is one way to do this. Illustrating this shift, in November 2022, French President Macron announced he would host the summit for a New Global Financing Pact ("Summit") in June 2023 to consider practical solutions to "unsustainable" injustices, including Bridgetown, citing the concerns of the Global South as a "fair debate" [55]. This announcement followed an extraordinary moment when Macron, while chairing a panel discussion, received a public and blistering rebuke from his fellow panelists—leaders from the Global South.[2]

It would be unfair, however, to conclude that Bridgetown's rising appeal is merely the product of the time. With ongoing economic uncertainty, there remain limits to how far the World Bank and its shareholders, the world's biggest economies, are willing to go.

With these constraints in mind, Mottley arguably contributed to Bridgetown's increased acceptability by advocating more extreme and seemingly expensive policy positions. This helped make Bridgetown appear more moderate by comparison (an example of the so-called "McKibben effect" referenced in Step 3).

For instance, at the climate talks in Glasgow in November 2021, Mottley had called for the IMF to issue 500 billion annually in so-called Special Drawing Rights—a reserve asset of the IMF issued primarily to the world's wealthiest countries.[3] Per Mottley's plan, these funds would then be re-channeled to support the needs of

---

[2] This exchange took place at the Paris Peace Forum in November 2022. In President Macron's presence, President Umaro Embalo of Guinea Bissau lashed at the alleged tendency of Western countries to do as they please in Africa. "Yes, we are poor, but we still have dignity," he said. "There should be mutual respect," he added. Di Rama, the prime minister of Albania, slammed his country's European neighbors for ignoring the plight of small countries at the height of the pandemic. "Without China, Turkey, and Russia—without the vaccines that they sent, we could not have survived." The president of the International Crisis Group Ms. Comfort Ero, who is of Nigerian parentage, added, "The chicken has come home to roost for Western countries." She stressed that African countries did not need Western lectures on sovereignty and independence.

[3] At the time of writing, 500 billion in Special Drawing Rights (SDRs) was the equivalent of US$670 billion. See currency converter: https://coinmill.com/SDR_USD.html#SDR=500.

developing countries.[4] The proposal was dead on arrival, as much as Mottley's sentiment struck a chord with the world leaders in the room. Regrouping with Persaud, Mottley refined the Bridgetown proposals, including Pause Clauses, to make them fit what they felt was acceptable. They pitched Pause Clauses as a meaningful change that could be implemented quickly and without much if any additional cost. Despite dragging their feet on whether to introduce them in preceding years, the World Bank and Western countries suddenly saw their appeal. By agreeing to offer them, they could demonstrate their responsiveness to the moment while working on longer-term solutions that require more money and which, therefore, take longer for countries, most notably the US, to approve.

Ultimately, Mottley's success to date in large part reflects her successful navigation of a moment when the current world order is increasingly "desperate and open to innovations to save itself" [56]. Historically, the West had resisted changing the game's rules for decades, favoring minor resource redistribution over genuine shifts in power. Mottley, in constant communication with leaders from both the West and Global South, recognizes that we may be at a point where the former is more willing than ever to reshape the rules for the future.[5] And she is not about to let this opportunity go to waste.

Mastering the Art of Storytelling

"Our world stands at a fork in the road, one no less significant than when the United Nations was formed in 1945. But then, the majority of countries here did not exist; we exist now. The difference is we want to exist 100 years from now."
—Prime Minister Mottley of Barbados [57]

---

[4] The argument is that Wealthy nations' Special Drawing Rights mostly sit on their balance sheets unused. In contrast, developing countries could leverage them to access cheap and affordable financing. While great in theory, however, the US Congress has so far not agreed to any redistribution of the US SDRs. See Cashman 2022.
[5] While some of this comfort arises from the fact that these ideas don't necessarily require immediate financial investments, the preference for these solutions (by at least some countries in the Global South) may also stem from their potential to unlock more funds in the long term compared to traditional charity dollars.

If you search for Mottley's speeches on Google or YouTube, you'll quickly notice her mastery of storytelling. This skill has propelled Bridgetown up the global agenda. There are a few takeaways to note.

First and foremost, Mottley is a master of *showing* and not just *telling* the impact of climate change. In her speech, considered her "global breakout speech at the climate talks in Glasgow, Scotland, in 2021," she humanized the story of climate change in powerful ways [58]. A particularly memorable moment came when she described a 2 degrees Celsius rise in global temperature as a "death sentence" for island and coastal communities. It attracted the attention of world leaders, as seen in a decisive moment when she left the talks hand in hand with US President Joe Biden.

Figure 6.1   Mottley leaves COP26 speech in Glasgow, hand in hand with Biden.
Source: Mia Amor Mottley, 2021, Facebook. https://www.facebook.com/SupportMiaMottley/photos/a.595099133890966/4647819648618874

Secondly, in a bid to connect her ideas to audiences worldwide, Mottley's speechcraft is almost always anchored in the shared experience of the global climate crisis. It is never just about Barbados alone. For example, in a speech to finance ministers at the 2023 World Bank spring meetings, advocates and philanthropists in Washington, DC, Mottley vividly described the impact of Cyclone Freddy—the strongest and longest living tropical cyclone ever recorded at the time, which claimed over 1,000 lives in Malawi alone [59]. The room fell silent as they listened to her recount its impact in intricate detail. She highlighted how whole villages and farms were wiped out, 5 million were left on the brink of hunger and a cholera epidemic—the country's deadliest ever—resulted in 1,700 deaths. The country lacked the money to respond and recover even as it was paying nearly a quarter of its annual revenue in debt payments [60]. Through these stories, she illustrates how Bridgetown's proposals, including Pause Clauses, could improve the lives of billions worldwide. As a result, it is perhaps unsurprising that Bridgetown has gained support from more than 60 countries in the Global South, representing more than 1.7 billion people whose economies suffered over $525 billion in losses due to man-made global warming between 2000 and 2019 [61].

Hyper-aware, however, that institutions such as the World Bank are accountable to their shareholders, primarily wealthy nations, Mottley also ensures her message resonates with the citizens of the Global North, many of whom also share the South's anxiety about the climate crisis. She understands that countries of the Global North are ultimately accountable to their citizens, whom she must reach. Thus, during that same visit to Washington mentioned above, Mottley urged Americans: "For the first time, challenges faced by impoverished nations affect us all. Look at Florida. It's underwater! We can't ignore it any longer. How many more lives must be lost before we unite to act?" To these audiences, Mottley also deploys analogies they can understand and relate to. For example, she compares the potential relief of Pause Clauses to that granted to US homeowners on their mortgage repayments during the pandemic. She points out that wealthy nations found the means to pay for such relief, often through massive stimulus programs, because it was right, necessary, and possible.

By making her message relatable and transcending national divides, Mottley has become a global leader in the climate justice movement, connecting with diverse audiences, from remote Pacific populations to young climate activists in Europe. This widespread popularity, in turn, gives her considerable influence and power in the eyes of leaders of the Global North and the World Bank. After all, while politicians in Washington or Paris may not care much for the views of the Global South, they take the opinions and demands of their constituents seriously. This is undoubtedly one of the reasons at least why Macron sought Mottley's participation and endorsement of his Summit in June 2023.[6] Similarly, British Labour Leader Keir Starmer, recognizing Mottley as "much sought-after," requested a meeting with her at the 2023 UN Climate Talks in Dubai.[7] In a telling sign, Starmer utilized this meeting to strengthen his claims to his constituents that a Labour-Led British Government would "lead from the front" on climate change [62].

Figure 6.2   A popular image shared by climate activists leading up to Macron's Summit in June 2023.
Source: Global Goals, 2023. https://www.globalgoals.org/uncategorised/world-leaders-urged-to-listen-to-mia.

---

[6] Indeed, while officially Mottley was just a participant at the summit, so visible was she in the communications and staging around it that many media resorted to describing her as a co-host or referred to the summit as the "Mottley/Macron Summit." See for example: Kyte 2023.
[7] I was involved in initial exchanges between Mottley's team and UK Labour to help set up the meeting in Dubai. See also Harvey 2023.

A third takeaway from Mottley's storytelling is her focus on *how* her solutions are realistic and actionable, drawing practical inspiration from wealthier nations' own experiences. For example, in a speech to the UN, she points out how Western creditors granted Germany a reprieve on debt repayments after World War II to support its economic recovery [63]. Similarly, in the same speech, she points out that the UK was allowed to take on long-term, low-interest debt to fund its post-war recovery after World War I. As she points out, it took until 2014 for London to ultimately retire the last of that debt. This allowed it to fund other essential priorities in the meantime, most notably establishing the UK's National Health Service (NHS), without worrying about how it would foot its interest bills [64].[8] These historical narratives underscore Bridgetown's practicality and that its ideals are hardly radical or revolutionary, disarming potential critics. Implicit in such practical examples is also the notion that denying the Global South similar forms of relief would be both wildly hypocritical and unfair.

Ultimately, by grounding her stories in the mechanics of "how" and focusing on the practical solutions offered by Bridgetown, Mottley also offers audiences hope in addressing the most severe impacts of the climate crisis. Given governments are responsive to their citizens, she also reinforces the message that this possibility is something each of us as individuals can influence. "We're at a stage right now where everything causing us challenges is global," Mottley tells an audience in New York. "So, if we can link between individual action and global consequences, then we're going in the right direction" [65].

---

[8] Interestingly, few Britons would give up the NHS today, but the Conservative government was very opposed on the grounds that it would bankrupt the country. But the incoming Clement Atlee–led government (1948-1951) understood the country would not be able to win the peace over there without economic security here. To quote the economist Keynes, who told Britons in the middle of WWII through the BBC while bombs exploded overhead, "If it is possible, then we can afford it."

Pragmatic Idealism

"We will be friends of all, satellites of none."
—The late Errol Barrow, former Prime Minister of Barbados

Sitting in her office in Bridgetown, Barbados, Mottley quotes from Adam Smith's *Wealth of Nations*: "It is not from the benevolence of the butcher, the brewer, or the baker that we expect our dinner, but from their regard to their own interest."[9] In many ways, this encapsulates Mottley's approach to brokering support for Bridgetown. She understands that successful implementation requires give and take, and it necessitates working with those with whom she may disagree ideologically to create progress. Most of all, it means not giving in to the constraints of the purity test outlined in Chapter 2, where one is forced into a binary choice between demonstrating absolute loyalty to the "tribe" and embracing change, even if it is imperfect. In this, she proves a courageous commitment to pragmatism.

This can be seen in Mia Mottley's collaboration with France's President Macron, despite the West's vast unpopularity with the Global South. Following Macron's commitment to host a summit in mid-2023 mentioned earlier, Mottley worked closely with France to encourage other countries and leading financial institutions to participate. Momentum began to build. In the weeks before and during the summit, leading economies such as the US, UK, and France all came out and committed to offering Pause Clauses [66]. This culminated in the moment mentioned at the start of this chapter, with the World Bank also pledging to follow suit at the 20,000-person Power Our Planet event in front of the Eiffel Tower.

Immediately after this announcement, Mottley thanked Macron in front of the audience, acknowledging the substantial political capital he had invested in the summit. However, due to Macron's unpopularity domestically, the crowd started booing and chanting,

---

[9] This was from an exchange the author had with Mottley in April, 2023 in Bridgetown, Barbados.

"Macron must go." Finding herself on the opposite side of the climate movement, in which she is considered a leader, Mottley faced a crucial decision. She could have taken the easier path and backtracked on her words. Instead, she challenged the crowd. Speaking above the booing, she stated, "My friends, trust me, I want you to know that the one person in the G7 who has stood up for the planet has been President Macron. So, whether we like it or not, that's our reality." The crowd settled and then cheered.

This story exemplifies the significance of private candor and public support in building trust with key decision-makers. Leading up to the summit, Mottley and her partners did not see eye to eye with Macron on every issue, and there were moments of frustration with the summit's organization from those involved in Bridgetown. Moreover, the summit did not secure commitments to all aspects of Bridgetown. However, throughout, Mottley conveyed her disagreements and concerns privately. After all, Macron had agreed to organize the summit and invested time and energy to make it a success in a way that other leaders had not. This, by itself, was instrumental in advancing Bridgetown's policy proposals. Therefore, she reasoned that she would defend him publicly and support his efforts. "I want to thank President Macron for his courage. He has broken away from the pack he has!" She said in a speech two months before the Summit. If she had chosen to be more critical publicly, she might have jeopardized their productive working relationship. Even worse, she may not have made any progress.

There are numerous other examples of Mottley's pragmatism. She spends time, for example, traveling to Washington, DC, to meet with Republican senators such as Lindsay Graham and Bill Cassidy. Not to chastise them for their lack of climate credentials but to offer counsel. Suppose they are apprehensive about China's rise and influence in the Global South, Mottley reasoned with them. In that case, they should spend time understanding and responding to the South's needs to earn more respect and goodwill toward the US. Bridgetown offered them a pathway to do this.

Similarly, Mottley understands the importance of working within institutions rather than burning them down. Following Barbados's removal of the British monarch as its head of state, Mottley could have taken Barbados out of the Commonwealth—the association of former British colonies—in protest at its controversial legacy of colonialism and slavery. Instead, she doubled down on her engagement in it, recognizing it as a valuable vehicle to build support for Bridgetown, helping to pressure countries such as the UK to endorse aspects of it. After all, most of the Commonwealth members are from the Global South. She has even nurtured a relationship with its head, King Charles, who she respects on a personal level. "He gets it," she tells me.

Finally, in her efforts to garner support and endorsements for Bridgetown, Mottley leveraged her growing platform and prominence as a leader in the broader global climate justice movement. She used this to support other policy proposals that could benefit countries beyond her own. For instance, at the Global Citizen Now conference in New York in April 2023, she called on wealthy nations to fulfill their commitment to provide US$100 billion annually in climate financing for developing countries. It is telling that she did this knowing that most of this funding would primarily benefit the poorest countries rather than those like hers, which, although vulnerable to climate change, are considered middle-income.[10] Additionally, she advocated for increased funding for the World Bank, emphasizing that it could intensify its climate change efforts without diverting resources from poverty alleviation. This approach not only bolstered Bridgetown's appeal among developing countries but also countered allegations that Bridgetown aimed to divert funds from poorer nations simply to support the reconstruction of 5-star resorts on her island.[11] As Mottley pointed out, the full implementation of

---

[10] Or in some cases they are even considered high-middle-income. See https://blogs.worldbank.org/opendata/new-world-bank-group-country-classifications-income-level-fy24.

[11] I have seen a transcript of at least one influential meeting where such allegations were made.

Bridgetown would ultimately expand available resources, benefiting not only poor countries but also those at risk of becoming impoverished due to climate change.

Leverage Your Partners' Strengths

"The power of one, if fearless and focused, is formidable, but the power of many working together is better."
—Gloria Macapagal Arroyo, 14th President of the Philippines
(2001–2010)

An effective policy entrepreneur identifies their leverage point and quickly discerns how to complement their approach through partnerships. Mottley consistently considers her strengths and limitations of being the leader of a small island independent nation. As the prime minister of one of the world's 193 sovereign nations, no matter how small, Mottley can gain access to the most influential people in the world. As I write this, Mottley has just participated in a gathering of leaders from the Americas, including figures such as President Biden and Prime Minister Justin Trudeau of Canada.

Yet, Mottley is also acutely aware of her influence's limits. From time to time she has publicly expressed her frustration. "I have to come here like I am a protestor, having been elected by a country—not once, but twice—and I'm being told that I have no right to speak at the World Bank's highest tables." But Mottley also understands how such constraints can be complemented.

As we've seen, Mottley understood the importance of having a leader from a wealthy nation, such as President Macron of France, agree to host a dedicated summit supporting many Bridgetown ideals. This was crucial to attract the participation and interest of high-profile leaders, such as the president of Brazil, Lula da Silva, US Treasury Secretary Janet Yellen, and Chinese Premier Li Qiang. However, she also recognized that convening a diverse group of partners was necessary to ensure that Bridgetown gained enough traction so that governments of wealthy nations felt pressure from their citizens.

In advance of the summit, Mottley convened various civil society organizations and foundations in July 2022, seeking their support for the Bridgetown Initiative and the broader climate justice agenda. The Rockefeller and Open Society Foundations were among the first to rally behind Bridgetown, having helped organize and participate in this original retreat that coalesced and developed its strategy. They committed substantial capital for public campaigns, encouraging countries and institutions such as the World Bank to implement Bridgetown proposals. Mottley herself said she could "think of few better allies than Rockefeller" [67]. Founded over a century ago from the proceeds of Standard Oil, the Rockefeller Foundation has pledged to divest its endowment from fossil fuels and allocate US$1 billion toward climate solutions, aligning well with the climate justice ideals of Bridgetown [68].

Furthermore, with the backing of these foundations, groups such as Global Citizen agreed to mobilize millions of global citizen advocates worldwide, urging them to call on their governments and the World Bank to support Bridgetown policy proposals. In the lead-up to the summit, over 250,000 actions, such as tweets, emails, letter-writing, and phone calls, were taken by citizens in support of this effort. Over 80 NGOs and think tanks, including the ONE Campaign and the Pandemic Action Network, endorsed the call to action. Additionally, organizations with technical expertise on policy ideas, such as the Centre for Disaster Protection, provided valuable evidence-based briefs and technical advice to policymakers considering supporting Pause Clauses.

The campaign also enjoyed the support of some of the world's most prominent artists. Mottley herself had discussions with Billie Eilish's mother, inviting the singer to join her at the summit in Paris. In the days leading up to the World Bank's announcement of its intention to support Pause Clauses, Barbadian superstar Rihanna also leveraged her social media platform to call out Ajay Banga and Janet Yellen, urging them to support Mottley's agenda. This collective effort provided a flashpoint for generating further pressure on attendees. It also offered a highly visible platform to highlight the promises made by powerful institutions, including the World Bank, to set an example.

Savoring the commitments toward Pause Clauses at Macron's summit, Mottley pays tribute to the power of partnership behind Bridgetown, making it clear that it was bigger than any individual or idea. Speaking to a reporter ahead of Banga's announcement, she corrects reports that credit her and Persaud for Bridgetown's success. This is an "inclusive process," she exclaims, involving other countries, organizations, and civil society. That is the spirit of Bridgetown [69].

Know Your Endgame

"Anyone who has followed her [Mottley] or who knows her will understand that if she picks up an issue, such as the finance question, she will follow it to its conclusion fearlessly" [70].

—Chloé Farand, *Climate Home News*

Mottley's Bridgetown achieved significant breakthroughs at the summit in June 2023, with the US, UK, France, Spain, the World Bank, and others all agreeing to offer Pause Clauses by the end of 2025, with some promising to offer them as early as 2023 [71]. In October 2023, Canada followed suit.

However, several issues emerged in the summit's immediate aftermath regarding how such promises would be adequately implemented and the extent of their real-world impact. One of the most crucial issues was whether Pause Clauses would be applied retrospectively to all loan agreements a country had with the World Bank or only to new agreements. Given the debt distress many countries were already under, a decision to apply them solely to new loans would have had limited impact, yet this seemed to be the direction the World Bank was at first planning to take [72].

True to her pragmatic approach, Mottley exhibited tenacity in her follow-up efforts, employing a dual-track process of public shaming alongside private discussions in which her tone was persuasive rather than bludgeoning.[12] According to one observer with inside knowledge of these meetings, "The original World Bank proposal had several shortfalls, and [she] would not let them go unaddressed." She fought vigorously for adjustments, ensuring important details that could affect the Pause Clauses' efficacy did not slip through her fingers. After all, "those who give up achieve nothing" [73].

Tenacity aside, however, sustaining the momentum, partnerships, and influence of Bridgetown was also imperative to extracting the changes Mottley sought. Crucially, she secured financial support from a private foundation to facilitate the establishment of a Bridgetown Initiative secretariat, equipped to delve into and track the technical details as institutions implemented their promises (after all, Mottley was still the prime minister of a country and had countless other demands on her time at any one moment). Additionally, by the end of 2023, Mottley had been nominated as the next Chair of the V20, a coalition of climate-vulnerable world leaders, including President Ruto of Kenya, President Akufo-Addo of Ghana, and President Macky Sall of Senegal, all of whom had endorsed Bridgetown.[13] This support also added much-needed institutional capacity for tracking delivery and advocating for full implementation.

Thanks to these collective efforts, less than six months after the initial announcement, the World Bank, during the UN climate talks in Dubai in December 2023, has outlined several ways it will enhance the implementation of Pause Clauses [74]. It has extended the number of countries offered Pause Clauses from 12 to 45. If triggered, the clauses will pause loan payments for two years with no conditions attached to how countries use the money. Crucially, it has also committed to introducing them into new *and* existing loan agreements, which would be significant for those nations

---

[12] This approach mirrored her participation in meetings the Rockefeller Foundation organized for Mottley behind the scenes at the Fall 2022 and Spring 2023 IMF/WB Meetings meant to advance the Bridgetown proposals on a very practical level.

[13] Known as the Vulnerable Twenty (V20) Group: https://www.v-20.org/members.

already saddled with high debt repayments, such as Barbados. In total, the new clauses cover US$9.5 billion in existing World Bank loans; up to US$500 million payments could be paused across all eligible loan contracts in the event of disaster. In a further boost, in October 2023, the credit rating agency Moody's also said they would not consider the triggering of Pause Clauses as an act of default, which should help continue to normalize their use even further in debt agreements with the private sector [75].

Conclusion

Pause Clauses are, of course, not a silver bullet to the growing climate and debt crisis.[14] Much of the other solutions proposed by Bridgetown— now in its second iteration—have yet to be implemented or even committed to. For instance, countries already facing crushing debt levels still need to negotiate some form of broader debt relief, such as cancellation. As Mottley herself has noted, wealthy nations currently appear willing only to implement the parts of Bridgetown that don't incur immediate upfront costs.[15] Even as far as Pause Clauses are concerned, as of the time of writing, the World Bank has not yet extended Pause Clauses to cover other disasters, such as pandemics, as called for by Bridgetown.

Mottley and Bridgetown is also not without their critics. Some observers point out the potential risks involved in her pragmatic realpolitik approach such as her choice to engage with all countries, including those some might perceive as having dubious moral standings. Others have argued that Barbados's domestic sustainable footprint is still developing, and rather than encouraging international

---

[14] Only 2.2% of international crisis financing for planning and preparing for shocks across the five years 2017–2021 is pre-arranged, and of this small amount, just 3.7% reached low-income countries between 2017 and 2021. See Plichta and Poole 2023.
[15] Moreover, while there has been some movement and interest, particularly at the recent climate talks in Dubai on other Bridgetown proposals such as taxation, the transformative financial commitments it calls for, such as $1 trillion in new affordable lending, still seem distant.

companies to explore Barbadian oil and gas opportunities, it should be doubling down on boosting its green credentials in order to walk the talk in global discussions [76].

Regardless of the merits and shortcomings of these criticisms however, it is undeniable that the approach taken by Mottley and the partnerships behind Bridgetown has already delivered. In her words, it has provided "a record of action." It has likely also laid the foundation for future policy breakthroughs. At the very least, it is a powerful illustration of how a clear and realistic policy agenda can help facilitate common ground on a potentially divisive issue. Her approach involves powerful storytelling, connecting with broad audiences, and effectively leveraging complementary coalitions and networks. As a result, assuming the momentum of Bridgetown continues and those who have made promises are held accountable, numerous climate-vulnerable countries will be able to respond to future disasters without worrying about how to pay their bills.

It is fitting that Bridgetown takes its name from a historic bridge that has, in one form or another, stood the test of time in what is today Barbados's capital. With her message deeply rooted in a strong sense of justice, Mottley could have quickly become a polarizing figure, exacerbating divisions between the Global North and South. Such an approach, anchored solely in blame, might have even been advantageous for her domestic politics. However, Mottley has made it her mission instead to build bridges wherever she can, never losing sight of the real difference she could make in people's lives [77]. Through Bridgetown, her calls for climate justice have gone "from being a symbol of moral outrage to a serious possibility". In a world in dire need of bridge builders, it is perhaps of little surprise that Mottley has been touted as a frontrunner for the next Secretary-General of the United Nations [78].

Perhaps more than anything else, Mottley's unique style of policy entrepreneurship demonstrates the prudence of embracing compromise and incremental breakthroughs when you can get them—a win is a win, after all—while not losing sight of the bigger picture. In this sense, Bridgetown is a path, not a milestone, and even in our divided world, we *can* walk it together, one step at a time.

7 | Finding One World: Lessons in Collective Action

"What is the UN, you might ask? Well, the very least we can say is that it is there, and it goes on. That is far more than nothing. It is, in fact, a huge collective enterprise. It is our best answer to the question of who the 'we' is" [1].
                                —Adam Tooze, historian and podcaster

A six-year-old boy looks up as he hears distant gunfire, signaling the approaching enemy with death and destruction in tow.

His parents conceal their fear, maintaining a semblance of normalcy until the war intensifies. With barely any belongings in hand, the boy, his younger brother, his father, and his nine-month-pregnant mother join the mass exodus from the city. Amid terror and excruciating pain, the boy's mother gives birth to a baby sister on the roadside. There is no time to recover; without a moment to lose, the family presses forward again. They soon reach their grandparents' house at a forest's edge to wait out the conflict. They look on in fear as bombs rain down on distant towns and villages.

Months go by. A coalition of countries united under one organization's flag intervenes, ending the conflict and bringing aid, food, and even school materials. The boy sees the organization's flag soaring high on a building—a "blue and white flag, with a globe cradled by the olive branches of peace," symbolizing safety and hope. Devouring the schoolbooks provided, the boy reads a message on their last page, "This textbook was printed with generous assistance from the UN."

The UN's operations rescued the boy's country, paving the way for him and his fellow students to rebuild their lives in improvised classrooms.

Decades later, South Korea, once completely ravaged by war, stands as one of the world's wealthiest economies—a testament to the transformative power of the UN. As the boy had sat in those makeshift classrooms, he knew he would one day repay the favor. More than 70 years later, Ban Ki-moon, the eighth Secretary-General of the United Nations, reflects that global solidarity "saved my country, and I believe it can save our world."[1]

****

The Challenge: Our Divided Nations

Today, as we grapple with the pressing challenges of runaway climate change, biodiversity loss, regional conflicts and casualties, and the enduring calamities of poverty and hunger, it is only natural to approach this chapter skeptically. Things, after all, are going from bad to worse.

Just as I concluded writing this chapter, war broke out between Israel and Hamas following the latter's shocking terrorist attacks on October 7, leaving more than 1,400 dead.[2] In the ensuing conflict that followed, as of writing, more than 10,000 people in Gaza have

---

[1] This is a summarized version of the story Ban tells in greater detail in his personal memoir. See Ban 2020.
[2] Hamas is designated as a terrorist organization by several countries, including the United States, the European Union, Canada, Israel, and others.

already been killed, with allegations of war crimes on both sides. The death toll will likely be far greater and horrifying by the time this book is released. The UN Security Council, designed to address such conflicts, faced its usual paralysis, with one great powers' veto following another. Richard Gowan, a longtime UN observer interviewed for this chapter, acknowledges that criticism of the UN "is hardly new." However, he also expressed concern that the UN appears "more rudderless than ever" and that the present conflict could deal "a significant blow to the UN's credibility" [2].

And yet . . . we blame the UN for the world's present trajectory at our peril. While the UN has evident faults, primarily due to geopolitical limitations ingrained at its inception, it remains crucial for humanity's survival. The UN provides a unique forum for addressing the numerous challenges in which all countries share an interest in cooperation. This is evident in the trust and support it continues to enjoy (miraculously so, given the bad press it gets), even as it falls short of expectations [3].

This recognition stems from the understanding, shared by many who identify as global citizens, that cooperation is essential—both in our daily lives and when addressing challenges that know no borders. Frustrating as it may be, working together is our only viable option if we aim to implement practical solutions to global challenges. History has shown, as seen with the fate of the UN's pre–World War II predecessor, the League of Nations, that abandoning such collaborative efforts is a risk we cannot afford [4].[3]

While cooperation in our personal lives may involve simple agreements, structured institutions such as the UN are essential for finding common ground on a larger scale [5]. The alternative—an "everyone for themselves" approach—is a recipe for disaster and, in today's divided world, akin to a suicide pact.

---

[3] While it's fair to acknowledge that the old League made many meaningful contributions to facilitating global cooperation, such as spreading new standards in medicine and industrial legislation, amid the turmoil of the 1930s, it cannot escape the judgment, as Steiner points out, that it ultimately failed to act as a substitute for great-power politics that gave way to World War II.

While much of the world's population appears to understand the value of such institutions, our daily news is full of stories that focus solely on their dismal performance.[4] Much like the European Union in the run-up to Brexit, the UN faces constant criticism.

Yet beneath the radar, and notwithstanding its many weaknesses, the UN at its best provides valuable insights into how to address our implementation crisis regarding global challenges. The following examples are fundamentally stories of "how"—narratives filled with hope, resilience, pragmatism, and collaboration. They demonstrate that far from being the root of our current woes, institutions of global cooperation such as the UN are often the only thing standing between some semblance of order and anarchy, between humanity and destruction.

To the extent that the UN does have failings—and there are many—they often stem, as we will see, from the weaknesses of national governments that constrain its full potential. Fortunately, these stories also demonstrate how innovative policy entrepreneurship can circumvent these limitations, providing solutions to challenges ranging from extreme poverty to climate change. Ultimately, they offer a glimpse into what is achievable if we rededicate ourselves to realizing former US President Harry Truman's vision of a "Republic of the World" [6].

Policy Entrepreneurship in Action: Finding One World

Know Which Stakeholders Matter and How to Appeal to Them

"We [need to] influence cabinet rooms, **boardrooms**, and living rooms."
—Simon Stiell, Executive Secretary of the United Nations Framework Convention on Climate Change ("UNFCCC")

---

[4] According to a Glocalities survey, 46% to 77% of individuals in each country support the idea of international institutions, such as the UN, having enforcement powers and the ability to promote global order, with only 4% to 18% in disagreement. Most people in surveyed nations, including the US (57%), view the UN as a legitimate entity on par with their own national government. This sentiment, even transcending political divides, reflects a desire to strengthen the UN to prevent countries from engaging in bullying tactics against others. See Global Nation 2023.

The UN was established as a place for nation-states to convene, find common ground, settle disputes, and address the shared challenges of our time. And yet, the world looks remarkably different from when it was founded in 1945. For example, big corporations are just as, and in some cases more, powerful and influential than the leaders of many nation-states [7–9]. And with that increased influence, they have also profoundly affected the world, including being significant contributors to greenhouse gas emissions [10–11].

As the world races against time to prevent runaway climate change, government actions progress sluggishly, with outright resistance from some. This raises fundamental questions: Can the world's largest businesses, cities, and universities be motivated to compensate for this shortfall, even when they are not legally obligated to do so? Even when many have reportedly waged a decades-long campaign against efforts to compel them to act? And how does the UN evolve—beyond its traditional nation-state-focused mandate—to persuade them otherwise?

By 2020, the UN had long recognized its unique convening role in accelerating action from significant non-state actors. After all, any government's ability to hit national climate targets largely depends on the efforts of companies, cities and universities. Accordingly, beginning in 2016, the UN had already started to appoint high-level champions to serve annually to urge non-state actors to take climate action. This built on prior efforts going back to 2000 when former UN Secretary-General Kofi Annan launched the UN's first initiative, the UN Global Compact, to promote responsible business practices.

Even so, while years of public shaming and increased technical support had succeeded in getting countless companies to take more significant notice, only a few companies had made commitments at the required scale.

Leveraging the unique credibility afforded by their UN mandate, the then high-level champions, Gonzalo Muñoz, a Chilean entrepreneur and Nigel Topping, a British non-profit leader known for private sector partnerships, launched the Race to Zero campaign in 2020. Building on the groundwork laid by various integrity frameworks and standards, the campaign's core objective is to rally businesses, universities and local governments to reduce emissions [12–13].

The campaign's premise is that if it can convince a critical mass of at least 20% of these players, to sign up, it will help countries reach a "point of no turning back" ("Breakthrough Ambition") [14]. In other words, governments will have greater political cover and face less resistance to introducing regulations necessary to compel holdout stakeholders to take action. This is how we shift society to reduce emissions.

Constantly undergoing continuous improvement, the Race to Zero campaign provides a robust road map to prevent climate targets from being undermined by greenwashing [15–17]. This is especially important, given that some corporations have made false claims about their sustainability efforts in recent years [18]. This has made it difficult for consumers to distinguish between what is legitimately green and what is not, eroding public confidence in corporate claims more broadly. Thus, one of the goals of the Race to Zero campaign is to prevent companies from simply creating shiny commercials about their climate commitments and instead align all their corporate operations with science-based targets [19]. In other words, to move from talk to action. This requires developing transparent short-term reduction targets that can be used by all stakeholders, including shareholders and civil society, to hold them accountable.

In signing up for the Race to Zero, participants must commit to halving their emissions by 2030 as part of a larger mission to achieve net-zero emissions by 2050. Their approach must result in actual emission reductions; offsetting alone ("paying to pollute") won't cut it. Committed stakeholders are also required to publish clear timelines and regular reports. At the same time, targets must be verified by UN-accredited climate scientists [20].

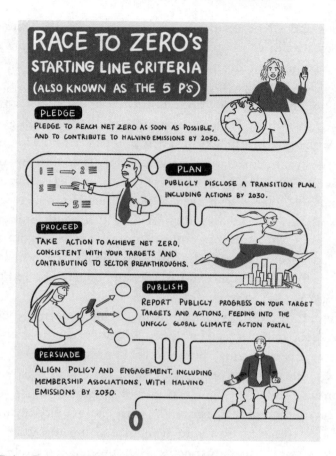

Figure 7.1   Race to Zero's Starting Line Criteria
Source: "Taking Stock of Progress—September 2022: First joint progress report across UN-backed global climate campaigns: Race to Resilience and Race to Zero." UNFCCC.

Since its inception, the Race to Zero campaign has influenced thousands of stakeholders—including some of the world's largest companies—to sign up by successfully appealing to their self-interest. This process is twofold.

First, the campaign promotes a compelling body of data and facts to underscore why taking action on climate change is not just a moral imperative but also firmly in the best interest of businesses. Campaign champions and advocates make companies aware of the risks they face if they are not adequately prepared. For example, they warn that those companies that do not move fast enough will eventually be forced to do so anyway, as incoming mandatory regulation and reporting requirements catch up with the urgency of climate change.

They also point out the economic benefits that will accrue to businesses that take early action. They point to a study, for instance, showing a strong correlation between financial performance and reduced emissions [21]. As an example of this, in 2020 Walmart stated it had been able to achieve hundreds of millions in annual cost savings through sustainable measures like installing LED light bulbs [22]. In the years since, the emissions from its operations have continued to fall as it adds solar panels to its buildings, installs electric vehicle charging stations for its customers and asks its suppliers to also reduce their emissions [23].

Second, the campaign identifies and recruits effective messengers to appeal to relevant stakeholders. Notable champions include advocates with substantial business backgrounds, such as Michael Bloomberg (former mayor of NYC and American billionaire and philanthropist) and Marc Benioff (CEO of Salesforce, which set ambitious reduction targets). It also works with civil society organizations to provide credible platforms to recognize companies that lead the way publicly. For instance, during the 24-hour streamed Global Citizen Live in 2021, featuring renowned artists such as Elton John and Coldplay, 13 of the world's largest companies officially committed to the Race to Zero campaign [24].

These collective efforts have yielded enormous results. Today, it stands as the largest-ever alliance committed to hitting net-zero carbon emissions by 2050. As of June 2023, the campaign boasts signatories from over 9,000 companies and more than 1,000 cities [25]. From small businesses in Spain to universities in Pakistan to wineries in Chile, commitments span the globe [26]. One campaign partner reported that, by December 2022, its approved Race to Zero corporate signatories had collectively pledged to reduce annual emissions by 76 million tons—an amount surpassing Switzerland's entire yearly emissions twice over [27].

In terms of follow-through, another partner report shows that companies with approved targets collectively reduced emissions from their operations and energy consumption by 12% in 2020 alone [28].

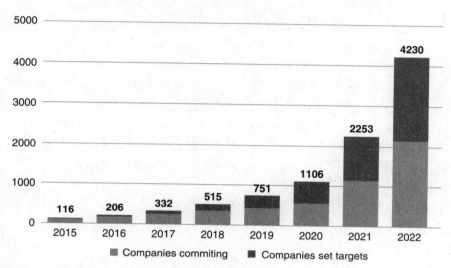

Figure 7.2 Cumulative number of companies with approved targets and commitments between 2015 and 2022.
Source: "SBTi Monitoring Report 2022." Science Based Targets 2022.

The campaign is not without criticism, with some accusing the UN of overstepping its mandate and others suggesting it might inadvertently take the pressure off and further alienate governments from the official UN climate process, the so-called "UN COP talks" [29]. In other words, rather than being complementary, it risks distracting from the "main event" [30].[5] Other critics point out the shortfalls of self-regulated voluntary action, emphasizing the need for full regulatory oversight to eliminate the risk of greenwashing [31].

With respect to these last points, however, the campaign's ultimate validation arguably lies in the fact that, driven by the

---

[5] In an email exchange, Michael Franczak of the International Peace Institute pointed out to me that this fear is grounded in how recent decades saw a major retreat of developed countries from those forums and a downgrading of their legislative and normative powers.

voluntary efforts of thousands of businesses ("the ambition loop"), the world's major economies including the US and the European Union have either introduced or are in the process of implementing regulations and rules to strengthen corporate climate action [32–33]. Without this plethora of corporate targets, regulators may have taken much longer to act. To reach this point, the campaign's success has been propelled by its strategic framing of sustainability as both a savvy business decision and a moral imperative. Ultimately, it serves as an example of how institutions can effectively sidestep obstacles—in this case, the slow pace of government action—to spur meaningful action and accelerate the race to zero.

Mastering the Art of Timing

"No one talked about divisive politics on this day. No nation abstained. It was a rare moment when the United Nations was truly united" [34].

—Ban Ki-moon, referring to the day when the SDGs were adopted (September 25, 2015)

In 2015, the world's governments transcended geopolitical and ideological divides to adopt two groundbreaking agreements:

1. The Paris Agreement on Climate Change symbolized a shared commitment to keep temperature rises below 2 degrees (Celsius) and preferably 1.5 degrees to avoid climate catastrophe.
2. The UN Sustainable Development Goals (SDGs) is a comprehensive set of 17 goals to tackle poverty, inequality, hunger, and public health challenges. This encompassed a unanimous and historic agreement to set a deadline for eradicating extreme poverty by 2030.

As the euphoria of these breakthroughs has faded away, giving rise to new divisions, it is easy to look back on them as mere products of their time. That, irrespective of the challenging issues involved in their negotiations, their passage was more or less assured due to the good luck in timing. Ban Ki-moon himself, who oversaw both processes as UN Secretary-General, has said: "There was never a question—not even for a minute—that the Millennium Development Goals (the forerunner of the SDGs) would continue in some form after the mandate expired in 2015" [35–36]. Indeed, their agreement came not long after the UN's ability to forge consensus peaked in the early 2010s.

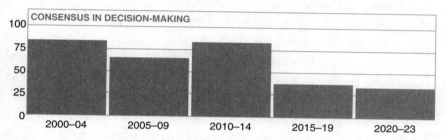

Figure 7.3 Score from the *2023 Global Solidarity Report* showing the collapse in the consensus of decision-making at the UN since 2015. *Source:* "Global Solidarity Report," 56. Global Nation. 2023. The score represents the percentage of UN decisions agreed by consensus that did not go to vote or veto.

However, those involved in the challenging work of diplomacy know there is no such thing as good luck regarding timing. A good diplomat creates good timing through skill, instinct, and proactiveness. Above all, they are hyper-aware that negotiations typically operate in a brief window of opportunity. They know they must step in and drive the process to a conclusion before this window closes.

Most importantly, good diplomats look for ways to control the timing of negotiations in a manner most advantageous to achieving consensus. At a certain point in the process, the person leading a negotiation must make an informed gamble—a big bet—and pull the trigger on when to impose a deadline. If they pick the right moment, "delegations will almost always join the group rather than capsize an agreement" [37]. After all, no one wants to be held publicly responsible for torpedoing essential agreements.

Ban and the diplomats he appointed were masterful policy entre-preneurs in the negotiation of the SDGs and the Paris Agreement. These included, among others, Amina Mohammed of Nigeria, who served as Ban's special advisor on the SDGs, and Christiana Figueres of Costa Rica as head of the UNFCCC. There are several films and books about the critical role these leaders played that I highly recom-mend readers check out.[6]

The SDGs dealt with significant contentious issues that required countries to find common ground. For example, there was disagree-ment on who would pay for their implementation; wealthy nations had to be assured they would not be on the hook to fund it all.[7] Nonetheless, in 2012, Ban Ki-moon gave governments just two weeks at a summit in Brazil to agree, in principle, to negotiate new develop-ment goals to end poverty by 2030. In his book *Resolved*, Ban describes the moment he abruptly took a gambit to bring debate to a close, winning authority from world leaders to agree on a new set of goals by September 2015. As he expresses in his own words, "Negotiations go down to the wire. Always. No matter how much time is allotted, no matter how anodyne the subject, people will find it necessary to debate a point until it's time to come together or pull the plug" [38].

---

[6] In September 2023, a documentary was released, showcasing Mohammed's relent-less efforts to build consensus and secure the adoption of the goals. The negotiations themselves could fill an entire book. A significant factor contributing to the success of the SDGs was the extensive global multi-stakeholder consultations. Notably, robust outreach and engagement with global civil society played a crucial role in bolstering support for the negotiations and lending broad-based credibility to this ambitious project. See UN Office of Partnerships 2023; for an overview of Figueres' role, check out the book she coauthored with her advisor Tom Rivett-Carnac: Figueres and Rivett-Carnac 2020.

[7] Other points of disagreement included the idea that the SDGs would apply equally and universally to all citizens, rich and poor alike, across all 193 UN countries; the US, in particular, is susceptible to any UN goal, mandate, or target that it might perceive as infringing on its sovereignty. Strong views in support and against "peace" being included as a goal also existed; some countries were worried peace might become a precondition for receiving humanitarian aid.

The following three years were dedicated to grueling negotiations on the details. Numerous negotiators and advocates played pivotal roles in these negotiations, capitalizing on the deadline Ban had secured to break through deadlocks. David Donoghue of Ireland, one of the two co-facilitators of the SDG negotiations, explained that the clear September 2015 deadline forced everyone's hand, making it a "now or never" situation.

Based on his experience working on the Good Friday Agreement (which was discussed in Chapter 2), Donoghue understood the power of timing and deadlines. In that negotiation, the US, Irish, and UK governments had imposed Good Friday in 1998 as a final deadline and were adamant they could not dedicate the same level of time and effort beyond that. Another opportunity would have to wait another generation or two if they failed.

Applying this insight to the SDGs, Donoghue and his Kenyan counterpart confronted a situation where progress seemed to stall, and negotiators resorted to delay tactics. In response, they strategically introduced their own "triggering events" or "phony reasons" to maintain momentum [39]. For example, they informed negotiators that all meeting rooms were booked in one instance to prevent discussions from dragging on. This adept use of deadlines and inventive measures proved instrumental in keeping the negotiation process on track.

When the SDGs were finally "gaveled" into existence in September 2015, the South African ambassador used his remarks to invoke the memory of Nelson Mandela: "It always seems impossible until it is done." For two whole minutes, applause filled the room.

★★★★★★★

Securing the Paris Agreement by November 2015 was even more arduous. The negotiations took place against the looming 2016 US election, which would have significant implications for US commitment depending on the outcome. Ban and UN negotiators used the US election as a triggering event to generate urgency. After all, an agreement without the largest economy and biggest historic emitter was not credible. Ban's proposition was thus clear: agree by the end of 2015 or risk losing the opportunity to agree anything at all. He traveled the world, met with leaders, and convinced them that getting something, even if not everything they wanted, was better than nothing. In late 2015, leaders celebrated another historic, albeit imperfect, agreement in Paris.

★★★★★★

Years on, we know the impact of these two agreements has not been smooth sailing, and it remains to be seen at the current moment of writing if their promises will be achieved fully, in part, or not at all. However, the flurry of creative diplomacy in the lead-up to 2015 deserves its place in the canons of history. These two agreements were far from certain. Ultimately, the skillful mastering of timing proved critical.

Know Your Endgame

"Organizations are incorporeal; they have no will, no mind, no soul. They live only through human beings who implement them" [40].
—John Foster Dulles, former US Secretary of State (1953-1959)

The main criticism of the UN today is its inability to hold nations accountable. Whether addressing crimes of aggression or upholding climate commitments, the UN faces near-daily attacks. Paradoxically, this lack of power stems from the UN's original design, shaped by the pragmatic interests of the victorious countries of WWII. The real surprise, however, isn't its failure to live down to its founders' expectations; it's the fact that it has exceeded them. Despite its imperfections, the UN has found innovative and creative approaches to hold countries accountable for crucial aspects of its mission. These developments inevitably get overshadowed by the frequent deadlock in the UN's executive body, the Security Council, but they do exist. They illustrate that progress can occur within institutions marked by deep divisions, improving people's lives, even amid a sometimes frustrating process.

Wrongdoing occurs at all levels of governance, from the local to the global. Everyday examples include receiving fines for running red lights and individuals being charged, tried, and imprisoned for attempted armed burglary. In this case, the critical question is whether and how institutions such as the UN can prevent impunity to maintain order and justice.

In the same vein, we are concerned about the UN's capacity to hold its members accountable for committing acts of aggression against other member countries and fulfilling their promises to address pressing global issues.

Let's consider three examples of how the UN has been able to do this with varying levels of success before examining *how* these evolutions occurred.

War and Conflict

The UN General Assembly ("Assembly") is the primary deliberating body for 193 member states. The victorious powers who designed the UN initially intended it to be little more than an annual advisory body for smaller states to let off steam [41–42]. Power was meant to be concentrated in the UN Security Council ("Council"), dominated by the veto-wielding power of its five permanent members.[8] In essence, if any of these powers decided to invade a small country, they were effectively given free rein to shut down any criticism of their actions in the Council by applying the veto. Impunity, at least for a select few, was thus a natural outcome of the WWII victorious powers' desire to ensure a UN system that would not challenge their national prerogatives.

On the one hand, the UN system was built to resist any changes that could challenge this prerogative. The Council and the exclusive power of the veto are virtually immune from any reform. As one

---

[8] These being: Russia, United Kingdom, France, United States, and China.

former Russian ambassador reportedly put it, "We created this structure after WWII, so if you want to make all these changes, you need WWIII" [43].

Nonetheless, notwithstanding these built-in limitations, the General Assembly has gradually amassed significant power that challenges these original intentions, including encroaching on the Council's hitherto exclusive oversight of peace and security matters. This includes the authority to recommend the imposition of sanctions and to create investigative bodies and tribunals to address serious crimes—powers once deemed beyond the Assembly's scope [44]. In other words, the General Assembly has actively sought to fill the power vacuum created by a Security Council that is often in gridlock [45].

These developments are evident in the UN's response to the Russia-Ukraine war. In this instance, Gowan has argued that "the UN system as a whole has done its job in terms of demanding accountability and identifying the aggressor" [46–47]. For example, the Assembly passed resolutions condemning Russia's actions with substantial majorities, suspended Russia from the UN Human Rights Council, and established a register to compile compensation claims for potential trials related to the war in Ukraine [48]. Additionally, the Human Rights Council has established a commission of inquiry for war crimes [49].[9]

By actively shaping the UN's response to conflict and war, an area initially reserved for the great powers in the Council, the Assembly can prevent some of the world's most powerful countries from acting with impunity. Some commentators suggest this shift sets the stage for further expansion of the Assembly's power in the coming years. For example, it could be granted the authority to bring a challenge to suspend the Russian delegation from UN participation, endorse diplomatic and economic sanctions, and establish a tribunal to prosecute Russian leaders for the crime of aggression [50]. Time will tell if this

---

[9] On April 7, 2022, it adopted a resolution suspending the rights of membership of Russia in the Human Rights Council. See UN 2022 (adopted by a vote of 93 in favor, 24 against, 58 abstentions).

becomes a reality. The Israel–Hamas conflict may provide further cause for the Assembly to flex its muscles. Ultimately, the longer the Council continues to be constrained by paralysis, the more pressure will build on the more inclusive Assembly to usurp its place.

Climate Change

The architects of the Paris Agreement were far from naive. They understood that short-term electoral considerations would inevitably constrain the actions of nation-states, potentially leading to a "Tragedy of the Horizon" [51]. To address this, they embedded a threefold approach to ensure the long-term goals of the Paris Agreement would be implemented over time. These steps include:

1. **Built-in moments** for reinforcing and revising individual countries' emission reduction targets at global climate summits every five years. We witnessed the first of these moments at the Glasgow summit in 2021.
2. **The Global Stocktake ("GST")** is a preemptive and built-in periodic review of the world's collective efforts toward achieving the Paris Agreement's long-term goals. The first GST was published in September 2023. It identifies the current implementation gap and provides a recommended path forward, with countries agreeing on how to respond to its findings.
3. **Enhanced transparency**, requiring each state to report on the status of target implementation and subject themselves to peer review. Starting in 2024, countries must submit reports every two years.

The underlying premise of these mechanisms is that they collectively serve as a trigger for generating public pressure and focusing the attention of world leaders. This approach gives climate activists a fighting chance to set the agenda in favor of ambitious action, although countries can still respond with insufficient commitments. However, the architects of these mechanisms ultimately hoped that serving as a basis to name and shame those countries failing to meet their obligations would incentivize them to enhance their commitments.

In the end, thanks to the pressure created by these mechanisms, the world is closer to the goal of limiting warming to 1.5 degrees Celsius since preindustrial times. While the promises made at Glasgow weren't sufficient, they did lead to an increase in the ambition of national targets compared to what existed before. By the conclusion of the Glasgow conference, countries representing almost 65 percent of global GDP had increased their emission reduction targets in line with what is required to avoid temperature rises above 1.5 degrees [52].

The first ever GST published in 2023 showed significant progress contrary to expectations—in 2010, the expected temperature rise by 2100 was 3.7°C–4.8°C, but by the end of 2022, it was 2.4°C–2.6°C, and if all countries fulfill their long-term pledges, it could be reduced to 1.7°C–2.1°C [53].

The world remains in a race against time. Should the world succeed in avoiding catastrophic climate change, we will likely owe a significant debt to the policy entrepreneurs who designed these accountability mechanisms to ratchet up ambition over time.

Sustainable Development

At first glance, the accountability process for the SDGs may seem questionable. Without a standardized guideline, countries submit a voluntary and subjective review plan to the UN yearly on their progress. Some countries, such as the US, have even chosen not to submit any reviews. Consequently, it's perhaps unsurprising that, at the halfway mark in 2023, only 12% of the goals had been implemented [54].

However, this is only part of the story. Ambassador Donoghue highlights the significance of having a designated yearly moment for countries to report their progress on the SDGs. This process, he tells me, has cemented citizens' expectations for their governments to effectively address their development needs. They have become, in effect, the minimum benchmark against which the governments are held accountable by both their citizens and each other. It's now widely expected that the SDGs, particularly those yet to be fulfilled, will continue in some form beyond the 2030 deadline. Even the Trump administration which pulled back from several UN process never seriously proposed dropping America's support for the SDGs. This marks a noteworthy shift, considering past concerns about encroachment on state sovereignty.

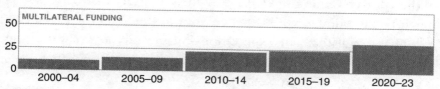

Figure 7.4 Score from the *2023 Global Solidarity Report* shows an overall increase in government funding for global institutions since 2000 when the Millennium Development Goals (the predecessor to SDGs) launched.
Source: "Global Solidarity Report," 56. Global Nation. 2023. The score represents aid given to multilateral institutions like the UN as a percentage of aid committed by wealthy nations.

One outcome of this shift in expectations is the increased financial contributions to the UN and its affiliated development programs. While these contributions may only partially meet the SDG investment needs, they indicate that countries are slowly moving in the right direction.[10] This is another noteworthy development, given the initial hesitations about who would pay for implementing the SDGs.

The worldwide response to the COVID-19 pandemic illustrates this transformation. International aid to UN appeals reached record levels [55]. Sub-Saharan Africa began vaccinating its population just two months after the UK—an impressive, though morally insufficient, achievement compared to historical precedents where such gaps in response times were measured in years or decades.[11] British historian Adam Tooze contrasts this with the early 20th-century

---

[10] See Conclusion for further discussion on scope of SDG investment needs, estimated to be in the trillions.

[11] Indeed, by the end of April 2021, nearly every country had introduced the vaccine. See The Delivery 2023.

response to the Spanish flu, where wealthy nations stood by and let tens of millions quietly die in countries such as India.[12] This response, which met with little public outcry, would be unthinkable today in which governments have—through the SDGs—unanimously agreed to the idea of health for all. Indeed, as Jonathan Glennie, co-founder of the Global Nation think tank told me, "The fact that there was so much public outrage with the inequities of the COVID-19 vaccine rollout is a sign that our expectations for global cooperation are so much higher than they were in the past."

★★★★★★★★

These admittedly glass-half-full examples of closing the implementation gap between vision and reality are reliant on several methods as discussed below.

Creative Legal Methods

Usually, it comes down to a few pioneering policy entrepreneurs willing to try something new and look for ways to push the parameters of UN processes to set new precedents. The UN's history "is full of heroic individuals and their improbable and creative ideas that have pushed the project forward" [56]. For example, a former UN ambassador of Liechtenstein—one of the UN's smallest countries—is credited with galvanizing the Assembly's taking of a historic step to establish and preserve evidence of international crimes in Syria to assist future trials, the first instance of its kind [57].

Public Shaming

Over time, countries have increasingly embraced public shaming of perceived aggressors and wrongdoers, even when it appears to go against their direct interests. For example, many Gulf countries, though

---

[12] This explanation from Tooze took place in a panel discussion during the 2023 Spring World Bank meetings.

not traditional democracies, publicly supported Ukraine in UN votes during Russia's initial invasion, despite having substantial trade surpluses with Russia [58]. In this context, Ukraine's democratic status was not the primary driver; rather, it was a shared commitment to upholding the sanctity of UN member state sovereignty. This is unsurprising given that membership in the UN has become virtually synonymous with the idea of state sovereignty, with 99% of all internationally recognized states being UN members.[13] Thus, despite its many criticisms, the UN has achieved a degree of legitimacy unparalleled in the 5,000 years of history of diplomacy and agreement-making.

The increased prominence of consensus-style UN forums, brought about by the UN's enlarged membership over several decades, has further bolstered countries' ability to shame others. Unlike the Security Council, which acts at the behest of great powers, alternative forums provide countries with an unfettered platform to speak truth to power. For example, the UN's intergovernmental process for negotiating government action on climate change operates by consensus, with each member having an equal vote. As most of its 190-plus members are developing countries, great powers cannot dominate climate negotiations as they do on security issues in the Council. This power dynamic, perhaps unexpected when the UN was founded with only 50 member states, has drawbacks like any consensus-based decision-making body. Still, it ensures that leaders such as Prime Minister Mottley and regional alliances such as the Association of Small Island States cannot be easily sidelined.[14]

---

[13] Note there are 11 disputed states in addition to the 195 that are not UN member states though many have ties and connections with respective UN agencies. The remaining two countries are both UN permanent observer states.

[14] As Michael Franczak noted to me, this contrasts with other institutions such as the IMF and the World Bank, where wealthy nations enjoy disproportionate or even effective veto power. Illustrating this point, in a discussion I attended, Prime Minister Mia Mottley once mentioned that the only way for her to air her views was to speak at forums on the margins of World Bank meetings. She felt that she had no seat at the official table where decisions were being made. This might largely explain why Mottley's "breakout speech" occurred at the COP26 UNFCCC discussions in Glasgow (see Chapter 6). Besides being an effective and timely speech, she was given an equal seat at the table. See Franczak 2023.

Monitoring, Consultation, and Reporting

In addition to various reporting mechanisms, including SDG voluntary reviews, expert panels addressing greenwashing, and the GST under the Paris Agreement, UN membership itself allows states to monitor and consult each other. The value of this should not be underestimated. It is the most enduring example of how the UN pursues its endgame.

Today, all major powers have chosen to remain engaged with the UN, despite significant disagreements or departures from specific UN agencies or agreements. Presumably, they recognize that the value of staying, and the legitimacy it bestows, outweigh the benefits of leaving. For instance, despite facing significant criticism within UN circles, Russia clearly recognizes the continued benefits of remaining at the UN table. Rather than retreating, it is actively trying to rejoin UN bodies such as the UN Human Rights Council (which it lost out to Bulgaria and Albania in votes) [59]. Moreover, while some Western politicians liken China's rise to that of Nazi Germany in the 1930s, unlike such past examples, China is trying to work within and influence the international system rather than creating a new one outside it [60].

Pragmatism and Cooperation

In our divided world, we have forgotten that making mutual concessions is a hallmark of every significant agreement or diplomatic effort. No one gets everything they want. Remember those who negotiated the Good Friday Agreement in Chapter 2.

In today's era, however, there's a growing tendency for groups and individuals to be subjected to a purity test, forcing them into a binary choice. On the one hand, they are pressured to show loyalty to their tribe, even if it means saying no to any incremental progress if we don't get everything we want. Conversely, if they embrace only marginally imperfect change, they risk being labeled a traitor or an outcast by their tribe with potentially serious consequences.

Remarkably, countries engaged in the UN system have primarily avoided being forced into making such binary choices. Few nations seriously advocate for Russia's departure from the UN, especially not Russia itself.[15] Similarly, countries disappointed by the lack of follow-through on global aid or climate commitments have not left the UN in protest.[16] As a result, even when disputes or conflicts arise between some members, as in the case of the Russia-Ukraine war, the UN continues to find consensus on other critical issues. These include unanimously condemning the Taliban's regressive policies on women and girls in Afghanistan while agreeing to channel aid to struggling Afghans [61]. Consensus rates in UN decision-making have improved since reaching their lowest point in the post–Cold War era in 2018 [62]. And it remains far from its lowest ever point in 1959 during the Cold War when the Council passed just one resolution for a whole year [63]. As Gowan told me in the spring of 2023, "While the Security Council maintains a steady state of dysfunction, it is not functioning any worse than before the [Russia-Ukraine] conflict" [64].

Of course, none of this guarantees a positive future. In the aftermath of the Israel-Hamas conflict, Gowan noted that throughout the second half of 2023, "Russia has acted as a spoiler with increasing frequency" [65]. For instance, it vetoed a renewal of a Council resolution from 2014 to provide aid to Syria.

Moreover, the entire system could rapidly unravel if one or more countries were to withdraw permanently. Germany's exit

---

[15] The obvious exception is Ukraine itself and a few lone US diplomats. See responses to this here arguing that excluding Russia would "ultimately make war more likely." See Stocker 2022.

[16] Arguably, they have acted in the opposite way and leaned further into the UN. One historical example: In the 1970s, developing countries initially hesitated to engage in environmental politics, viewing it as a game for the wealthy or a Northern tactic to exclude them. Michael Franczak of the International Peace Institute highlighted that Canadian diplomat and businessman Maurice Strong persuaded them to participate. He approached leaders such as Indira Gandhi, emphasizing that if they didn't define environmental protection on their terms, developed countries would do it for them. As a result, the Group of 77 (G77) came together, ensuring that discussions on the environment wouldn't neglect development. The Kenyan delegation even lobbied successfully to establish the United Nations Environ-ment Programme (UNEP) in Nairobi instead of Geneva, aiming for more equitable technology transfer in the future. See Franczak 2023.

from the League of Nations, prompted by criticism over its acts of aggression, was preceded by Costa Rica's departure due to dissatisfaction with the League's handling of a border dispute with Panama [66]. As the GOP nomination fight kicked off in the fall of 2023, at least one US presidential candidate suggested the US should consider leaving the UN [67]. While momentarily appeasing domestic audiences, such a move would profoundly undermine the UN's legitimacy as the primary forum for countries to discuss major international issues. It could trigger the beginning of a domino effect. Fortunately, most countries have let pragmatic instincts guide them, recognizing the diverse nature of their interests in an increasingly multipolar world.

★★★★★

Conclusion

"The Crisis of Today is the history of tomorrow."
    —Eleanor Roosevelt, First US Delegate to the UN

As with every example in this book, the UN remains a work in progress. As of the time of writing, the UN faces some of its most significant existential challenges in nearly eight decades. Despite this, and perhaps much better than some of its founders imagined, the UN has not been entirely without success in bridging the gap between its ideals and reality. This success, however imperfect, is perhaps why the UN continues to command a level of trust akin to, and in some cases exceeding, that of national governments [68].

Despite sustained criticism, or perhaps because of it, public opinion also appears to be firmly on the side of strengthening the UN, including its powers of enforcement against transgressors, as well as the type of bold reforms needed to achieve many of the SDGs and Paris Agreement's aspirations [69–70]. People recognize, at least for now, that the solution to our implementation crisis regarding many transnational challenges is not retreating from an imperfect and flawed system of global cooperation but doubling down on it. To riff off the words of Marcus Aurelius, the impediment to action is the key to advancing action; what stands in the way must become the way.

This moment will not last indefinitely, and missed chances can lead to repercussions that tarnish support and legitimacy—a reputation the UN has upheld for eight decades. The swiftest path, after all, to eroding public support and isolationism is through disappointment. We are at an inflection point where we can change history's trajectory for better or worse. Much depends on how we respond in coming years, including the physical survival of entire nations. But I would not count the UN out.

Conclusion: Being Part of the Solution in a World on Fire

"Start where you are. Use what you have. Do what you can."
—Arthur Ashe, American tennis player and civil rights activist

There is a stark difference between my unwavering belief in the *potential* for change and the often disappointing reality. It's a recognition that two things can be true simultaneously. Many people worldwide still maintain an enduring and resilient faith in the promise of democratic governance and international institutions such as the UN. Such faith persists even as people harbor concerns about their current performance [1].

So many of us worldwide feel an urgent need for systemic policy change to address challenges such as the climate crisis, biodiversity loss, financial upheaval, wars, unprecedented waves of refugees, and pervasive poverty.[1] However, the gap between the demands of the

---

[1] In the wealthiest G7 countries, over 50% of people believe that we must fundamentally change our economic approach to tackle global crises such as climate change, cost of living, and equitable global development. See Club of Rome 2022.

179

present moment and the commitments our leaders are willing to make is widening. An even more immense gulf exists between what our leaders have promised to do and what they have delivered.[2] Instead of fostering "good politics," many leaders amplify divisions, contributing to our profound implementation crisis [2].

The symptoms of this crisis have left many powerless and disillusioned, but hope for a better way still lingers. In a race against time, we must bridge these ambition gaps, expectation gaps, performance gaps, or whatever term you prefer before it is too late. If left unchecked, disillusionment leads to fear, resulting in a vicious cycle where people seek security in populism and exclusion. These divisive forces are less conducive to nurturing solidarity and cooperation—precisely what we need more of now. In facing these challenges, effective policy entrepreneurship emerges as a crucial approach, offering the skills and tools to bridge these gaps and implement powerful solutions.

This is not a new phenomenon. Nor are the approaches that make up the art of policy entrepreneurship. They are as old as power itself. History is full of policy entrepreneurs who demonstrated the ability to ideate and change the status quo. Going back to ancient Rome and beyond, elites and rulers of all types envisioned bold goals, harnessed strategic framing, leveraged diverse coalitions, and made unusual alliances.[3] They translated theory into action to create real-world impact during times of crisis. Often, solutions were implemented, and even entire institutions were built at a breakneck pace. The chaos created by bank runs in the early 1900s led to the creation of the Federal Reserve to establish economic stability in the US [3]. The UN's inception was negotiated in two months, and the World Bank's in even less time—just three

---

[2] The One Campaign's Climate Finance Files highlight one example: between 2013 and 2021, almost two-thirds of the developed world's pledged climate finance, a total of $343 billion, either went unreported as spent or had minimal connection to climate goals. See ONE Campaign, The, 2023.

[3] Aspiring policy entrepreneurs today can learn a lot by looking at how Roman emperors developed and implemented innovative policy solutions. See Strauss 2019.

weeks—as the Second World War raged. Since then, it has transformed an initial $20 billion contribution from wealthy nations into $800 billion in investments, significantly improving the lives of millions worldwide [4].

Policy entrepreneurs from bygone eras were often profoundly unpopular in their times and accused of betraying their tribes. Despite this, the lasting impact of their ideas, whether perfectly or imperfectly implemented, continues to resonate today. Many of their stories, although frequently overlooked, bear a striking resemblance to contemporary debates.

Past Successes in Policy Entrepreneurship

Today, perspectives on the relationship between society and business diverge. Some insist enterprises should exclusively serve shareholder interests, deriding regulatory "woke" efforts focused on corporate sustainability.[4] Others welcome greater government oversight of corporate supply chains, viewing them as necessary to provide investor certainty and accelerate sustainability efforts [5]. While terms such as "woke capitalism" are relatively new, the underlying debate about the relationship between the state and the market is not. And each time it has flared up, it has been resolved by disruptive policy entrepreneurship, albeit not without controversy.

In the 1930s, facing the Great Depression, Franklin D. Roosevelt (FDR) sought a policy road map to prevent a future economic crisis. With the evident malfunctioning of the free enterprise system that had led to the 1929 stock market crash, FDR wanted businesses to be more responsive to the public interest. Convening his infamous "brains trust," a small group of innovative advisors, FDR's administration introduced tighter coordination over business activity. As part of its New Deal, massive social spending funds were disbursed to

---

[4] Such criticism has been leveled, for example, at regulations requiring companies to disclose supply chain information related to their carbon footprint. See Georgiev 2022, 50.

support local and state planning efforts. By 1936, all states, except one, had a state planning board dealing with everything from agriculture to conservation efforts, public housing, and water pollution [6]. Often, they had the power to discipline exploitative behavior. These boards were crucial in implementing extensive social and economic policies that helped lift America out of the Depression. But their coordination helped attract private investment as well.

Backlash nonetheless emerged after their creation; it intensified in the 1940s with the onset of the Cold War era. The term "planning," sounding too much like something the Soviets would do, was derided as "socialist" [7]. FDR's visionary planning tsar and brain trust member, Rexford Tugwell, known as "Rex the Red" by his detractors, was criticized as un-American and Communist and hounded out the administration [8]. National planning boards were dissolved, and state boards appeared as if they would suffer the same fate.

The reality was far different. Planning boards were, over time, often simply rebranded as "economic development corporations" rather than abolished altogether [9]. Their functions had become too essential. This shift in terminology represented a classic case of pulling the policy ropes sideways (see "Step 3: Mastering the Art of Timing"), where an issue is moved from one polarized dimension—free-market capitalism versus planned economy—into another less ideological contentious spectrum. Economic development, after all, was about "partnering" with the private sector and attracting investments for economic growth [10]. This seemed "more American, something everyone could get behind" [11].[5] The underlying work was often similar, leveraging the power of the state to direct private enterprise to achieve societal objectives.

Today, the legacy of FDR and Tugwell's solutions lives on in the form of countless economic development corporations in towns and states across the US. They still play a crucial role in driving private investment to achieve public objectives. Companies invest billions of dollars in clean energy and electric vehicle manufacturing thanks to

---

[5] For more info see Balisciano 1998.

federal and state tax credits and economic development plans. The labeling of "wokeism" against companies investing in such green projects is less apparent than one might expect. Indeed, 60% of all investments connected with the Inflation Reduction Act have so far, as at the time of writing, been in Republican states [12]. Perhaps for all the talk about "woke capitalism," not much will change in the way of substance regarding private sector investment. Except, perhaps, for another rebranding exercise.

Past Failures in Policy Implementation

Of course, those in power have not always succeeded at policy entrepreneurship. These failures range in severity. Long before he became president and took on robber barons and railway tycoons, a young Theodore Roosevelt served as New York City police commissioner in the 1890s.[6] He responded to the plea of celebrated photojournalist Jacob Riis, who had exposed the pervasive poverty, congested living conditions, inadequate sanitation, surging crime, and police corruption in the Lower East Side.[7] The pair infamously stalked the streets undercover at night to enforce tenement safety codes and catch corrupt police officers. Roosevelt even set his sights on stopping saloons from selling beer on Sundays, a policy he was less successful at implementing! While the outcome of this implementation failure was likely minimal (other than on Roosevelt's bruised ego), others have been far more consequential for humanity.[8]

---

[6] Theodore Roosevelt's battle with the robber barons in the early 1900s was an early iteration of the debate over the proper relationship between the state and the market. See Berfield 2020.

[7] Motivated by Riis's groundbreaking use of flash photography to reveal the grim truths of New York's slums, Roosevelt and city officials took action. They shut down the most overcrowded lodging houses and launched reforms to housing policies. See Stamp 2014; Zacks 2012.

[8] For a great and entertaining overview of Roosevelt's efforts to enforce this unpopular law in the face of rampant corruption, see Zacks 2012. In any case, the episode helped make Roosevelt immensely popular, and he would redeem himself just a few years later when he became president with many landmark achievements that still leave their mark on America today.

At the end of World War I, after negotiating the formation of the ill-fated League of Nations (the "League") in Paris for six months, then–US President Woodrow Wilson faced a challenge in securing Congressional approval for US membership. A group of Republicans proposed a deal: they would support US entry into the League on the condition that a crucial element, requiring Congressional approval for automatic military action when the territorial independence of a member is threatened, be amended. They felt such a condition would unacceptably infringe US sovereignty. Faced with the option of compromise, Wilson insisted on an all-or-nothing approach.[9] He refused to budge even when it became clear the alternative was the US not being involved in the League at all.[10] The vote failed, and without US participation, the League never truly took off and was powerless to prevent geopolitical tensions from rising again.

Wilson's righteousness, prioritizing the purity of his vision over impact, contrasts starkly with the birth of the UN. In contrast, two decades—and one bloody war later—FDR was willing to compromise on the same crucial points Wilson was not. He even gained the support and endorsement of his former Republican opponent for the presidency, Wendell Willkie, who toured the US advocating for America to join a new global international organization.[11] They recognized that the US being at the table of such an institution, notwithstanding any compromises needed to secure consensus in the Congress, was fundamental to preventing another war.

In other cases, those in power did not even attempt to deploy the levers of policy entrepreneurship to rectify policy failures. This is evident in events such as the Great Irish Famine, also known as the Potato Famine, which resulted in mass starvation and over a million deaths in the 19th century. While the potato blight was a natural

---

[9] Indeed, Wilson expressed his "hope that the friends and supporters of the League will vote against" the Republicans' proposed compromise. See McMillan 2003, 492.
[10] Wilson dared them "to break the heart of the world." In doing so, he won the battle but lost the war to end all wars. See McMillan 2003, 489.
[11] See Zipp 2020 for an account of Willkie's world tour.

disaster that destroyed the country's primary food source, the British government's response is often criticized for being inadequate and even exacerbating the disaster by continuing to export grain and cattle from Ireland while people starved [13].[12] Former British Prime Minister Tony Blair would issue an apology a century and a half later.[13] Similarly, farmlands across the US Great Plains were afflicted by severe drought in the Dust Bowl of the 1930s, leading to social and economic upheaval. Today, it is widely regarded as a self-inflicted policy failure [14]. The unsustainable farming practices and policies at the time, including extensive plowing and monoculture farming, contributed to severe soil erosion, producing a human-created environmental catastrophe. It wasn't until Tugwell's (yes, the same Rexford Tugwell mentioned previously) spearheading of the new Soil Conservation Service in 1933 that much of this damage was reversed [15].

From Elites to Everyday Citizens

Fortunately, we don't need to wait solely for elites to "save" us today—some of whom might be more concerned with influencing and shaping policy change that benefits *their* ends over society's. While the tools and levers of policy entrepreneurship were traditionally reserved for those in positions of power, often rendered invisible to most of society, today, they are accessible to all of us—in the sunlight, with the sunlight.

Today, anyone can play the role of a policy entrepreneur within their respective spheres of influence—be it in business, government, entertainment, philanthropy, nonprofits, or communities. This book, influenced by the experiences of countless individuals and organizations, aims to equip everyone to overcome society's present implementation crisis in ways that foster trust and are less polarizing. It

---

[12] Indeed, Ireland was allegedly producing twice as much food as was needed. See O'Neill 1952.

[13] While not a formal apology, the acknowledgment that not enough has been done was interpreted as an "implicit apology." See Berg 2021.

guides us in envisioning bold and audacious policies, identifying novel and creative ways to build connections, networks, and consensus, and implementing real-world impact.

In the face of the stark reality that we have achieved only 12% of the SDGs by the halfway mark to 2030, it is tempting to feel overwhelmed and question the possibility of meaningful change. However, the missing piece in this narrative is the tremendous potential for powerful action between now and 2030 that each of us can have. There is still a lot worth fighting for.

Consider the progress against polio, once afflicting 350,000 annually in the late '80s, now on the brink of eradication with only 6 cases of wild polio reported in 2021.[14] Similarly, Gavi, the Vaccine Alliance—an innovative public-private global health partnership—has already vaccinated one billion children in the past two decades [16]. These ventures depend on relatively little spending by the governments of wealthy nations. Dollar for dollar, however, you would be hard-pressed to find another area of government spending with such a life-saving impact. As these initiatives seek more funding in the coming years, each of us can play a role in encouraging governments to contribute more.

Take for instance, the inspiring story of Kristina Crawford. After participating in Global Citizen's Ambassador program, she returned to her home, the Isle of Man, with a population of 85,000. Despite the absence of an established aid program, Kristina, in collaboration with the local Rotary Club, mobilized 2,000 locals to sign a petition. Their collective efforts convinced the Isle of Man's local government to commit £90,000 over three years to support the global polio program. Stories like Kristina's abound, showcasing the transformative potential of individual commitment and collective action.

Also, consider the issue of climate change. Political strategist, author, and podcaster on climate solutions Tom Rivett-Carnac articulates the transformative potential of our actions eloquently. He

---

[14]As of writing there were just six cases of wild polio virus in 2023. See latest updates at Polio Global Eradication Initiative n.d.

recounts a poignant moment when one of his children questioned the significance of their actions. "You have the biggest chance in all of human history," Carnac replied, "to live an incredibly meaningful life." What he was getting at was that today's citizens have more power to effect change thanks to the tools at our disposal than any previous generation. Because of the existential scale of climate change, our actions today will influence people's lives in the coming 5, 50, or even 500 years. As Carnac puts it, it is "an incredible gift" to be part of *the* generation capable of positively impacting history [17].

In pursuing change, it is not always possible to know exactly the end destination or how to overcome our implementation inexperience. And that is okay. Remember from Chapter 1 the power of simply having a bold, audacious goal. Ultimately, we don't always need to know how we will reach the destination to start the journey; taking that first step, that initial action, and witnessing its impact can help overcome anxiety and catalyze further action. Whether writing a letter or composing an email, reaching out to someone who hasn't responded, or even resending a text message, there's always a meaningful action within our reach. There is always something we can do. And do not worry about being perceived as bothersome. Unapologetically prioritize and advocate for your cause, seizing every opportunity to advance it. As one former politician once advised me: "You can achieve a lot and influence many people simply by showing up." Remember that the individuals we aim to influence are often busy, and our cause will likely slip their minds if we are not persistent.

Consider the policy entrepreneurs in the preceding chapters. Grassroots activists in South Africa, unwavering in their commitment to addressing period poverty, held their government accountable by continuing to ask questions. Similarly, trade union officials in Collie, Western Australia, refused to give up after being initially rebuffed, deciding to 'keep the story going' by continuing to have conversations until everyone was on board with a just transition. Mia Mottley of Barbados shows grit and endurance, balancing domestic responsibilities as a national leader with a punishing travel schedule to ensure her people are front and center in the corridors of global power.

Finally, as UN Secretary-General, Ban Ki-moon was forthright, relentless, and direct in chasing down presidents and prime ministers until they agreed to accept his initiatives.

Without these policy entrepreneurs punching above their weight with determination and resilience, the outcomes in this book might have been very different. South African activists might not have secured the means to keep more girls in school, the community of Collie, Western Australia, might have been seeking a new town to call home, and Prime Minister Mottley would have been just another leader calling the alarm on climate change without making any impact. There might be no Paris Climate Agreement or even the UN today.

These examples provide a glimpse into the myriad stories of meaningful policy change unfolding around us. By applying the approaches from this playbook, we can create more stories of hope and impact. As we move forward, new challenges will arise in the next decade, but the tools and levers described in this book will continue to be relevant, even as circumstances evolve. Consider the following far from exhaustive examples:

1) Leveraging AI's Potential for Good

The demand for AI regulation will continue to build in the coming months and years as these technologies integrate further into our daily lives, with the associated risks and benefits becoming increasingly evident. Author Ian Bremmer has argued we will likely soon live in a "technopolar world" with tech companies as the new superpowers affecting all aspects of our lives [18]. A significant challenge is to implement policies that bring these companies within a common framework that aligns nations' and regional blocs' distinct regulatory approaches [19]. Ensuring these technologies benefit the broader population rather than a select few will also be essential.

In applying the playbook to this challenge, policy entrepreneurs might grapple with the following questions:

- Know Your Policy Goal: What does good AI regulation look like from the perspective of governments, technology companies, and everyday citizens? How do you get the balance right between protecting the public interest and enabling innovation?
- Embrace Pragmatic Idealism: What mutual concessions need to be agreed to, for example, between China and the US, as AI developments feed into broader geopolitical rivalries to get consensus around global agreements? Can it be confined within the prism of "managed strategic competition," as former Australian Prime Minister Kevin Rudd outlines, or will it form the basis of the next arms race? [20].
- Know Your Endgame: How do you implement an accountability framework that is agile enough to respond to the as-yet-unknown and novel ways AI technologies might rapidly develop? If regulation is too slow to develop, how do you hold wrongdoers of voluntary corporate pacts accountable for violations?

Work is already underway to address many of these questions, with President Biden announcing a new executive order on AI in October 2023 [21]. However, these efforts are still in their early stages. One fact is clear: getting these policy solutions right in the coming AI era could significantly enhance our institutions' capacity to deliver solutions to major challenges at all levels. This includes better performance in areas such as energy security and breakthroughs in medical research, which can typically take generations. In short, proper governance of AI technologies has the potential to help address the overall implementation crisis at the heart of this book.

2) Unlocking the Hidden Promise of Blockchain

American crypto entrepreneur Sam Bankman-Fried's downfall in December 2022 was widely viewed as the end of the cryptocurrency boom era. It marked the conclusion of a tumultuous period during which cryptocurrency values soared during the COVID-19 pandemic, only to plummet dramatically in 2022. And yet, one should be mindful of not throwing the baby out with the bathwater. After all, the sudden popularity of cryptocurrencies, even if based on misplaced beliefs, was largely driven by a significant lack of trust in traditional financial institutions, including central banks and regular fiat currency—the everyday money we use, like dollar bills or euros, issued by governments.

If we needed a reminder of how fragile the banking sector was, it came in early 2023 when a sudden rush of customers withdrawing their deposits at Silicon Valley Bank resulted in the second-largest bank failure in US history. Similarly, frustrated by barriers to the free flow of money, high transaction costs, volatile currencies, and high inflation rates, citizens globally continue to demand a new system that allows money to move freely and effortlessly across borders [22]. This desire is especially resonant with marginalized communities living in vulnerable or oppressed conditions for whom cross-border remittances are a major source of income.

Momentum is already building in some areas, such as high transaction costs, to rebuild trust and modernize the existing financial system. In October 2023, the Biden-Harris administration announced new efforts to crack down on hidden and surprise fees to bring down costs for American consumers [23]. Elsewhere, Shift4, an American payment processing company, announced a new partnership with the fundraising platform Give Lively to "make it easy and affordable for nonprofits to adopt modern donation methods."[15] It is expected to benefit at least 8,000 charities through transaction fees. Nonetheless, more work is required at the systemic level.

In applying the playbook to this challenge, policy entrepreneurs might grapple with the following questions:

- Know Your Policy Goal: What is a good policy goal that allows people to safely store and transfer their money at little cost across borders? What policies will limit communities' exposure to the economic instability caused by currency fluctuations? What policies would help reduce remittance transaction costs

---

[15] As said by Shift4 CEO Jared Isaacman. See Give Lively 2023.

from as high as 6.5% to 3%, as targeted in the SDGs, which could save migrants and their families up to US$16 billion per year? [24].

- Know Which Stakeholders Matter and How to Appeal to Them: How do you convince relevant stakeholders, such as central banks, to support and strengthen new platforms to increase financial inclusion and protect the most vulnerable?
- Embrace Pragmatic Idealism: What mutual concessions need to be made between offering greater freedom of choice and accepting that no monetary or financial system is completely devoid of risk?
- Know Your Endgame: How can blockchain policies strengthen accountability and safeguard against any new transfer system being used for nefarious purposes by repressive governments? These include tracking down marginalized communities or systems being used to fund terrorist or other criminal activities.

3) Tapping into Private Wealth to Meet the SDG Investment Needs

Despite increased global aid levels in recent years, the SDGs remain underfunded. Estimates vary, but achieving them is usually estimated to be US$2.5–US$3.5 trillion.[16] Several policy proposals are on the table, including the Bridgetown Initiative's recommendations, to unlock additional lending from institutions such as the World Bank, as championed by Prime Minister Mia Mottley of Barbados (see Chapter 6). Yet, one obvious and under-tapped source is private wealth. As Tom Hall of UBS Philanthropy says, "There's US$103 trillion in the wealth management industry alone. And growing. Now, there's a new billionaire created every week in Asia. So there's lots of money out there" [25].

In the process of writing this book, a friend told me that maybe there were approaches to systemic change that did not need to rely on

---

[16] Some estimates are even higher. See UNCTAD 2023.

policy change. Their example was billionaire philanthropy and investment. And yet, even here, we see that harnessing and deploying such
capital necessitates policy solutions at some level. Money in pension
and sovereign wealth funds will not flow to address the world's biggest
challenges without assurance of adequate returns given the fiduciary
duties such funds owe their clients. In many cases, however, such assurance is unavailable, or the investment is considered too risky. This partly
explains why even some billionaires advocate policy measures to help
incentivize investments in sustainable development [26].

Meanwhile, a "generosity crisis" exists as charitable giving continues to fall [27]. Too many philanthropic assets sit idle with little
incentive to be deployed. As Hall further notes, "Why isn't it [private
wealth] already flowing into philanthropy? That's the question.
I always ask myself—Why aren't people giving?" [28].

In applying the playbook to this question, policy entrepreneurs
might grapple with the following questions:

- Know Your Goal: What policy goals can incentivize private
  sector wealth to invest in the SDGs at scale? Hall suggests we
  should look at ways to create an "impact economy" to, in part,
  ensure communities are rewarded for the genuine public good
  benefits they provide [29]. For example, a value should be
  assigned to the work done by communities that protect our
  forests and lower deforestation. And the people who benefit
  from that work in the form of reduced carbon emissions should
  pay for it. What is the right policy goal to create this 'impact
  economy'? Is it, for example, to implement a carbon price that
  would force investors and companies to pay the true cost of
  their carbon footprint? [30].
- Embrace Pragmatic Idealism: How do we ensure we're not letting a stubborn commitment to ideological purity get in the
  way of impact? For example, communities that conserve our
  vital natural resources can be compensated by selling carbon
  credits. But billions of potential investment dollars in such
  communities allegedly fell through after some of these projects

were accused of greenwashing in 2023. Indigenous groups argued that they were being punished for the actions of a few [31]. How do we strike a more pragmatic balance that allows communities to generate much-needed funds while minimizing the risk of greenwashing? What mutual concessions are we willing to make?

- Leverage Your Partners' Strengths: How can limited philanthropic assets or even government resources be used to leverage the deployment of private investment? Philanthropic giving in the US amounts to roughly US$500 billion annually [32]. It is a hefty sum but far short of what is needed to address the world's problems. Used properly, however, it could help leverage the deployment of trillions of private sector capital by making investing profitable in developing countries [33]. Equally, can such assets be used to insulate some government programs from the political cycle? Can philanthropy be used to strike a deal with the government whereby the philanthropist takes the risk of paying for the project if it fails, but if it succeeds, the government agrees to scale it nationally? [34]. Alternatively, can they be used to incentivize governments to spend public money so that it is spent on the right things?

- Know Your Endgame: Can philanthropy be used to ensure government funding is spent on things that work? Hall further notes that about US$32 trillion in public money globally a year is spent on policies such as health and education [35]. The question is whether this money is spent on the right policies. Is it being spent on policies that are delivering results? Should philanthropy invest in the policy entrepreneurial capacity of nonprofits to ensure accountability of government spending? Finally, without government regulations, can new integrity codes of conduct and blockchain technology help minimize the risk of practices such as greenwashing in a new "impact economy"?[17]

---

[17]An example of such a voluntary standard is the Equitable Earth Initiative. See Equitable Earth Initiative n.d.

4) Putting Citizens at the Heart of Governance

Criticism of the UN and other institutions is soaring. But so, too, is technology and other means of connection. We all experienced this through the COVID-19 pandemic. We were further apart than ever before, but in some ways, we were closer than ever, too. Can this be leveraged to give citizens greater involvement in our governance structures? What would that look like? Ireland once again offers us some insight.

In 2016, the Republic of Ireland took a significant step toward formalizing citizen-led consensus building by establishing the Citizens' Assembly [36]. This assembly, consisting of 100 citizen members, was tasked with deliberating on various significant topics, with the issue of abortion being particularly contentious. For over 25 years, the issue had been marked by public debates and referendums. The unique approach of the Citizens' Assembly allowed for a mature and informed discussion, enabling citizens to lead the process. Ultimately, this initiative led to a constitutional amendment legalizing abortion and legislative changes on this highly charged topic that unified rather than divided the country.

In applying the playbook to this question, policy entrepreneurs might grapple with the following questions:

- Know Your Goal: What goals might lead to creating citizen assemblies at a global level? What policies are needed to ensure citizens are educated and equipped to be able to contribute adequately to them?
- Know Which Stakeholders Matter and How to Appeal to Them: Are governments even essential for citizen assemblies to function? Are there other institutions that matter just as much or even more so, where this could be influential in setting the policy agenda?
- Leverage Your Partners' Strengths: What other networks might be helpful to leverage and to the credibility of such an exercise? Many initiatives already exist that could be tapped into. For example, the Global Town Hall discussion, co-hosted annually between

Global Citizen and the Foreign Policy Community of Indonesia, brings together 28,000+ participants from 131 countries, including Papua New Guinea, Sudan, Somalia, Tanzania, Iran, Cuba, Costa Rica, Bangladesh, and more [37]. Might these citizens themselves have unique policy ideas to contribute? What is the best forum to solicit these?

■ Know Your Endgame: In the absence of a government agreeing to act on the recommendations, as in the case of the Irish citizen assembly, how does it create change? How do you track whatever comes out of the exercise to ensure it creates an impact?

■ Communicate Stories of Success: Might sharing examples of consensus in and of itself hold value as a power motivator?

★★★★★★★★★★★★★

We live in a world on fire. Each passing day brings new negative headlines, highlighting how dire our situation is, how divided we've become, and how deep our troubles run. But remember, nothing is inevitable. We are not prisoners of fate. While we can't predict the future with certainty, we have the power to shape it.

Beneath the surface, people are tirelessly working to make a difference in their own ways, albeit unevenly and gradually. These are all worthy endeavors. However, to tackle our challenges, we urgently need systemic policy change. We need effective policy entrepreneurs to deliver and see through implementation over the long term. This necessity persists even in the face of society's inclination toward the immediate gratification of "taking down the other"—a preference for feeling safe, righteous, certain, and right.

We don't need more people who want to prove they can win an argument—with the help of ChatGPT, anyone can do that. What we truly need are those who want to change *our* world. This path is less traveled. Armed with this playbook, I hope more people will choose to navigate this route and actively contribute to turning ideas into impact.

Epilogue

A few weeks before finishing this book, I found myself on a Facetime call with a 105-year-old World War II veteran named Len [1].

Len was born in England in 1917, the youngest of seven children, four of whom died early on ("A lot of children died in those days."). He married the love of his life on November 11, 1939. Shortly after, Len was sent to France as war descended across Europe.

Len recalled his time as a British soldier in France in mid-1940, just as the German blitzkrieg was overwhelming the country. He described to me in intimate detail the moment two hundred German Luftwaffe planes appeared over a hill in front of him, blocking out the sky.

Finding an abandoned car ("It was an American one. A real beauty! I thought 'that'll do.'"), Len managed to make it to one of the last boats leaving the port of Calais. English spitfires engaged German aircraft overhead as the ship carefully navigated mine-infested waters.

Upon his return to English shores, he was stationed as a lone soldier to look after a small village. Len described how he soon found himself rallying the villagers to respond to an incoming group of German paratroopers falling from the sky. "I had a few bullets, and they had pitchforks."

I asked Len whether at that moment—when France had fallen, when Europe had been overrun by tyranny and fascism, and when it looked like Britain might be next with invasion seemingly imminent—he thought it was all over.

"No," Len responded instantly, "we said to each other, 'We haven't got much, but we'll give it a go. We're not running away. We'll give it a go.'"

When we think of the challenges we face today, they can seem overwhelming, leaving us feeling paralyzed and powerless. And yet, while we are in the danger zone, we are not yet at breaking point [2].

Today, we have far more than Len and his fellow soldiers had at that dark moment in 1940. They were willing to risk so much with much less to depend on. How will we rise to meet the present moment? Will we make full use of all of the formidable array of tools and levers at our disposal to live a meaningful life?

By the time this book comes out my daughter will have been born. What will her generation say of us? Will they say we ran away, or will they say that we "gave it a go?" Only we can write the answer to that.

Acknowledgments

Any flaws in this book reflect my imperfections. All the good insights, however, are due to the chorus of supporters who gave so much advice and support along the way.

Thomas Kalil, a former advisor in the Clinton and Obama administrations, likened the challenges of teaching effective policy entrepreneurship to "learning to ride a bicycle rather than memorizing the quadratic formula" [1]. Writing this book certainly felt like an unwieldy task on multiple occasions. This was especially so since I wrote most of this book in a compressed time—mere months—and in a sprint to submit the manuscript before my daughter was born. Much of it was written while working simultaneously on several intense campaigns. It would not have been possible without countless friends, experts, and colleagues' invaluable contributions, understanding, and patience.

I owe a great deal of thanks to Global Citizen. I have worked with the organization for the better part of the last 15 years. It has profoundly influenced my life and undoubtedly shaped many perspectives I have shared in this book. I thank my fellow co-founders, Simon Moss and Hugh Evans, for their continued support and guidance. I also want to thank all my colleagues who expressed enthusiasm for this project, especially those who, in their own time, volunteered to read drafts, offered feedback, or otherwise inspired me in some way: Nikola Ivezaj, Friederike Röder, Liz Agbor-Tabi, Rubén Escalante Hasbún, Annabel Lee McShane Bickford, Mwandwe Chileshe, Joe Skibbens, Jordan Devon, Lucas Turner, and Aaron Holtz.

I want to thank former colleagues and great friends who took the time to review and share thoughts or else encourage me to write something that appears in this book, including Madge Thomas, Talia Fried, Ivana Kvesic, Ryan Gall, Julia Frifield, Sophie Barbier, Ivana Kvesic, Elana Broitman, Lindsay Hadley, and Caitria Mahoney.

I especially owe much debt to Mike Hoffman of Changing Our World for his incredible mentorship, friendship, and support. He was a champion of this project from the start and offered much-needed encouragement when needed most. I also want to thank Christian Santiago and Emma Bearison of Changing Our World for reviewing and helping to improve different parts of this book. I'm grateful, too, for the generous support of Kathleen Ventrella, John Damonti, Andrea Pfanzelter, and Craig Cohon, who formed the "marketing committee" for this project.

My thanks to Idris and Sabrina Elba for graciously contributing the Foreword to this book and for championing the campaigns we collaborated on.

For the chapter "Advancing Access: Equal Education for All," I owe particular thanks to the following for taking the time to speak with me: Candice Chirwa, Nokuzola Ndwandwe, and Sipiwo Matshoba of the South African Department of Women, Youth & Persons with Disabilities in the Presidency who convened a special consultation of local and regional stakeholders to go over questions we had. I also want to thank Emily Isaacman for her help researching critical statistics on the state of period poverty in the world. Thanks to Dr. Phumzile Mlambo-Ngcuka, former deputy president of South Africa, for reviewing this chapter. Finally, to Paula Shugart and Harnaaz Kaur Sandhu of the Miss Universe Organization for inspiring the creation of the Global Menstrual Equity Accelerator.

For the chapter "Empowering a Community: Just Transition beyond Coal," I owe special thanks to Alex Cassie, Jodie Hanns, Mick

Murray, Jayde Rowlands, and Steve McCartney for taking the time to share their experiences. I also thank Ben Wyatt and Mark Read for making the necessary connections. Thanks to Carl Pope of Bloomberg's Beyond Coal initiative, who was very generous in walking me through the ins and outs of how to close a coal mine in a just way.

For the chapter "Building Bridges: Small and Mighty in a Warming World," I owe a big thanks, first and foremost, to Prime Minister Mia Mottley of Barbados for being the inspiration behind this story and for her friendship, partnership, and leadership. She gives many of us hope right now. I also thank her special envoy for climate, Avinash Persaud, and Karima Degia, deputy director of the Bridgetown Initiative Unit, for giving me feedback. I extend my gratitude to Shakira Mustapha of the Centre for Disaster Protection. Special thanks also to Theodore Talbot, who generously provided thoughtful feedback even after he departed from the Centre. I extend my gratitude to Eric Pelofsky of the Rockefeller Foundation, who informed me of positive developments regarding the implementation of Pause Clauses during the final editing of this book. Many thanks to the copy editors for their patience with this last-minute addition!

For the chapter "Finding One World: Lessons in Collective Action," I thank Richard Gowan for sharing his glass-half-full analysis of the UN system. This was a hard one to write, and I am grateful to those who reviewed what I had written and gave much-needed guidance, including Ambassador David Donoghue and Ban Ki-moon, the eighth UN secretary-general.

Some people reviewed significant parts of this book and gave extensive feedback. I am incredibly grateful and cannot wait to return the favor. Thank you, Maha Aziz, Frank Van Gansbeke, Monika Froehler, Akram Azimi, and Gbenga Akinnagbe!

I would also like to thank all those who fact-checked segments at various times, spent time explaining a particular concept, sent helpful references my way, and, in other ways, offered inspiration: Márcia Balisciano (who supplied the Benjamin Franklin quote at the start of this book and alerted me also to the story of the state planning boards, which is featured in the conclusion!), Rosalind McKenna, Guillaume Grosso, Kindred Motes, John Concannon (who taught me there is no word for "no" in the Irish language), Peter Schurman (who first introduced me to the concept of the "Overton window"), Patrick Grace, Phil Harvey, Jennifer Jones, Michelle Goldstone (whose dad, David, also inspired me to get involved in my first big campaign on polio eradication), Tom Hall, Nicole Sebastian, Hassan Damluji, Jonathan Glennie, Espen Gullikstad, Ambassador Mustafa Osman Turan, Jill Wilkins, Mike Lake (for alerting me to the backlash against the phrase "just transition" in Alberta, Canada!), Alex Rafalowicz, Ambassador Kevin Rudd, Idee Inyangudor, Ambassador Dino Patti Djalal, Ambassador Nigel Siegel, Jad Daley, Joseph McMahon, Terri Bowles, Madalina Vlasceanu, Arrey Obenson, David McNair, Elizabeth Li, Jeff Brez, Julia Gillard, Zeid Ra'ad Al Hussein, Jimena Leiva Roesch, Michael Franczak, Anote Tong, Sant Kumar, Martijn Lambert, Gavin Gramstad, Tim Shirk, Craig Cohon, and Katra Sambili.

To my agent Jill Marsal and editors at Wiley, Brian Neill, Kristi Bennett, Lori Martinsek, Aldo Rosas, Rene Caroline, Deborah Schindlar, and Ranjith Kumar—thank you!

This book was only possible because I was introduced to the idea of policy entrepreneurship. A body of academic research exists on this term, but I owe much debt to my former professor at the University of Western Australia, Bruce Stone. I still recall sitting across from him in his office in mid-2012, trying to explain what we had just achieved with The End of Polio campaign. "So, you're essentially a policy entrepreneur," Bruce replied. He then described policy entrepreneurs to me as he saw them: creative individuals who embrace risk-taking, employ innovative and disruptive tactics and exhibit strong leadership to set the policy agenda. I hope I have done you proud, Bruce!

In closing, I want to thank all members of my family for being so supportive, including and especially my mum, dad, and sister—Jane, Mark, and Kelly—for all their continued encouragement. I wrote much of the first part of this book while traveling with my folks for a week in the Caribbean. I am grateful, as always, for their patience. Mum even set up a Facetime with Len, whose story I feature in the epilogue. He is currently a resident at the aged care facility where she works.

Finally, and most importantly, I want to truly thank my wife, Xinyi, for being an incredibly supportive life partner. She read every word of this book and gave me honest but fair feedback every step of the way. As I write this, we are two weeks out from the birth of our daughter, Miki, and Xinyi is still up with me late in the night reviewing my final chapter. Thank you, Xinyi, you are the love of my life!

You can reach me on social media (Instagram, X) as @micksheldrick. Connect with me, too, on LinkedIn and Facebook. Subscribe to my weekly newsletter on Substack: michaelsheldrick.substack.com.

As a final call to action, I encourage everyone interested in building a better world to visit globalcitizen.org or download the Global Citizen app and register as a global citizen.

Annex: Summary: Eight Steps for Policy Entrepreneurship

The Visionary: Setting the Foundation for Change

1. Know Your Policy Goal

- Having a clear policy goal is essential for turning intentions into impact.
- Many well-intentioned initiatives lack a clear policy goal, leading to wasted resources and lost momentum.
- Defining an explicit policy goal involves identifying the challenge, conducting thorough research, and using SMART criteria (specific, measurable, achievable, relevant, and time-bound).
- Clear policy goals empower advocates and leaders to allocate resources efficiently and build strong support networks.
- "Naive audacity" and visionary goals can catalyze support, helping to overcome a shortfall in implementation skills and experience.

2. Know Which Stakeholders Matter and How to Influence Them

- Identifying key stakeholders with the authority to implement policy goals is crucial for success.
- Accessing high-profile decision-makers can be challenging, so consider influential figures within their network. This may include advisors, donors, colleagues, peers, and representatives of beneficiaries. Engaging with future leaders who may not hold power yet but will likely do so is also strategic.
- Be friendly and authentic. This is crucial to building long-term relationships. Take the time to invest in them.
- Identify the most legitimate and credible messenger who will resonate with key stakeholders.
- Engagement from like-minded individuals is often more persuasive.
- Be targeted in your outreach!
- Make it easy for key stakeholders to help you by doing any necessary prep work such as drafting documents, correspondence, talking points, and speeches.
- Strategic framing seeks to align policy goals with stakeholders' self-interest, motivating action. Reframing issues to align with self-interest can lead to powerful shifts.

3. Mastering the Art of Timing

- Understanding the Overton window:
  - The Overton window defines the range of policies generally acceptable to most people at a given time.
  - It can change gradually due to evolving societal norms or rapidly due to a crisis.
  - Polling data can help determine whether a policy is within the Overton window.
  - Survey providers such as the Open Society Barometer provide insights into sentiments on policy issues related to global challenges.

- Shifting the Overton window:
  - Policies outside the Overton window require convincing segments of the public to support them.
  - Strategies include pushing for extreme policy positions (e.g., the "McKibben effect" on climate policy), incremental "gateway" changes (e.g., support for child health as a way to boost support for foreign aid as a whole), and pulling policy "ropes" sideways (e.g., how British abolitionists leveraged geopolitical considerations during the war to end the transatlantic slave trade).
  - Be ready to respond to crises. Politicians will often be on the lookout for timely solutions. As former British Prime Minister Harold Macmillan said when asked what had the biggest impact on his government: "Events, dear boy, events."

4. Mastering the Art of Storytelling

- Humans think in stories, making storytelling crucial for making sense of the world.
- Storytelling helps build trust and rapport, especially in times of division and crisis.
- A well-told story can establish connections and partnerships where other methods may fail.
- Storytelling helps cut through the noise and aids understanding in complex situations.
- Missed opportunities:
  - Many leaders miss opportunities in policy due to a lack of understanding of the power of storytelling.
  - Focusing on statistics rather than building a genuine connection can hinder progress.
  - Stories of heroism and resilience can resonate more than a list of facts.
- Telling a memorable story:
  - Emphasize the *why* and *how* rather than the *who*, *what*, or *when*.
  - Sharing motivations humanizes intentions and fosters open dialogue.

- Crafting compelling narratives:
  - Focus on solutions, avoiding excessive emphasis on problems.
  - Ground the narrative in shared values to connect with the audience.
- Demonstrating change and momentum:
  - Showcase stories of people contributing to solutions and overcoming difficulties.
  - Provide evidence of momentum building behind proposed solutions.
- Show, don't just tell:
  - Humanize stories by focusing on individuals to demonstrate the importance of the narrative.
- Authenticity and credibility:
  - People can discern genuine enthusiasm.
  - Be truthful and supported by credible evidence, acknowledging and addressing any learnings from failures.

The Diplomat:
Catalyzing Impact through Pragmatism

5. Embrace Pragmatic Idealism

- Concessions and compromises are essential for real change.
- Successful breakthroughs involve no party getting everything they want.
- Courage in accepting imperfect settlements:
  - Advocating for compromise is challenging in a polarized world.
  - Yet, accepting imperfect settlements often drives agendas forward (however frustrating it might feel at the time!)
- Tips and pitfalls in pragmatic idealism:
  - Avoid the purity test:
    - Pressure to demonstrate unwavering loyalty to tribal beliefs.
    - This can hinder necessary trade-offs and progress.
  - Engage with everyone: this includes the importance of engaging with adversaries for progress.
  - Adhere to "do no harm" principle:

- Negative consequences can occur in pursuit of moral causes.
- Assess the potential harm and seek input from those directly impacted.
    - Leverage existing (imperfect) institutions. Instead of pursuing an unrealistic utopia, strive for optia—the best possible outcome based on the tools and levers at our disposal.
- Rejecting or undermining institutions increases conflict and is counterproductive in the long run.

6. Leveraging Your Partners' Strengths:

- Figure out your leverage point first, and then examine how to complement this.
- Partnerships can help secure access, credibility, funding, electoral power, and more.
- Building trust is essential for coalition building.
- Leveraging philanthropic giving for policy entrepreneurship:
    - Traditional reluctance to fund policy advocacy.
    - Emphasize impact and return on investment rather than how money gets spent.
    - Establish these principles for philanthropic partnerships:
        - Emphasize long-term engagement and flexible funding.
        - Align reporting requirements and outcomes with policy goals.
        - Take funders on a journey to see themselves as cocreators of solutions.

The Implementer: Enforcing Accountability and Follow-Through

7. Know Your Endgame

- Understand how to ensure sustained implementation. Challenges that can disrupt policy delivery include premature celebration, change in leadership, and new crises. Three approaches hold commitment makers accountable:
    - Legal avenues:
        - Contracts: Establishing clear, legally binding agreements.

- Regulation and government rules: Using government-set rules and regulations.
- Creative legal methods: Exploring innovative legal approaches such as court actions to establish new precedents.
- Non-legal avenues:
  - Public shaming: Mobilizing public opinion to drive accountability.
  - Monitoring, consultation, and reporting: Tracking progress and reporting impact regularly.
  - Third-party verification: Involving independent third parties to authenticate claims.
  - Renegotiation on reasonable terms: Consider renegotiation or third-party intervention when difficulties arise.
- Sustaining policy implementation for the long term:
  - Develop a succession plan and secure long-term funding and resources.
  - Establish a dedicated advocacy organization to oversee ongoing efforts.

8. Communicate Stories of Success

- Real stories give us hope. They show us that our actions matter.
- Give credit to partners and funders to foster long-term loyalty.
- Share lessons learned to provide blueprints for others.
- Avoid premature victory claims and engage in honest, constructive conversations if progress is only half achieved.

Endnotes

Foreword

1. Food and Agriculture Organization of the United Nations. "The State of Food Security and Nutrition in the World 2023". https://www.fao.org/documents/card/en/c/cc3017en.

Prologue

1. Jay, J., and G. Grant. 2017. *Breaking through Gridlock: The Power of Conversation in a Polarized World*. Berrett-Koehler Publishers.
2. International Rice Research Institute. n.d. "Golden Rice FAQs." https://www.irri.org/golden-rice-faqs.
3. Sengupta, S., H. Howard, and D. Erdenesanaa. 2023. "Climate Protesters March on New York, Calling for End to Fossil Fuels." *The New York Times*. September 17, 2023.
4. Ramos-Horta, J. 2022. President East Timor. "Op Ed: For a Fraction of Australia's Fighter Jet Budget, I'd Leave East Timor's Fuel in the Ground." José Ramos-Horta. October 5, 2022. https://ramoshorta.com/op-ed-for-a-fraction-of-australias-fighter-jet-budget-id-leave-east-timors-fuel-in-the-ground/.
5. Scheiber, N. 2021. "The Achilles' Heel of Biden's Climate Plan? Coal Miners." *The New York Times*. December 8, 2021.
6. Cotovio, V., L. Paddison, and S. Noor. 2023. "Amazon deforestation at six-year-low in Brazil after plunging 66% in July." CNN,

August 4, 2023. https://www.cnn.com/2023/08/04/americas/amazon-deforestation-brazil-climate-intl/index.html.

7. World Economic Forum. 2023. "For First Time, Women Represented in All Parliaments of the World." April 12, 2023. https://www.weforum.org/agenda/2023/04/for-first-time-women-represented-in-all-parliaments-of-the-world/.

8. Partners in Health. 2023. "Good News in Global Health." July 28, 2023. https://www.pih.org/article/good-news-global-health.

9. Global Nation. 2023. "Global Solidarity Report." https://globalnation.world/global-solidarity-report.

10. Open Society Foundations. 2023. "Open Society Barometer." September 2023.

11. Ibid.

12. Guterres A. 2023. Interview by Christiane Amanpour, CNN. September 18, 2023. https://www.cnn.com/videos/world/2023/09/18/exp-united-nations-antonio-guterres-intw-091801pseg3-cnni-world.cnn.

Introduction

1. UN. 2023b. "Warning Over Half of World Is Being Left Behind, Secretary-General Urges Greater Action to End Extreme Poverty, at Sustainable Development Goals Progress Report Launch." SG/SM/21776, April 25, 2023. https://press.un.org/en/2023/sgsm21776.doc.htm.

2. Global Nation. 2023. "Global Solidarity Report." https://globalnation.world/global-solidarity-report.

3. Open Society Foundations. 2023. "Open Society Barometer." September 2023.

4. Glocalities. 2022. "Generation Z—Gen Z Marketing." November 29, 2022.

5. Bhanumati, P., M. De Haan, and J. W. Tebrake. 2022. "Greenhouse Emissions Rise to Record, Erasing Drop During Pandemic."

IMF Blog. June 30, 2022. https://www.imf.org/en/Blogs/ Articles/2022/06/30/greenhouse-emissions-rise-to-record-erasing-drop-during-pandemic.

6. Denning, G. 2023. *Universal Food Security: How to End Hunger While Protecting the Planet.* Columbia University Press.

7. Kingdon, J. 2010. *Agendas, Alternatives, and Public Policies* (2nd ed.). New York, NY: Pearson.

8. Mintrom, M. 2019. "So You Want to Be a Policy Entrepreneur?" *Policy Design and Practice* 2, no. 4, 307–323. https://doi.org/10. 1080/25741292.2019.1675989.

9. Glocalities. 2023. "Harvesting Solar Power Five Times More Favored Than Burning Fossil Fuels." September 15, 2023. https:// glocalities.com/reports/harnessingsolarpower.

10. Kalil, T. 2017. "Policy Entrepreneurship at the White House: Getting Things Done in Large Organizations." *Innovations: Technology, Governance, Globalization* 11, no. 3–4 (2017): 4–21.

11. Dalio, R. 2021. *Principles For Dealing With the Changing World Order: Why Nations Succeed and Fail.* Avid Reader Press/Simon & Schuster.

12. Open Society Foundations. 2023. "Open Society Barometer." September 2023.

13. Global Nation. 2023. "Global Solidarity Report." https:// globalnation.world/global-solidarity-report.

14. Ibid.

15. Zahra, T. 2023. *Against the World: Anti-Globalism and Mass Politics Between the World Wars.* W. W. Norton & Company.

16. Barber, M. 2016. *How to Run a Government: So that Citizens Benefit and Taxpayers Don't Go Crazy.* Penguin.

17. Jay, J. J., and G. Grant. 2017. *Breaking through Gridlock: The Power of Conversation in a Polarized World.* Berrett-Koehler Publishers.

18. Reilly, K. 2018. "'Fight Our Tribal Mindset.' Read Justin Trudeau's Commencement Address to NYU Graduates." *Time.* May 16, 2018. https://time.com/5280153/justin-trudeau-nyu-commencement-2018-transcript.

Part 1

1. Hogan, A. 2008. *Moving in the Open Daylight: Doc Evatt, an Australian at the United Nations,* 50. Sydney University Press.
2. Kalil, T. 2017. "Policy Entrepreneurship at the White House: Getting Things Done in Large Organizations." *Innovations: Technology, Governance, Globalization* 11, no. 3–4 (2017): 4–21.
3. Kingdon, J. 2010. *Agendas, Alternatives, and Public Policies* (2nd ed.). New York, NY: Pearson.
4. Kalil, T. 2017. "Policy Entrepreneurship at the White House: Getting Things Done in Large Organizations." *Innovations: Technology, Governance, Globalization* 11, no. 3–4 (2017): 4–21.
5. Ibid.
6. Mintrom, M. 2019. "So You Want to Be a Policy Entrepreneur?" *Policy Design and Practice* 2, no. 4, 307–323. https://doi.org/10.10 80/25741292.2019.1675989.
7. Levinson, B. 2013. "Policy Entrepreneurs: The Power of Audacity." *The Regulatory Review.* May 21, 2013. https://www.theregreview .org/2013/05/21/21-levinson-policy-entrepreneurs/.

Chapter 1

1. Kalil, T. 2017. "Policy Entrepreneurship at the White House: Getting Things Done in Large Organizations." *Innovations: Technology, Governance, Globalization* 11, no. 3–4 (2017): 4–21.
2. SDG2 Advocacy Hub. n.d. "Bringing People Together to Achieve Good Food for All." https://sdg2advocacyhub.org/.
3. FFNPT. n.d. "Fossil Fuel Non-Proliferation Treaty." https:// fossilfueltreaty.org.
4. Sheldrick, M. 2023. "Ajay Banga and the World Bank: An Opportunity for Transformational Progress on Climate and Poverty." *Forbes.* February 24, 2023. https://www.forbes.com/ sites/globalcitizen/2023/02/24/ajay-banga-and-the-world-bank-an-opportunity-for-transformational-progress-on-climate-and-poverty/?sh=48e832cf5576.

5. Roser, M. 2022. "Malaria: One of the Leading Causes of Child Deaths, but Progress Is Possible and You Can Contribute to It." OurWorldInData.org. https://ourworldindata.org/malaria-intro duction.

6. Murray, W. H. 1951. *The Scottish Himalayan Expedition*. U.K/J. M. Dent & Sons Ltd.

7. Obenson, A. 2021. *Bridging the Opportunity Gap*. Xlibris.

8. Glocalities. 2022. "Generation Z—Gen Z Marketing." November 29, 2022.

9. Kalil, T. 2017. "Policy Entrepreneurship at the White House: Getting Things Done in Large Organizations." *Innovations: Technology, Governance, Globalization* 11, no. 3–4 (2017): 4–21.

10. GPEI. 2015. "Commonwealth Leaders and Polio Survivors Unite for Polio-Free World." November 30, 2015. https://polioer adication.org/news-post/commonwealth-leaders-and-polio-survivors-unite-for-polio-free-world/.

11. GPEI. 2018. "Commonwealth Leaders Affirm Commitment to End Polio." April 27, 2018. https://polioeradication.org/news-post/commonwealth-leaders-affirm-commitment-to-end-polio/.

12. Mintrom, M. 2019. "So You Want to Be a Policy Entrepreneur?" *Policy Design and Practice* 2, no. 4, 307–323. https://doi.org/10.1080/25741292.2019.1675989.

13. Cohen, G. L. 2003. "Party Over Policy: The Dominating Impact of Group Influence on Political Beliefs." *Journal of Personality and Social Psychology* 85, no. 5 (2003): 808–822. https://doi.org/10.1037/0022-3514.85.5.808.

14. Mintrom, M. 2019. "So You Want to Be a Policy Entrepreneur?" *Policy Design and Practice* 2, no. 4, 307–323. https://doi.org/10.1080/25741292.2019.1675989.

15. McAdam, D., J. D. McCarthy, and M. N. Zald (Eds.). 1996. *Comparative Perspectives on Social Movements: Political Opportunities, Mobilizing Structures, and Cultural Framings*, 262. Cambridge Studies in Comparative Politics. Cambridge: Cambridge University Press, 1996. https://doi.org/10.1017/CBO9780511803987.

16. Money Talk Research. n.d. "Interactive Dashboard." https://moneytalksresearch.org/interactive-dashboard.

17. Vlasceanu, M., K. Doell, J. Bak-Coleman, J. J. van Bavel, et al. 2023 "Addressing Climate Change with Behavioral Science: A Global Intervention Tournament in 63 Countries." PsyArXiv. November 20. https://doi.org/10.31234/osf.io/cr5at.

18. Busby, J. W. 2007. "Bono Made Jesse Helms Cry: Jubilee 2000, Debt Relief and Moral Action in International Politics." *International Studies Quarterly* no. 51 (2007): 247–275. https://repositories.lib.utexas.edu/bitstream/handle/2152/61793/Bono_Jesse.pdf.

19. McPherson, A. 2015. *The World and U2: One Band's Remaking of Global Activism.* Rowman & Littlefield, 2015.

20. Ibid.

21. AceShowbiz. 2018. "In an Interview with Jenna Bush, the U2 Frontman Recalls His First Meeting with the Former U.S. President Back in 2002 when He Tried to Convince the Latter to Join Fight against AIDS in Africa." December 3, 2018. https://www.aceshowbiz.com/news/view/00129518.html.

22. White House, The. 2023. "Statement from President Joe Biden on the 20th Anniversary of the U.S. President's Emergency Plan for AIDS Relief (PEPFAR)." January 28, 2023. https://www.whitehouse.gov/briefing-room/statements-releases/2023/01/28/statement-from-president-joe-biden-on-the-20th-anniversary-of-the-u-s-presidents-emergency-plan-for-aids-relief-pepfar/.

23. UNICEF. 2023. "Accelerating Progress on Safe Sanitation and Hygiene for All: Countdown to 2030." March 24, 2023. https://knowledge.unicef.org/wash/accelerating-progress-safe-sanitation-and-hygiene-all-countdown-2030.

24. Kar, K., and R. Chambers. 2008. "Handbook on Community-Led Total Sanitation: Approach Guidelines." The Sanitation Learning Hub. March 2008. https://sanitationlearninghub.org/resource/handbook-on-community-led-total-sanitation.

25. Mahapatra, R. 2023. "Is Open Defecation Back in India?" *Down To Earth*. July 9, 2023. https://www.downtoearth.org.in/news/water/is-open-defecation-back-in-india--90483.

26. Conceptually. n.d. "The Overton Window." https://conceptually.org/concepts/overton-window.

27. Open Society Foundations. 2023. "Open Society Barometer." September 2023.

28. Jang, Y., Ph.D. 2020. "Survey Data: Reliability and Validity? Are They Interchangeable?" Explorance. April 28, 2020. https://explorance.com/blog/survey-data-reliability-and-validity-are-they-interchangeable/.

29. Conceptually. n.d. "The Overton Window." https://conceptually.org/concepts/overton-window.

30. Ibid.

31. Roberts, D. 2017. "The McKibben Effect: A Case Study in How Radical Environmentalism Can Work." Vox. November 17, 2017. https://www.vox.com/energy-and-environment/2017/9/29/16377806/mckibben-effect.

32. Simpson, B., R. Willer, and M. Feinberg. 2020. "Radical Flanks of Social Movements Can Increase Support for Moderate Factions." *PNAS Nexus* 1, no. 3 (2020). https://doi.org/10.1093/pnasnexus/pgac110.

33. Davis, C. 2022. "Just Stop Oil: Do Radical Protests Turn the Public Away from a Cause? Here's the Evidence." The Conversation. October 21, 2022. https://theconversation.com/just-stop-oil-do-radical-protests-turn-the-public-away-from-a-cause-heres-the-evidence-192901.

34. Conceptually. n.d. "The Overton Window." https://conceptually.org/concepts/overton-window.

35. Marchildon, J. 2019. "How Global Citizens Helped a Health Organization Deliver Millions of Life-Saving Vaccines." Global Citizen. September 12, 2019. https://www.globalcitizen.org/en/content/gavi-canada-case-study/.

36. Inyangudor, I. 2023. Idee Inyangudor (Director of Policy and Stakeholder Relations - Office of the Minister of International

Development during the government of Stephen Harper, 22nd prime minister of Canada) in discussion with the author. October 2023.

37. Hanson, R. 2007. "Policy Tug-O-War." Overcoming Bias. May 23, 2007. https://www.overcomingbias.com/p/policy_tugowar html.

38. Hanson, R. 2019. "To Oppose Polarization, Tug Sideways." Overcoming Bias. March 13, 2019. https://www.overcomingbias. com/p/tug-sidewayshtml.

39. Stepp, Al., and C. Watney. 2022. "Progress Is a Policy Choice." Institute for Progress. January 20, 2022. https://progress.institute/ progress-is-a-policy-choice.

40. Bazelon, S., and M. Yglesias. 2021. "The Rise and Importance of Secret Congress." Slow Boring. June 21, 2021. https://www. slowboring.com/p/the-rise-and-importance-of-secret.

41. Oldfield, J. 2021. "Abolition of the Slave Trade and Slavery in Britain." British Library. February 4, 2021. https://www.bl.uk/ restoration-18th-century-literature/articles/abolition-of-the-slave-trade-and-slavery-in-britain.

42. Nix, K. 2015. "It's All in the Frame: Winning Marriage Equality in America." OpenDemocracy. September 8, 2015. https://www. opendemocracy.net/en/openglobalrights-openpage/ its-all-in-frame-winning-marriage-equality-in-america/.

43. Ibid.

44. Tribou, A., and K. Collins. 2015. "This Is How Fast America Changes Its Mind." *Bloomberg*. June 26, 2015. https://www. bloomberg.com/graphics/2015-pace-of-social-change.

45. Jordan, J. F. 2013. "Sanctions Were Crucial to the Defeat of Apartheid." *The New York Times*. November 19, 2013. https:// www.nytimes.com/roomfordebate/2013/11/19/sanctions-successes-and-failures/sanctions-were-crucial-to-the-defeat-of-apartheid.

46. Barnato, K. 2015. "Did the Fall of the Berlin Wall Help End Apartheid?" CNBC. July 17, 2015. https://www.cnbc .com/2015/07/16/did-the-fall-of-the-berlin-wall-help-end-apartheid.html.

otes.

47. *Independent*. 2011. "David Cameron Dismisses Aid Criticism." May 27, 2011. https://www.independent.co.uk/news/world/politics/david-cameron-dismisses-aid-criticism-2289947.html.
48. Klein, S., and T. Mason. 2016. "How to Win an Election." *The New York Times*. February 18, 2016. Video. https://www.nytimes.com/video/opinion/100000004216589/how-to-win-an-election.html.
49. Ibid.
50. Bowles, T. 2023. Email sent to author. October 25, 2023.
51. Ibid.
52. Open Global Rights. 2019. "A Guide to Hope-based Communications." https://www.openglobalrights.org/hope-guide.
53. Ibid.
54. Fruean, B. 2021. "Pacific Islanders Aren't Just Victims—We Know How to Fight the Climate Crisis." *The Guardian*. November 2, 2021. https://www.theguardian.com/commentisfree/2021/nov/02/pacific-islanders-fight-climate-crisis-cop26.
55. Ibid.
56. Bowles, T. 2023. Email sent to author. October 25, 2023.

Chapter 2

1. Figueres, C., T. Rivett-Carnac, and P. Dickson. 2022. "179: The Best of Times, the Worst of Times." Interview with Rory Stewart. *Outrage + Optimism* podcast (audio). November 23, 2022. https://www.outrageandoptimism.org/episodes/the-best-of-times-the-worst-of-times.
2. Dalio, R. 2023. "Principle of the Day." LinkedIn. March 2023. https://www.linkedin.com/posts/raydalio_principle oftheday-activity-7042514703725514752-IvWo.
3. Kalil, T. 2017. "Policy Entrepreneurship at the White House: Getting Things Done in Large Organizations." *Innovations: Technology, Governance, Globalization* 11, no. 3–4 (2017): 4–21.
4. Blair, T. 2023. "Lessons From Northern Ireland's Peace." Tony Blair Institute for Global Change. April 11, 2023. https://www.institute.global/insights/politics-and-governance/lessons-northern-irelands-peace.

5. Dhillon, N. 2023. "Remembering the Road to the Good Friday Agreement: 'People Knew History Was Being Made.'" Tony Blair Institute for Global Change. April 10, 2023. https://www.institute.global/insights/geopolitics-and-security/remembering-road-good-friday-agreement-people-knew-history-being-made.

6. Madden, A. 2023. "David Donoghue on a 'Miraculous' Moment and 'Emotional Blackmail' in Last Days of Good Friday Agreement Talks." *Belfast Telegraph*. April 3, 2023. https://www.belfasttelegraph.co.uk/news/northern-ireland/david-donoghue-on-a-miraculous-moment-and-emotional-blackmail-in-last-days-of-good-friday-agreement-talks/352983556.html.

7. Donoghue, D. 2022. *One Good Day: My Journey to the Good Friday Agreement*. Gill Books.

8. Blair, T. 2023. "Lessons From Northern Ireland's Peace." Tony Blair Institute for Global Change. April 11, 2023. https://www.institute.global/insights/politics-and-governance/lessons-northern-irelands-peace.

9. Grant, A. 2021. *Think Again: The Power of Knowing What You Don't Know*. Viking.

10. Pullella, P. 2020. "'Infidels': Ultra-Conservative Catholic Groups Slam Pope Francis over Inter-Faith Prayers." *National Post*. May 14, 2020. https://nationalpost.com/news/world/pope-joins-inter-faith-prayers-against-coronavirus-irks-ultra-conservatives.

11. Francis. 2023. "Address of His Holiness Pope Francis to the Conference of Parties to the United Nations Framework Convention on Climate Change (COP28)." Expo City, Dubai. December 2, 2023.

12. TV Show Transcripts. n.d. *The Diplomat*. "The James Bond Clause." Season 1, Episode 8. OurBoard TV Show Transcripts. https://tvshowtranscripts.ourboard.org/viewtopic.php?f=1820&t=62232.

13. FAO, IFAD, UNICEF, WFP, and WHO. 2023, "The State of Food Security and Nutrition in the World 2023: Urbanization, Agrifood Systems Transformation and Healthy Diets Across the Rural–Urban Continuum." Rome, FAO. https://doi.org/10.4060/cc3017en.

14. Rhodes, B. 2018. *The World as It Is: A Memoir of the Obama White House*. Random House.

15. GhanaWeb. 2021. "Australian Diplomat Who Helped Commission LGBTQ+ Office to Leave Ghana." December 11, 2021. https://www.ghanaweb.com/GhanaHomePage/NewsArchive/Australian-diplomat-who-helped-commission-LGBTQ-office-to-leave-Ghana-1421593.

16. Carbon Almanac. n.d. "Aiming for Optopia." https://thecarbonalmanac.org/aiming-for-optopia/.

17. Mikes, A., and S. New. 2023. "How to Create an Optopia?—Kim Stanley Robinson's 'Ministry for the Future' and the Politics of Hope." *Journal of Management Inquiry* 32, no. 3, 228–242. https://doi.org/10.1177/10564926231169170.

18. University of Pennsylvania. n.d. "Rockefeller Foundation President Raj Shah, M'02, GRW'05 Comes Home." Perelman School of Medicine, University of Pennsylvania. https://www.alumni.upenn.edu/s/1587/psom/index.aspx?sid=1587&gid=2&pgid=22000&cid=48287&ecid=48287&crid=0&calpgid=3450&calcid=8636.

19. Robinson, K. 2021. *The Ministry for the Future*. Orbit Books.

20. Robinson, K. 2023. "Paying Ourselves to Decarbonize." Noēma. February 21, 2023. https://www.noemamag.com/paying-ourselves-to-decarbonize/.

21. Mikes, A., and S. New. 2023. "How to Create an Optopia?—Kim Stanley Robinson's 'Ministry for the Future' and the Politics of Hope." *Journal of Management Inquiry* 32, no. 3, 228–242. https://doi.org/10.1177/10564926231169170.

22. Adrian, T., P. Bolton, and A. M. Kleinnijenhuis. 2022. "The Great Carbon Arbitrage." IMF Working Papers. June 1, 2022. https://www.imf.org/en/Publications/WP/Issues/2022/05/31/The-Great-Carbon-Arbitrage-518464.

23. Halm, I. 2023. "Big Oil Profits Soared to Nearly $200bn in 2022." Energy Monitor. February 8, 2023. https://www.energymonitor.ai/finance/big-oil-profits-soared-to-nearly-200bn-in-2022/.

24. Mikes, A., and S. New. 2023. "How to Create an Optopia?—Kim Stanley Robinson's 'Ministry for the Future' and the Politics of Hope." *Journal of Management Inquiry* 32, no. 3, 228–242. https://doi.org/10.1177/10564926231169170.

25. Raworth, K. 2018. *Doughnut Economics: Seven Ways to Think Like a 21st-Century Economist.* Chelsea Green Publishing.

26. Hayhoe, K. 2020. *Saving Us: A Climate Scientist's Case for Hope and Healing in a Divided World.* Atria/One Signal Publishers.

27. Robson, D. 2019. "The '3.5% Rule': How a Small Minority Can Change the World." BBC. May 13, 2019. https://www.bbc.com/future/article/20190513-it-only-takes-35-of-people-to-change-the-world.

28. Jones, J. 2023. Interview by author. Kiribati. March 30, 2023.

29. US EPA. n.d. "Greenhouse Gas Inventory." Chapter 6: "Land Use, Land-Use Change, and Forestry." https://www.epa.gov/sites/default/files/2020-04/documents/us-ghg-inventory-2020-chapter-6-land-use-land-use-change-and-forestry.pdf.

30. Pallotta, D. 2021. *Uncharitable: How Restraints on Nonprofits Undermine Their Potential.* Brandeis University Press.

31. Denning, G. 2023. *Universal Food Security: How to End Hunger While Protecting the Planet.* Columbia University Press.

32. Thompson, A., and A. Pitt. 2023. "Philanthropy and The Global Economy V3.0: Perspectives on the Future of Giving." Citi. October 2023. https://ir.citi.com/gps/vUSkZVZEY9B6wXtK8Vnpj8yxjsKMYGQvHXfR6MuSXc7M7D4DDYtIuSK9Jt%2F5wszyEE4rnXLUUVkxNEqzT1edTw%3D%3D.

33. Spectrum News. 2022. "Darren Walker: Philanthropy and the Push for Systemic Change." Spectrum News NY1. September 15, 2022. https://ny1.com/nyc/all-boroughs/you-decide-with-errol-louis/2022/09/15/darren-walker-philanthropy-and-the-push-for-systemic-change.

34. Alemanno, A. 2023. "The Lobbying for Good Movement." *Stanford Social Innovation Review* 22, no. 1, 36–43. https://doi.org/10.48558/1AES-X733.

35. Ibid.

Chapter 3

1. Kalil, T. 2017. "Policy Entrepreneurship at the White House: Getting Things Done in Large Organizations." *Innovations: Technology, Governance, Globalization* 11, no. 3–4 (2017): 4–21.
2. Mintrom, M. 2019. "So You Want to Be a Policy Entrepreneur?" *Policy Design and Practice* 2, no. 4, 307–323. https://doi.org/10.1080/25741292.2019.1675989.
3. Yuan, H., X. Wang, L. Gao, T. Wang, B. Liu, D. Fang, and Y. Gao. 2023. "Progress towards the Sustainable Development Goals has been slowed by indirect effects of the COVID-19 pandemic." *Communications Earth & Environment* 4, no. 1 (2023): 184.
4. Jones, J. 2023. Interview by author. Kiribati. March 30, 2023.
5. Ronald Reagan Presidential Library and Museum. n.d. "President's Private Sector Survey on Cost Control (Grace Commission)." https://www.reaganlibrary.gov/archives/topic-guide/presidents-private-sector-survey-cost-control-grace-commission.
6. Sikkink, Kathryn. Evidence for Hope: Making Human Rights Work in the 21st Century. Vol. 28. Princeton University Press, 2017. https://doi.org/10.2307/j.ctvc77hg2.
7. Korte, A. 2019. "Katharine Hayhoe Encourages Conversations to Build a Climate of Hope." American Association for the Advancement of Science. December 20, 2019. https://www.aaas.org/news/katharine-hayhoe-encourages-conversations-build-climate-hope.
8. Hawkins, S., D. Yudkin, M. Juan-Torres, and T. Dixon. 2018. "Hidden Tribes: A Study of America's Polarized World." The Hidden Tribes. More in Common. https://hiddentribes.us/media/qfpekz4g/hidden_tribes_report.pdf.
9. Open Global Rights. 2019. "A Guide to Hope-based Communications." https://www.openglobalrights.org/hope-guide.
10. Gyberg, V. B., and E. Lövbrand. 2022. "Catalyzing Industrial Decarbonization: The Promissory Legitimacy of Fossil-free Sweden." *Oxford Open Climate Change* 2, no. 1 (2022): kgac004. https://doi.org/10.1093/oxfclm/kgac004.

Chapter 4

1. SABC News. 2018. "President Cyril Ramaphosa Praises the 2018 Global Citizen Festival." YouTube. December 8, 2018. Video. https://www.youtube.com/watch?v=E5MNJJ0Fku8.

2. UNFPA South Africa. 2021. "Moving the Needle Forward for Menstrual Health Requires Multi-sectoral Partnerships." May 25, 2021. https://southafrica.unfpa.org/en/news/moving-needle-forward-menstrual-health-requires-multi-sectoral-partnerships.

3. Alvarez, A. 2019. "Period poverty." American Medical Women's Association. https://www.amwadoc.org/period-poverty.

4. Thinx and PERIOD. n.d. "State of the Period 2021: The Widespread Impact of Period Poverty on US Students." Commissioned by Thinx and PERIOD. https://period.org/uploads/State-of-the-Period-2021.pdf.

5. Tellier, S., and M. Hyttel. 2018. "Menstrual Health Management in East and Southern Africa: A Review Paper." UNFPA ESARO. May 2018. https://esaro.unfpa.org/en/publications/menstrual-health-management-east-and-southern-africa-review-paper.

6. Always. 2017. "The Always Confidence and Puberty Wave VI Study." November 2017; based on females aged 16–24 years old.

7. Davies, S., G. Clarke, and N. Lewis. 2021. "Period Poverty: The Public Health Crisis We Don't Talk About." Children's Hospital of Philadelphia. April 6, 2021. https://policylab.chop.edu/blog/period-poverty-public-health-crisis-we-dont-talk-about.

8. UNESCO. 2014. "Puberty Education & Menstrual Hygiene Management." UNESCO Digital Library. https://unesdoc.unesco.org/ark:/48223/pf0000226792.

9. World Bank. 2022. "Menstrual Health and Hygiene." May 12, 2022. https://www.worldbank.org/en/topic/water/brief/menstrual-health-and-hygiene.

10. Mucherah, W., and K. Thomas. 2017. "Reducing Barriers to Primary School Education for Girls in Rural Kenya: Reusable Pads' Intervention." *International Journal of Adolescent Medicine and Health* 31, no. 3 (2017). https://doi.org/10.1515/ijamh-2017-0005.

11. Phillips-Howard, P. A., G. Otieno, B. Burmen, F. Otieno, F. Odongo, C. Odour, E. Nyothach, N. Amek, E. Zielinski-Gutierrez, F. Odhiambo, C. Zeh, D. Kwaro, L. A. Mills, and K. F. Laserson. 2015. "Menstrual Needs and Associations with Sexual and Reproductive Risks in Rural Kenyan Females: A Cross-Sectional Behavioral Survey Linked with HIV Prevalence." *Journal of Women's Health* 24, no. 10 (2015): 801–811. https://doi. org/10.1089/jwh.2014.5031.

12. Crankshaw, T. L., M. Strauss, and B. Gumede. 2020. "Menstrual Health Management and Schooling Experience Amongst Female Learners in Gauteng, South Africa: A Mixed Method Study." *Reprod Health* 17, no. 1 (Apr 15, 2020): 48. https://doi .org/10.1186/s12978-020-0896-1.

13. Mwinemwesigwa, C. A., and A. Esparaz. n.d. "The Unique Way This Village Fights Period Poverty." Compassion. https://www .compassion.com/for-sponsors/stories/the-unique-way-this-village-fights-period-poverty.htm.

14. Devaki, R., D. Nelson, I. Silagy, S. Matshoba, and M. Mafico. n.d. "Menstrual Health Country Snapshot: South Africa." Days For Girls, WASH United and WaterAid. https://drive.google. com/file/d/15CCtf4FSONC6L4fbmIaTihOHyFKB W6Wr/view.

15. World Bank. 2022. "Policy Reforms for Dignity, Equality, and Menstrual Health." May 25, 2022. https://www.worldbank.org/ en/news/feature/2022/05/25/policy-reforms-for-dignity-equality-and-menstrual-health.

16. Editor's Desk. 2023. "South Africa's Menstrual Health Drive Takes over Global Citizen Festival." *Now in SA*. October 3, 2023. https://nowinsa.co.za/2023/editors-picks/south-africas-men strual-health-drive-takes-over-global-citizen-festival.

17. Mwinemwesigwa, C. A., and A. Esparaz. n.d. "The Unique Way This Village Fights Period Poverty." Compassion. https://www. compassion.com/for-sponsors/stories/the-unique-way-this-village-fights-period-poverty.htm.

18. MENstruation Foundation. n.d. "Ending Period Poverty." https://menstruation.foundation/who-we-are.

19. Crankshaw, T. L., M. Strauss, and B. Gumede. 2020. "Menstrual Health Management and Schooling Experience Amongst Female Learners in Gauteng, South Africa: A Mixed Method Study." *Reprod Health* 17, no. 1 (Apr 15, 2020): 48. https://doi.org/10.1186/s12978-020-0896-1.

20. South African Government News Agency. 2015. "Fight to Keep Young Girls at School." South African Government News Agency. July 22, 2015. https://www.sanews.gov.za/features/fight-keep-young-girls-school.

21. Letsoalo, I. 2019. "We Caught Up With Schoolgirls Impacted by Always' Sanitary Pad Programme in South Africa." Global Citizen. December 9, 2019. https://www.globalcitizen.org/en/content/always-pads-school-girls-periods-south-africa.

22. Devaki, R., D. Nelson, I. Silagy, S. Matshoba, and M. Mafico. n.d. "Menstrual Health Country Snapshot: South Africa." Days For Girls, WASH United and WaterAid. https://drive.google.com/file/d/15CCtf4FSONC6L4fbmIaTihOHyFKBW6Wr/view.

23. Department of Women, Youth and Persons with Disabilities, Republic of South Africa. 2023. "Presentation to Global Citizen: Sanitary Dignity Programme" (Zoom, October 11, 2023).

24. Ibid.

25. Ibid.

26. Chirwa, C. 2021. "I'm the 'Minister of Menstruation.' Here's How I'm Fighting Period Poverty in South Africa: Activist Candice Chirwa Shares Why She's so Passionate about Ending Period Poverty." Global Citizen. May 28, 2021. https://www.globalcitizen.org/en/content/activist-period-poverty-south-africa-candicechirwa.

27. Ibid.

28. Department of Women, Youth and Persons with Disabilities, Republic of South Africa. 2019. "Sanitary Dignity Implementation Framework." September 2019. https://drive.google.com/file/d/1mjg22IqEJ_oOMdwRVLwzPjZoTxI8MGWm/view.

29. FMCG News South Africa. 2019. "P&G SA Invests in Local Always Manufacturing Plant." Bizcommunity. November 5, 2019.

https://www.globalcitizen.org/en/content/activist-period-poverty-south-africa-candicechirwa/.

30. Kgame, M., L. Mogoatlhe, and I. Calderwood. 2019. "How Global Citizens & Activists Spurred South Africa to Improve Menstrual Health in Over 5,000 Schools." Global Citizen. May 28, 2019. https://www.globalcitizen.org/en/content/how-south-african-activists-and-global-citizens-he.

31. Department of Women, Youth and Persons with Disabilities, Republic of South Africa. 2023. "Presentation to Global Citizen: Sanitary Dignity Programme" (Zoom, October 11, 2023).

32. Global Citizen Festival. 2022. "Introducing the Global Menstrual Equity Accelerator | Global Citizen Festival: NYC." YouTube. September 25, 2022. Video. https://www.youtube.com/watch?v=Rk3G04G6hKg.

33. UNFPA South Africa. 2021. "Moving the Needle Forward for Menstrual Health Requires Multi-sectoral Partnerships." May 25, 2021. https://southafrica.unfpa.org/en/news/moving-needle-forward-menstrual-health-requires-multi-sectoral-partnerships.

34. Devaki, R., D. Nelson, I. Silagy, S. Matshoba, and M. Mafico. n.d. "Menstrual Health Country Snapshot: South Africa." Days For Girls, WASH United and WaterAid. https://drive.google.com/file/d/15CCtf4FSONC6L4fbmIaTihOHyFKBW6Wr/view.

35. Department of Women, Youth and Persons with Disabilities, Republic of South Africa. 2023. "Presentation to Global Citizen: Sanitary Dignity Programme" (Zoom, October 11, 2023).

36. Parliamentary Monitoring Group. 2020. "Sanitary Dignity Programme Implementation." Department of Women, Youth and Persons with Disabilities meeting report. October 13, 2020. https://pmg.org.za/committee-meeting/31175.

37. Department of Women, Youth and Persons with Disabilities, Republic of South Africa. 2023. "Presentation to Global Citizen: Sanitary Dignity Programme" (Zoom, October 11, 2023).

38. Devaki, R., D. Nelson, I. Silagy, S. Matshoba, and M. Mafico. n.d. "Menstrual Health Country Snapshot: South Africa." Days

For Girls, WASH United and WaterAid. https://drive.google.
com/file/d/15CCtf4FSONC6L4fbmIaTihOHyFKB
W6Wr/view.

39. Parliamentary Monitoring Group. 2022. "Department of Women,
Youth and Persons with Disabilities 2022/23 Annual Performance
Plan; with Minister." Department of Women, Youth and Persons
with Disabilities meeting report. May 24, 2022. https://pmg.org.
za/committee-meeting/35027.

40. Rossouw, L., H. Ross, and Bill & Melinda Gates Foundation.
2020. "An Economic Assessment of Menstrual Hygiene Product
Tax Cuts." *Gates Open Res* 2020. https://doi.org/10.21955/
gatesopenres.1116672.

41. Department of Women, Youth and Persons with Disabilities,
Republic of South Africa. 2023. "Presentation to Global Citizen:
Sanitary Dignity Programme" (Zoom, October 11, 2023).

42. UNFPA South Africa. 2021. "Moving the Needle Forward for
Menstrual Health Requires Multi-sectoral Partnerships." May 25,
2021. https://southafrica.unfpa.org/en/news/moving-needle-
forward-menstrual-health-requires-multi-sectoral-partnerships.

43. Department of Women, Youth and Persons with Disabilities,
Republic of South Africa. 2023. "Presentation to Global Citizen:
Sanitary Dignity Programme" (Zoom, October 11, 2023).

44. Rossouw, L., H. Ross, and Bill & Melinda Gates Foundation.
2020. "An Economic Assessment of Menstrual Hygiene Product
Tax Cuts." *Gates Open Res* 2020. https://doi.org/10.21955/
gatesopenres.1116672.

45. Devaki, R., D. Nelson, I. Silagy, S. Matshoba, and M. Mafico.
n.d. "Menstrual Health Country Snapshot: South Africa." Days
For Girls, WASH United and WaterAid. https://drive.google.
com/file/d/15CCtf4FSONC6L4fbmIaTihOHyFKB
W6Wr/view.

46. Borgen Project. 2021. "Period Poverty in South Africa." June
30. 2021. https://borgenproject.org/period-poverty-in-south-
africa.

47. Chirwa, C. 2023. Interview by author. Zoom. September 15, 2023.

48. Department of Women, Youth and Persons with Disabilities, Republic of South Africa. 2023. "Presentation to Global Citizen: Sanitary Dignity Programme" (Zoom, October 11, 2023).
49. Ndwandwe, N. 2023. *Interview by Author*. New York. September 18, 2023.
50. Chirwa, C. 2021. "I'm the 'Minister of Menstruation.' Here's How I'm Fighting Period Poverty in South Africa: Activist Candice Chirwa Shares Why She's so Passionate about Ending Period Poverty." Global Citizen. May 28, 2021. https://www.globalcitizen.org/en/content/activist-period-poverty-south-africa-candicechirwa.
51. Department of Women, Youth and Persons with Disabilities, Republic of South Africa. 2023. "Presentation to Global Citizen: Sanitary Dignity Programme" (Zoom, October 11, 2023).
52. UNFPA South Africa. 2021. "Moving the Needle Forward for Menstrual Health Requires Multi-sectoral Partnerships." May 25, 2021. https://southafrica.unfpa.org/en/news/moving-needle-forward-menstrual-health-requires-multi-sectoral-partnerships.
53. Ndwandwe, N. 2023. *Interview by Author*. New York. September 18, 2023.

Chapter 5

1. Roadtrippers. n.d. "Collie Essential Info." https://maps.roadtrippers.com/regions/collie/info.
2. Department of Climate Change, Energy, the Environment and Water. n.d.- "Latest NPI Emission Data: 2021–2022." Australian Government. https://www.dcceew.gov.au/environment/protection/npi/data/latest-data.
3. Cooban, A. 2023. "'Not Nearly Enough.' IEA Says Fossil Fuel Demand Will Peak Soon but Urges Faster Action." CNN. September 26, 2023. https://www.cnn.com/2023/09/26/energy/fossil-fuels-demand-peak-climate-action-iea/index.html.
4. Global Energy Monitor. 2023. "Boom and Bust Coal 2023: Tracking the Global Coal Plant Pipeline." April 2023. https://globalenergymonitor.org/report/boom-and-bust-coal-2023.

5. Quiggin, J. 2020. "Getting Off Coal: Economic and Social Policies to Manage the Phase-out of Thermal Coal in Australia." The Australia Institute. June 17, 2020. https://australiainstitute. org.au/report/getting-off-coal-economic-and-social-policies-to-manage-the-phase-out-of-thermal-coal-in-australia.

6. IEA. 2021. "Net Zero by 2050: A Roadmap for the Global Energy Sector." Paris, 2021. https://www.iea.org/reports/net-zero-by-2050.

7. IEA. 2022. "Coal 2022: Analysis and Forecast to 2025." Paris, 2022. https://www.iea.org/reports/coal-2022.

8. Global Energy Monitor. 2023. "Boom and Bust Coal 2023: Tracking the Global Coal Plant Pipeline." April 2023. https://globalenergymonitor.org/report/boom-and-bust-coal-2023.

9. Celebi, M., L. Lam, J. Grove, and N. Northrup. 2023. "A Review of Coal Fired Electricity Generation in the U.S." The Brattle Group. April 27, 2023. https://www.brattle.com/wp-content/uploads/2023/04/A-Review-of-Coal-Fired-Electricity-Generation-in-the-U.S..pdf.

10. IEA. 2021. "Phasing Out Unabated Coal: Current Status and Three Case Studies." October 2021. https://iea.blob.core .windows.net/assets/861dc94d-a684-4875-80fb-a1faaf914125/PhasingOutUnabatedCoal-CurrentStatusandThreeCaseStudies .pdf.

11. IMF. 2023. "Bangladesh: Requests for an Arrangement Under the Extended Fund Facility, Request for Arrangement Under the Extended Credit Facility, and Request for an Arrangement Under the Resilience and Sustainability Facility-Press Release; Staff Report; and Statement by the Executive Director for Bangladesh." *IMF Staff Country Reports* 2023, 066 (2023),A001.https://doi.org/10.5089/9798400232206.002.A001.

12. Islam, S. 2021. "Bangladesh Scraps Plans for 10 Coal-fired Power Plants." *Nikkei Asia.* July 8, 2021. https://asia.nikkei.com/Politics/International-relations/Bangladesh-scraps-plans-for-10-coal-fired-power-plants.

13. Global Energy Monitor. 2023. "Boom and Bust Coal 2023: Tracking the Global Coal Plant Pipeline." April 2023. https://globalenergymonitor.org/report/boom-and-bust-coal-2023.

14. Rising, J, M. Dumas, S. Dicker, D. Propp, M. Robertson, and W. Look. 2021. "Regional Just Transitions in the UK: Insights from 40 Years of Policy Experience." Environmental Defense Fund. December 2021. https://www.edf.org/sites/default/files/documents/UK_Report_Case_Study.pdf.

15. Nyathi, M. "United Position Needed on Future of Komati." *Mail & Guardian*. October 30, 2023. https://mg.co.za/the-green-guardian/2023-10-30-presidential-climate-commission-says-a-united-position-is-needed-on-the-future-of-power-stations.

16. Topping, N. "Germany Can End Coal Power Much Earlier than 2038." Climate Home News. January 29, 2019. https://climatechangenews.com/2019/01/29/germany-can-end-coal-power-much-earlier-2038.

17. Connolly, K. 2022. "5 Lessons from South Africa's Just Transition Journey." World Resources Institute. September 1, 2022. https://www.wri.org/technical-perspectives/5-lessons-south-africas-just-transition-journey.

18. Oei, P.-Y., H. Brauers, and P. Herpich. 2019. "Lessons from Germany's Hard Coal Mining Phase-out: Policies and Transition from 1950 to 2018." Taylor & Francis Online. November 28, 2019. https://doi.org/10.1080/14693062.2019.1688636.

19. Karp, P. 2018. "Matt Canavan Castigates Fossil Fuel Opponents for Using 'Highly Objectionable' Term 'Just Transition.'" *The Guardian*. March 28, 2018. https://www.theguardian.com/australia-news/2018/mar/28/matt-canavan-castigates-fossil-fuel-opponents-for-using-highly-objectionable-term-just-transition.

20. Thurton, D. 2023. "Ottawa Must Scrap Polarizing Term 'Just Transition': Alberta Environment Minister." CBC. January 8, 2023. https://www.cbc.ca/news/politics/ottawa-just-transition-alberta-environment-1.6704486.

21. McCartney, S. 2023. Interview by author. Google Meet. October 25, 2023.

22. Ibid.

23. Ibid.

24. Ibid.

25. IEA. 2022. "Coal in Net Zero Transitions: Strategies for Rapid, Secure, and People-centered Change." Paris, 2022. https://www.iea.org/reports/coal-in-net-zero-transitions.

26. Mah, A. 2023. "The Labour Movement Origins of 'Just Transition.'" *Our Times Magazine.* May 30, 2023. https://ourtimes.ca/article/the-labour-movement-origins-of-just-transition.

27. IEA. 2021. "Net Zero by 2050: A Roadmap for the Global Energy Sector." Paris, 2021. https://www.iea.org/reports/net-zero-by-2050.

28. Vorrath, S. 2019. "W. A. Councils Demand 'True to Science' 50% Renewable State Target." Renew Economy. May 31, 2019. https://reneweconomy.com.au/w-a-councils-demand-true-to-science-50-renewable-state-target-97322.

29. Clean Energy Council. 2023. "Clean Energy Australia: Report 2023." https://assets.cleanenergycouncil.org.au/documents/Clean-Energy-Australia-Report-2023.pdf.

30. International Labour Organization. n.d. "Frequently Asked Questions on Just Transition." https://www.ilo.org/global/topics/green-jobs/WCMS_824102/lang--en/index.htm.

31. Quiggin, J. 2020. "Getting Off Coal: Economic and Social Policies to Manage the Phase-out of Thermal Coal in Australia." The Australia Institute. June 17, 2020. https://australiainstitute.org.au/report/getting-off-coal-economic-and-social-policies-to-manage-the-phase-out-of-thermal-coal-in-australia.

32. Cassie, A. 2022. "Just Transition: Lessons from a Living Process." 2022 Harold Peden Lecture at Australian Society for the Study of Labour History. Perth, Australia. November 22, 2022. https://www.unionswa.com.au/peden_lecture_2022.

33. Ibid.

34. Ibid.

35. McCartney, S. 2023. Interview by author. Google Meet. October 25, 2023.

36. Ibid.

37. Bennett, E. 2018. "Climate of the Nation 2018." The Australia Institute. September 2018. https://australiainstitute.org.au/wp-content/uploads/2020/12/180911-Climate-of-the-Nation-2018-PRINT.pdf.

38. Morison, E. 2023. "Climate of the Nation 2023." The Australia Institute. September 2023. https://australiainstitute.org.au/wp-content/uploads/2023/09/Climate-of-the-Nation-2023-Web.pdf.

39. Quicke, A., and S. Venketasubramanian. 2022. "Climate of the Nation 2022." The Australia Institute. November 2022. https://australiainstitute.org.au/wp-content/uploads/2022/11/Climate-of-the-Nation-2022.pdf.

40. Rowland, J. 2023. Interview by author. Google Meet. October 25, 2023.

41. Cassie, A. 2022. "Just Transition: Lessons from a Living Process." 2022 Harold Peden Lecture at Australian Society for the Study of Labour History. Perth, Australia. November 22, 2022. https://www.unionswa.com.au/peden_lecture_2022.

42. *ChangeMakers*. 2022. "Alex Cassie—ChangeMaker Chat: Just Transition." *ChangeMakers: Stories of People Changing the World*, podcast audio. December 16, 2022. https://changemakerspodcast.org/alex-cassie-changemaker-chat-just-transition.

43. Parkinson, G. 2022. "Western Australia Sets New Renewables Record of 81%—in World's Biggest Isolated Grid." Renew Economy. November 17, 2022. https://reneweconomy.com.au/western-australia-sets-new-renewables-record-of-81-in-worlds-biggest-isolated-grid.

44. Synergy. n.d. "Synergy's Generation Transformation." https://www.synergy.net.au/About-us/Vision-and-values/Generation-transformation.

45. Government of Western Australia. 2022. "State-owned Coal Power Stations to Be Retired by 2030." June 14, 2022. https://web.archive.org/web/20220714095132/https://www.mediastatements.wa.gov.au/Pages/McGowan/2022/06/State-owned-coal-power-stations-to-be-retired-by-2030.aspx.

46. Cassie, A. 2022. "Just Transition: Lessons from a Living Process." 2022 Harold Peden Lecture at Australian Society for the Study of

Labour History. Perth, Australia. November 22, 2022. https://www.unionswa.com.au/peden_lecture_2022.

47. Bourke, K. 2023. "WA Government Spends Millions More to Keep Ageing Griffin Coal Mine Running." Australian Broadcasting Corporation. June 13, 2023. https://www.abc.net.au/news/2023-06-14/wa-government-spends-millions-more-to-keep-griffin-coal-mine-run/102474704

48. Smith, S. "The Local Heroes Battling to Steady Collie's Wobbles as Town Transitions to New Future." *The West Australian*. March 20, 2019. https://thewest.com.au/business/mining/the-local-heroes-battling-to-steady-collies-wobbles-as-town-transitions-to-new-future-ng-b881128240z.

49. Murray, N. 2023. Interview by author. Zoom. March 17, 2023.

50. Smith, S. "The Local Heroes Battling to Steady Collie's Wobbles as Town Transitions to New Future." *The West Australian*. March 20, 2019. https://thewest.com.au/business/mining/the-local-heroes-battling-to-steady-collies-wobbles-as-town-transitions-to-new-future-ng-b881128240z.

51. Ibid.

52. Murray, N. 2023. Interview by author. Zoom. March 17, 2023.

53. McCartney, S. 2023. Interview by author. Google Meet. October 25, 2023.

54. Ibid.

55. Ibid.

56. Cassie, A. 2023. Email sent to author. September 19, 2023.

57. Ibid.

58. Cassie, A. 2022. "Just Transition: Lessons from a Living Process." 2022 Harold Peden Lecture at Australian Society for the Study of Labour History. Perth, Australia. November 22, 2022. https://www.unionswa.com.au/peden_lecture_2022.

59. McCartney, S. 2023. Interview by author. Google Meet. October 25, 2023.

60. Ibid.

61. Ibid.

62. Rowland, J. 2023. Interview by author. Google Meet. October 25, 2023.

63. Ibid.

64. Government of Western Australia. 2022. "State-owned Coal Power Stations to Be Retired by 2030." June 14, 2022. https://web.archive.org/web/20220714095132/https://www.mediastatements.wa.gov.au/Pages/McGowan/2022/06/State-owned-coal-power-stations-to-be-retired-by-2030.aspx.

65. Cummin, J. 2018. "Mining in Collie: A Strong Future." *The Australian Mining Review*. December 7, 2018. https://australianminingreview.com.au/features/mining-in-collie-a-strong-future.

66. Mercer, D. 2023. "WA's Push for 2030 Coal Exit Draws Broad Warnings the Power System 'May Not Cope.'" Australian Broadcasting Corporation. February 7, 2023. https://www.abc.net.au/news/2023-02-08/plans-to-end-coal-in-wa-by-2030-face-growing-pressure/101940540.

67. Rowland, J. 2023. Interview by author. Google Meet. October 25, 2023.

68. Government of Western Australia. 2023. "$708 Million to Power WA's Renewable Energy Boom." November 17, 2023. https://www.wa.gov.au/government/media-statements/Cook-Labor-Government/%24708-million-to-power-WA%27s-renewable-energy-boom-20231117#:~:text=The%20Cook%20Government%20will%20invest,a%20global%20renewable%20energy%20powerhouse.

69. Government of Western Australis. 2023c. "Cook Government Takes Major Step with Climate Change Legislation." November 30, 2023. https://www.wa.gov.au/government/media-statements/Cook-Labor-Government/Cook-Government-takes-major-step-with-climate-change-legislation-20231130.

70. Murray, N. 2023. Interview by author. Zoom. March 17, 2023.

71. Ibid.

72. Government of Western Australia. 2023. "$1 Billion Contracts Awarded for Kwinana and Collie Big Batteries." September 19, 2023. https://www.wa.gov.au/government/media-statements/Cook-Labor-Government/$1-billion-contracts-awarded-for-Kwinana-and-Collie-big-batteries-20230919.

73. Hanns, J. Interview by author. Zoom. May 21, 2023.

74. Murray, N. 2023. Interview by author. Zoom. March 17, 2023.

75. McCartney, S. 2023. Interview by author. Google Meet. October 25, 2023.

76. Cassie, A. 2023. Email sent to author. September 19, 2023.

77. FitzSimons, P. 2019. *The Catalpa Rescue*. Constable.

78. Toscano, N., and E. Bagshaw. 2017. "Despair as Last Australian Car-Maker Exits Manufacturing." *Stuff*. October 14, 2017. https://www.stuff.co.nz/motoring/news/97881597/despair-as-last-australian-carmaker-exits-manufacturing.

79. Rowland, J. 2023. Interview by author. Google Meet. October 25, 2023.

80. Ibid.

81. Global Energy Monitor. 2023. "Boom and Bust Coal 2023: Tracking the Global Coal Plant Pipeline." April 2023. https://globalenergymonitor.org/report/boom-and-bust-coal-2023.

82. IEA. 2023. "Net Zero Roadmap: A Global Pathway to Keep the 1.5 °C Goal in Reach." Update. https://iea.blob.core.windows.net/assets/4d93d947-c78a-47a9-b223-603e6c3fc7d8/NetZeroRoadmap_AGlobalPathwaytoKeepthe1.5CGoalin Reach-2023Update.pdf.

83. UNFCCC. n.d.- "Race-to-Zero Breakthroughs: Transforming Our Systems Together." UNFCCC. https://racetozero.unfccc.int/wp-content/uploads/2021/02/Race-to-Zero-Breakthroughs-Transforming-Our-Systems-Together.pdf.

84. Kuykendall, T. 2021. "5 Asian countries building 80% of new coal power – Carbon Tracker." *S&P Global Market Intelligence*. June 30, 2021. https://www.spglobal.com/marketintelligence/en/news-insights/latest-news-headlines/5-asian-countries-building-80-of-new-coal-power-8211-carbon-tracker-65232956.

Chapter 6

1. Greenidge, K. BusinessBARBADOS. https://www.businessbarbados.com/articles/barbadospositions-itself-as-best-in-class.

2. Vigilance, C., and J. L. Roberts. (Eds.). 2011. *Tools for Mainstreaming Sustainable Development in Small States.* Commonwealth Secretariat. https://doi.org/10.14217/9781848591042-en.

3. Carter, S. T., and E. F. Hansen. 2023. *The History of Barbados: Caribbean Jewel.* Independently published.

4. AFP. 2023. "'We Only Have This Planet': Barbados PM Urges Unified Climate Finance Response." AFP. June 23, 2023. https://www.france24.com/en/live-news/20230623-we-only-have-this-planet-barbados-pm-urges-unified-climate-finance-response.

5. World Bank. 2023. "World Bank Group Announces Comprehensive Toolkit to Support Countries After Natural Disasters." June 22, 2023. https://www.worldbank.org/en/news/factsheet/2023/06/22/comprehensive-toolkit-to-support-countries-after-natural-disasters.

6. Franczak, M. 2023. (Dr. Franczak is a Research Fellow in the division of Peace, Climate, and Sustainable Development at the International Peace Institute, IPI). Email to the author. December 18, 2023.

7. AFP. 2023. "'We Only Have This Planet': Barbados PM Urges Unified Climate Finance Response." AFP. June 23, 2023. https://www.france24.com/en/live-news/20230623-we-only-have-this-planet-barbados-pm-urges-unified-climate-finance-response.

8. Global Citizen. 2023 "PM Mia Mottley & World Bank's Ajay Banga on Climate Promises | Power Our Planet: Live in Paris." YouTube. June 26, 2023. Video. https://www.youtube.com/watch?v=cK-guP_Z5Mo.

9. WMO. 2021. "State of the Global Climate 2020." World Meteorological Organization. No. 1264. https://library.wmo.int/records/item/56247-state-of-the-global-climate-2020.

10. WMO. 2023. "Economic Costs of Weather-related Disasters Soars but Early Warnings Save Lives." World Meteorological Organization. May 22, 2023. https://public.wmo.int/en/media/press-release/economic-costs-of-weather-related-disasters-soars-early-warnings-save-lives.

11. Mallucci, E. 2020. "Natural Disasters, Climate Change, and Sovereign Risk." Board of Governors of the Federal Reserve

System. December 18, 2020. https://www.federalreserve.gov/econres/notes/feds-notes/natural-disasters-climate-change-and-sovereign-risk-20201218.html.

12. Baarsch, F., J. R. Granadillos, W. Hare, M. Knaus, M. Krapp, M. Schaeffer, and H. Lotze-Campen. 2020. "The Impact of Climate Change on Incomes and Convergence in Africa." *World Development* 126 (February 2020). https://doi.org/10.1016/j.worlddev.2019.104699.

13. Persaud, A. 2021. "Debt, Natural Disasters, and Special Drawing Rights: A Modest Proposal." The Centre for Economic Policy Research. March 17, 2021. https://cepr.org/voxeu/columns/debt-natural-disasters-and-special-drawing-rights-modest-proposal.

14. Sheldrick, M. 2023. "Making Climate Finance Work For Real People." *Forbes.* April 17, 2023. https://www.forbes.com/sites/globalcitizen/2023/04/17/making-climate-finance-work-for-real-people-lessons-for-the-world-bank-from-fiji-and-barbados/?sh=18097e355a75.

15. AICCRA. 2023. "Drought tolerant crops provide relief for smallholder farmers in Kenya's drylands." March 9, 2023. https://aiccra.cgiar.org/news/drought-tolerant-crops-provide-relief-smallholder-farmers-kenyas-drylands.

16. Pala, C. 2020. "Kiribati's president's plans to raise islands in fight against sea-level rise." *The Guardian.* August 9, 2020.

17. UN. 2023. "United Nations Secretary-General's SDG Stimulus to Deliver Agenda 2030." United Nations. February 2023. https://www.un.org/sustainabledevelopment/wp-content/uploads/2023/02/SDG-Stimulus-to-Deliver-Agenda-2030.pdf.

18. Lustgarten, A. 2022. "Barbados Resists Climate Colonialism in an Effort to Survive the Costs of Global Warming." ProPublica, Co-published with *The New York Times Magazine.* July 27, 2022. https://www.propublica.org/article/mia-mottley-barbados-imf-climate-change.

19. Mooney, H., J. O. Prats, D. Rosenblatt, and J. Christie. 2021. "Why Have Caribbean Countries Been So Indebted, and What Can

They Do to Improve Outcomes?" IDB. March 10, 2021. https://blogs.iadb.org/caribbean-dev-trends/en/why-have-caribbean-countries-been-so-indebted-and-what-can-they-do-to-improve-outcomes/.

20. Munevar, D. 2018. "Background Paper On: Climate Change and Debt Sustainability in the Caribbean: Trouble in Paradise?" UNCTAD. November 7, 2018. https://unctad.org/system/files/non-official-document/tdb_efd2c01_Munevar_en.pdf.

21. Mazzucato, M. 2023. "A Mission-Orientated Strategy for Inclusive and Sustainable Economic Growth in Barbados." UCL Institute for Innovation and Public Purpose. November 2023. 2023. https://www.ucl.ac.uk/bartlett/public-purpose/sites/bartlett_public_purpose/files/barbados_report.pdf.

22. UN. 2023. "United Nations Secretary-General's SDG Stimulus to Deliver Agenda 2030." United Nations. February 2023. https://www.un.org/sustainabledevelopment/wp-content/uploads/2023/02/SDG-Stimulus-to-Deliver-Agenda-2030.pdf.

23. Franczak, M. 2023. (Dr. Franczak is a Research Fellow in the division of Peace, Climate, and Sustainable Development at the International Peace Institute, IPI). Email to the author. December 18, 2023.

24. Persaud, A. 2023. "Avinash Persaud: The Climate Crisis Is Expensive—Here's Who Should Pay for It." TED. July 2023. Video/ https://www.ted.com/talks/avinash_persaud_the_climate_crisis_is_expensive_here_s_who_should_pay_for_it?language=en.

25. UNFCCC. 2023. Conference of the Parties (COP). "Operationalization of the new funding arrangements, including a fund, for responding to loss and damage." November 29, 2023. https://unfccc.int/documents/634215.

26. Lakhani, N. 2023. "$700m pledged to loss and damage fund at Cop28 covers less than 0.2% needed." *The Guardian*. December 6, 2023. https://www.theguardian.com/environment/2023/dec/06/700m-pledged-to-loss-and-damage-fund-cop28-covers-less-than-02-percent-needed.

27. UN. 2022. "Barbados – Prime Minister Addresses United Nations General Debate, 77th Session (English)." YouTube. September 22, 2022. Video. https://www.youtube.com/watch?v=y4lUZK1Y JNo.

28. Lustgarten, A. 2022. "The Barbados Rebellion: Caribbean Nations Are Trapped between the Global Financial System and a Looming Climate Disaster. One Country's Leader Has Been Fighting to Find a Way Out." *The New York Times Magazine*. July 27, 2022. https://www.nytimes.com/interactive/2022/07/27/magazine/barbados-climate-debt-mia-mottley.html.

29. Harris, L. 2023. "Can Avinash Persaud Convince Capitalists to Embrace Green Growth?" *Foreign Policy*. June 17, 2023.https://foreignpolicy.com/2023/06/17/bridgetown-avinash-persaud-mia-mottley-green-growth/#cookie_message_anchor.

30. PBS. 2008. "The Lobotomist." January 21, 2008. https://www.pbs.org/wgbh/americanexperience/films/lobotomist/.

31. GEG. n.d. Groupe d'études géopolitiques (GEG). "Breaking the Deadlock on Climate: The Bridgetown Initiative." *After COP 27: Geopolitics of the Green Deal*, Issue #3. https://geopolitique.eu/en/articles/breaking-the-deadlock-on-climate-the-bridgetown-initiative.

32. Ibid.

33. Civillini, M. 2023. "World Bank to Suspend Debt Repayments for Disaster-hit Countries." Climate Home News. June 22, 2023. https://www.climatechangenews.com/2023/06/22/world-bank-debt-disaster-climate.

34. Ministry of Foreign Affairs and Foreign Trade, Barbados. 2022. "Natural Disaster & Pandemic Clauses Are Critical." December 9, 2022. https://www.foreign.gov.bb/natural-disaster-pandemic-clauses-are-critical.

35. Mustapha, S., T. Talbot, and J. Gascoigne. 2023. "Innovations in Sovereign Debt: Taking Debt Pause Clauses to Scale." Insight Paper. Centre for Disaster Protection: London.

36. Lustgarten, A. 2022. "The Barbados Rebellion: Caribbean Nations Are Trapped between the Global Financial System and a

Looming Climate Disaster. One Country's Leader Has Been Fighting to Find a Way Out." *The New York Times Magazine*. July 27, 2022. https://www.nytimes.com/interactive/2022/07/27/magazine/barbados-climate-debt-mia-mottley.html.

37. Civillini, M. 2023. "World Bank to Suspend Debt Repayments for Disaster-hit Countries." Climate Home News. June 22, 2023. https://www.climatechangenews.com/2023/06/22/world-bank-debt-disaster-climate.

38. Open Society Foundations. 2023. "Barometer in Context: Debt, Development, and Climate." Open Society Foundations. October 9, 2023. https://www.opensocietyfoundations.org/publications/barometer-in-context-debt-development-and-climate.

39. Contested Histories Initiative. 2021 "Admiral Nelson Statue in Barbados." Contested Histories Case Study #11 (April 2021). https://contestedhistories.org/wp-content/uploads/Barbados_Admiral-Nelson-Statue-in-Bridgetown.pdf.

40. Marshall, T. 2018. "The Most Controversial Statue in Barbados, Horatio Nelson." Ibuka. May 29, 2018.

41. Heblich, S., S. J. Redding, and H.-J. Voth. 2023. "Slavery and the British Industrial Revolution." National Bureau of Economic Research. August 2023. https://doi.org/10.3386/w30451.

42 Greenfield, P., F. Harvey, N. Lakhani, and D. Carrington. 2022. "Barbados PM Launches Blistering Attack on Rich Nations at Cop27 Climate Talks." *The Guardian*. November 7, 2022. https://www.theguardian.com/environment/2022/nov/07/barbados-pm-mia-mottley-launches-blistering-attack-on-rich-nations-at-cop27-climate-talks.

43. UNDP. 2021. "The Peoples' Climate Vote." January 26, 2021. https://www.undp.org/publications/peoples-climate-vote.

44. Open Society Foundations. 2023. "Barometer in Context: Debt, Development, and Climate." Open Society Foundations. October 9, 2023. https://www.opensocietyfoundations.org/publications/barometer-in-context-debt-development-and-climate.

45. International Energy Agency. 2023. "Net Zero Roadmap: A Global Pathway to Keep the 1.5 °C Goal in Reach." 2023 Update.

https://iea.blob.core.windows.net/assets/4d93d947-c78a-47a9-
b223-603e6c3fc7d8/NetZeroRoadmap_AGlobalPathwaytoKee
pthe1.5CGoalinReach-2023Update.pdf.

46. GEG. n.d. Groupe d'études géopolitiques (GEG). "Breaking the
Deadlock on Climate: The Bridgetown Initiative." *After COP 27:
Geopolitics of the Green Deal*, Issue #3. https://geopolitique.eu/
en/articles/breaking-the-deadlock-on-climate-the-bridgetown-
initiative.

47. Andreoni, M. 2022. "Al Gore Calls the World Bank Chief a
'Climate Denier.'" *The New York Times*. September 20, 2022.
https://www.nytimes.com/2022/09/20/world/americas/
world-bank-david-malpass-climate.html.

48. Van Staden, C. 2023. "Ajay Banga in Africa to Rally Support for
World Bank Leadership Amid Stand-off With China." China
Global South Project. March 7, 2023. https://chinaglobalsouth.
com/analysis/ajay-banda-in-africa-to-rally-support-for-
world-bank-leadership-amid-stand-off-with-china.

49. US Department of the Treasury. 2023. "READOUT: U.S.
Candidate for President of the World Bank Ajay Banga Visit to
the United Kingdom." March 12, 2023. https://home.treasury.
gov/news/press-releases/jy1336.

50. Djalal, D. P., and M. Sheldrick. 2023. "The Global South Is Tired
of the West's Disrespect." *Nikkei Asia*. June 17, 2023. https://
asia.nikkei.com/Opinion/The-Global-South-is-tired-of-the-
West-s-disrespect.

51. Puko, T. 2023. "Rich countries promised poor nations billions for
climate change. They aren't paying." *The Washington Post*. October
9, 2023. https://www.washingtonpost.com/climate-environ
ment/2023/10/09/rich-nations-pledged-poor-ones-billions-
climate-damages-they-arent-paying/.

52. Dearden, N. 2021. "Vaccine Apartheid: The Global South Fights
Back." *Al Jazeera*. September 30, 2021. https://www.aljazeera.
com/opinions/2021/9/30/vaccine-apartheid-the-global-
south-fights-back.

53. Akita, H. 2023. "Will anti-Westernism sweep Global South?" *Nikkei.* August 5, 2023. https://asia.nikkei.com/Spotlight/Comment/Will-anti-Westernism-sweep-Global-South.

54. Ibid.

55. Garric, A., and L. Stephan. 2022. "Emmanuel Macron Pushes for Climate Justice at COP27." *Le Monde.* November 8, 2022. https://www.lemonde.fr/en/environment/article/2022/11/08/emmanuel-macron-pushes-for-climate-justice-at-cop27_6003347_114.html.

56. Franczak, M. 2023. (Dr. Franczak is a Research Fellow in the division of Peace, Climate, and Sustainable Development at the International Peace Institute, IPI). Email to the author. December 18, 2023.

57. Farand, C. 2021. "Mia Mottley: The 'Fearless' Leader Pushing a Global Settlement for the Climate Frontlines." Climate Home News. November 18, 2021. https://www.climatechangenews.com/2021/11/18/mia-mottley-fearless-leader-pushing-global-settlement-climate-frontlines.

58. Mottley, M. 2021. "Speech: Mia Mottley, Prime Minister of Barbados at the Opening of the #COP26 World Leaders Summit." YouTube. November 1, 2021. Video. https://www.youtube.com/watch?v=PN6THYZ4ngM

59. Knickmeyer, E. 2023. "Slow Start on World Bank Reform Angers Climate-hit Countries." AP. April 17, 2023. https://apnews.com/article/climate-yellen-world-bank-kerry-barbados-603156bb7b3c672e8358675a32c8e22a.

60. World Bank. https://data.worldbank.org/indicator/GC.XPN.INTP.RV.ZS?locations=MW

61. V20. 2023. "Joint Declaration of the Climate Vulnerable Forum Heads of States and Governments, Ministers, and High-Level Representatives." The Vulnerable Twenty (V20) Group of Ministers of Finance of the Climate Vulnerable Forum. September 21, 2023. https://www.v-20.org/wp-content/uploads/2023/09/CVF-Leaders-Declaration_Adopted-21-September-2023.pdf.

62. Harvey, F. 2023. "UK would be a climate leader again under Labour, vows Starmer." *The Guardian*. December 4, 2023. https://www.theguardian.com/environment/2023/dec/04/keir-starmer-vows-to-make-uk-climate-leader-again-labour-cop28-rishi-sunak.

63. UN Affairs. 2022. "Barbados Prime Minister Mottley Calls for Overhaul of Unfair, Outdated Global Finance System." United Nations. September 22, 2022. https://news.un.org/en/story/2022/09/1127611.

64. Osborne, C. 2022. "The Barbadian Proposal Turning Heads at COP27." Foreign Policy. November 11, 2022. https://foreignpolicy.com/2022/11/11/cop27-un-climate-barbados-mottley-climate-finance-imf.

65. Sheldrick, M. 2022. "Mia Mottley, The Leader Disrupting Global Financial Institutions in the Name of People and the Planet." *Forbes*. June 7, 2022. https://www.forbes.com/sites/global citizen/2022/06/07/mia-mottley-the-leader-disrupting-global-financial-institutions-in-the-name-of-people-and-planet/?sh=6d7e30b86d31.

66. Civillini, M. 2023. "World Bank to Suspend Debt Repayments for Disaster-hit Countries." Climate Home News. June 22, 2023. https://www.climatechangenews.com/2023/06/22/world-bank-debt-disaster-climate.

67. Rockefeller Foundation, The. 2023. "The Rockefeller Foundation Commits Over USD 1 Billion to Advance Climate Solutions." September 15, 2023. https://www.rockefeller foundation.org/news/the-rockefeller-foundation-commits-over-usd-1-billion-to-advance-climate-solutions.

68. Ibid.

69. AFP. 2023. "'We Only Have This Planet': Barbados PM Urges Unified Climate Finance Response." AFP. June 23, 2023. https://www.france24.com/en/live-news/20230623-we-only-have-this-planet-barbados-pm-urges-unified-climate-finance-response.

70. Farand, C. 2021. "Mia Mottley: The 'Fearless' Leader Pushing a Global Settlement for the Climate Frontlines." Climate Home News. November 18, 2021. https://www.climatechangenews.com/2021/11/18/mia-mottley-fearless-leader-pushing-global-settlement-climate-frontlines.

71. Focus. 2023. "Summit for a New Global Financing Pact: Conclusions and Next Steps." Focus 2030. June 29, 2023. https://focus2030.org/Summit-for-a-New-Global-Financing-Pact-conclusions-and-next-steps.

72. Thurton, D. 2023. "Canada Offers to Pause Debt Repayments for Countries Hit by Natural Disasters." Canadian Broadcasting Corporation. October 18, 2023. https://www.cbc.ca/news/politics/trudeau-caricom-debt-natural-disasters-climate-1.7000644.

73. Mintrom, M. 2019. "So You Want to Be a Policy Entrepreneur?" *Policy Design and Practice* 2, no. 4, 307–323. https://doi.org/10.1080/25741292.2019.1675989.

74. World Bank. 2023. "World Bank Extends New Lifeline for Countries Hit by Natural Disasters." December 1, 2023. https://www.worldbank.org/en/news/factsheet/2023/12/01/world-bank-extends-new-lifeline-for-countries-hit-by-natural-disasters.

75. Mustapha, S. (@kira_mustapha). "Timely report from Moody's on impact of CRDCs/debt pause clauses on the creditors who offer them & the sovereign borrowers who request them, including bonds." X. November 2, 2023. https://x.com/kira_mustapha/status/1720113536687370722?s=20.

76. Wilkinson, B. 2023. "Barbados Thinks It Will Soon Find Oil." *The New York Amsterdam News*. March 2, 2023. https://amsterdamnews.com/news/2023/03/02/barbados-thinks-it-will-soon-find-oil.

77. Osborne, C. 2022. "The Barbadian Proposal Turning Heads at COP27." Foreign Policy. November 11, 2022. https://foreignpolicy.com/2022/11/11/cop27-un-climate-barbados-mottley-climate-finance-imf.

78. Fillion, S. 2023. "Who Could Lead the United Nations Next? This Caribbean Climate Leader Makes Diplomats 'Jump' with Excitement." CNN. September 29, 2023. https://www.cnn.com/2023/09/29/americas/united-nations-secretary-general-mia-mottley-intl-latam.

Chapter 7

1. Tooze, A. 2023. "Chartbook Carbon Notes #3 Four trillion dollars per annum—The shock of reality from sustainable development thinking." *Chartbook. Substack.* April 9, 2023. https://adamtooze.substack.com/p/chartbook-carbon-notes-3-four-trillion.

2. Gowan, R. 2023. "How the World Lost Faith in the UN." *Foreign Affairs.* November 9, 2023. https://www.foreignaffairs.com/israel/how-world-lost-faith-united-nations-gaza.

3. Global Nation. 2023. "Global Solidarity Report." https://globalnation.world/global-solidarity-report.

4. Steiner, Z. 2005. *The Lights That Failed. European International History, 1919–1933.* Oxford University Press.

5. Steiner, Z. 2013. *The Triumph of the Dark: European International History 1933–1939.* Oxford University Press.

6. Truman, H. S. 1966. *Public Papers of the Presidents of the United States: Harry S. Truman, Containing the Public Messages, Speeches, and Statements of the President, 1945–1953.* Government Printing Office.

7. Babic, M., E. Heemskerk, and J. Fichtner. 2018. "Who Is More Powerful—States or Corporations?" The Conversation. July 10, 2018. https://theconversation.com/who-is-more-powerful-states-or-corporations-99616.

8. Kamps, H. J. 2023. "When Companies Have More Influence than Countries." TechCrunch. June 29, 2023. https://techcrunch.com/2023/06/29/so-who-watches-the-watchmen.

9. Khanna, P. 2016. "These 25 Companies Are More Powerful Than Many Countries: Going Stateless to Maximize Profits, Multinational Companies Are Vying with Governments for

Global Power. Who Is Winning?" *Foreign Policy*. March 15, 2016. https://foreignpolicy.com/2016/03/15/these-25-companies-are-more-powerful-than-many-countries-multinational-corporate-wealth-power.

10. CDP. 2017. "New Report Shows Just 100 Companies Are Source of over 70% of Emissions." July 10, 2017. https://www.cdp.net/en/articles/media/new-report-shows-just-100-companies-are-source-of-over-70-of-emissions.

11. Generation Investment Management. 2021. "Listed Companies Account for 40% of Climate-Warming Emissions, Reveals New Research by Generation Investment Management." Generation Investment Management. October 11, 2021. https://www.generationim.com/our-thinking/news/listed-companies-account-for-40-of-climate-warming-emissions/.

12. Science Based Targets. n.d. "Ambitious Corporate Climate Action." https://sciencebasedtargets.org.

13. TCFD. n.d. "Task Force on Climate-related Financial Disclosures." https://www.fsb-tcfd.org.

14. UNFCCC. 2021. "Transforming Our Systems Together." United Nations Framework Convention on Climate Change. Race to Zero Breakthroughs. February 2021. https://racetozero.unfccc.int/wp-content/uploads/2021/02/Race-to-Zero-Breakthroughs-Transforming-Our-Systems-Together.pdf.

15. Carbon Market Watch. n.d. "Corporate Climate Responsibility Monitor 2023: Net Zero or Not Zero? Combating Corporate Greenwashing." https://carbonmarketwatch.org/campaigns/ccrm.

16. UN. n.d. "Integrity Matters: Net Zero Commitments by Businesses, Financial Institutions, Cities and Regions: Report from the United Nations' High-Level Expert Group on the Net Zero Emissions Commitment of Non-State Entities." https://www.un.org/sites/un2.un.org/files/high-level_expert_group_n7b.pdf.

17. UNFCCC. n.d.- "Race to Zero Criteria." United Nations Framework Convention on Climate Change. Race to Resilience: Race to Zero. https://racetozero.unfccc.int/system/criteria.

18. Sheldrick, M. 2022. "Corporate Net Zero Commitments: PR Project or Bold Action." *Forbes.* January 7, 2022. https://www.forbes.com/sites/globalcitizen/people/michaelsheldrick/?sh=e9 2f2bd6804f#:~:text=Corporate%20Net%20Zero% 20Commitments%3A%20PR%20Project%20Or%20Bold %20Action%3F.

19. Science Based Targets. n.d. "Ambitious Corporate Climate Action." https://sciencebasedtargets.org.

20. UNFCCC. 2022. "Taking Stock of Progress—September 2022: First Joint Progress Report Across UN-Backed Global Climate Campaigns: Race to Resilience and Race to Zero." UNFCCC. https://climatechampions.unfccc.int/wp-content/uploads/ 2022/09/Race-to-Zero-Race-to-Resilience-Progress-Report.pdf.

21. Bendig, D., A. Wagner, and K. Lau. 2022. "Does It Pay to Be Science-based Green? The Impact of Science-based Emission-reduction Targets on Corporate Financial Performance." Wiley Online Library. November 10, 2022. https://doi.org/10.1111/ jiec.13341.

22. Thomas, L. 2022. *Walmart changed the way it buys shopping bags and saved $60 million—and that's just one way it cut costs.* CNBC. https:// www.cnbc.com/2020/02/18/walmart-saves-millions-of-dollars-each-year-by-making-these-small-changes.html.

23. Tiseo, I. 2023. "Annual greenhouse gas emissions released by Walmart worldwide from 2015 to 2021." *Energy and Environment.* https://www.statista.com/statistics/531531/ carbon-emissions-worldwide-walmart/

24. Global Citizen. 2021. "GLOBAL CITIZEN LIVE CALLS FOR ACTION TO HALT CLIMATE CHANGE AND FOR WEALTHY COUNTRIES TO DELIVER ON $100B CLIMATE PLEDGE, $6B FOR FAMINE RELIEF, AND VACCINE JUSTICE." September 25, 2021. https://www .globalcitizen.org/en/enquiries/press/2021/global-citizen-live-calls-action-halt-climate-change-and-wealthy/.

25. UNFCCC. n.d.- "Who's In." Race to Resilience: Race to Zero. https://climatechampions.unfccc.int/join-the-race/whos-in.

26. Owen-Burge, C. 2022. "Global Campaigns Progress Report." UNFCCC. September 21, 2022. https://climatechampions. unfccc.int/team_member/global-campaigns-progress-report

27. Science Based Targets. 2022. "SBTi Monitoring Report 2022." https://sciencebasedtargets.org/reports/sbti-monitoring-report-2022.

28. UNFCCC. 2022. "Taking Stock of Progress—September 2022: First Joint Progress Report Across UN-Backed Global Climate Campaigns: Race to Resilience and Race to Zero." UNFCCC. https://climatechampions.unfccc.int/wp-content/uploads/2022/09/Race-to-Zero-Race-to-Resilience-Progress-Report.pdf.

29. Figueres, C., T. Rivett-Carnac, and P. Dickson. 2023. "205: How to Talk About Climate Change So People Will Listen." Interview with John Marshall. *Outrage + Optimism* podcast (audio). June 21, 2023.

30. Franczak, M. 2023. (Dr. Franczak is a Research Fellow in the division of Peace, Climate, and Sustainable Development at the International Peace Institute, IPI). Email to the author. December 18, 2023.

31. UN. n.d. "Integrity Matters: Net Zero Commitments by Businesses, Financial Institutions, Cities and Regions: Report from the United Nations' High-Level Expert Group on the Net Zero Emissions Commitment of Non-State Entities." https://www.un.org/sites/un2.un.org/files/high-level_expert_group_n7b.pdf.

32. Ibid.

33. UNFCCC. 2022. "The Pivot Point: Building the Groundswell of Voluntary Climate Action into Ground Rules for the Economy." UNFCCC. September 2022. https://climatechampions.unfccc.int/wp-content/uploads/2022/09/R2Z-Pivot-Point-Report-5.pdf.

34. Ban, K. 2020. *Resolved: Uniting Nations in a Divided World.* Columbia University Press.

35. Ibid.

36. UN. 2020. "Achieving Our Common Humanity: Celebrating Global Cooperation through the United Nations." United Nations Department of Global Communications. https:// euagenda.eu/upload/publications/achieving_our_common_ humanity.pdf.pdf.

37. Ban, K. 2020. *Resolved: Uniting Nations in a Divided World.* Columbia University Press.

38. Ibid.

39. Donoghue, D. 2023. Interview by author. Zoom. June 25, 2023.

40. Dulles, J. F. 1945. "The United Nations: A Prospectus." *Foreign Affairs.* October 1, 1945. https://www.foreignaffairs.com/articles/ united-nations-general-assembly-john-foster-dulles.

41. Buell Papers. 2010. "Raymond Leslie Buell Papers: A Finding Aid to the collection in Library of Congress." Manuscript Division, Library of Congress, Washington, DC. https://findingaids.loc.gov/ exist_collections/ead3pdf/mss/2011/ms011006.pdf.

42. Hearden, P. J. 2003. *Architects of Globalism: Building a New World Order During WWII,* 156. The University of Arkansas Press.

43. Scharf, M. P. 2023. "Power Shift: The Return of the Uniting for Peace Resolution." Case Western Reserve University. Faculty Publications. 2153. https://scholarlycommons.law.case.edu/ faculty_publications/2153.

44. Ibid.

45. Lopez-Castro, A., A. L. Dahl, and M. Groff. 2020. "The General Assembly: Reforms to Strengthen Its Effectiveness." In *Global Governance and the Emergence of Global Institutions for the 21st Century,* 81–106. Cambridge: Cambridge University Press.

46. Gowan, R. 2023. Interview by author. Zoom. May 5, 2023.

47. UN. 2023. "UN General Assembly Calls for Immediate End to War in Ukraine." United Nations. February 23, 2023. https:// news.un.org/en/story/2023/02/1133847.

48. Scharf, M. P. 2023. "Power Shift: The Return of the Uniting for Peace Resolution." Case Western Reserve University. Faculty Publications. 2153. https://scholarlycommons.law.case.edu/faculty_publications/2153.

49. Gowan, R. 2023b. Interview by author. Zoom. May 5, 2023.

50. Ibid.

51. Carney, M. 2015. "Breaking the Tragedy of the Horizon— Climate Change and Financial Stability, Speech by Mark Carney." Bank of England. September 29, 2015. https://www.bankofengland.co.uk/speech/2015/breaking-the-tragedy-of-the-horizon-climate-change-and-financial-stability.

52. Kerry, J. F. 2021. "The Glasgow Climate Summit Has Already Achieved Success. But Time Is Running Short." *The Washington Post*. November 3, 2021. https://www.washingtonpost.com/opinions/2021/11/03/glasgow-summit-climate-change-john-kerry.

53. UN Climate Change. n.d. "Global Stocktake." https://unfccc.int/topics/global-stocktake.

54. UN. 2023. "Secretary-General's Remarks to Launch the Special Edition of the Sustainable Development Goals Progress Report [as Delivered]." April 25, 2023. https://www.un.org/sg/en/content/sg/statement/2023-04-25/secretary-generals-remarks-launch-the-special-edition-of-the-sustainable-development-goals-progress-report-delivered.

55. Ahmad, Y., and E. Carey. 2021. "Development co-operation during the COVID-19 pandemic: An analysis of 2020 figures and 2021 trends to watch." OECD.

56. Whiting, A. 2017. "An Investigation Mechanism for Syria: The General Assembly Steps into the Breach." *Journal of International Criminal Justice* 15, no. 2 (2017): 231–237. https://doi.org/10.1093/jicj/mqx008.

57. Scharf, M. P. 2023. "Power Shift: The Return of the Uniting for Peace Resolution." Case Western Reserve University. Faculty Publications. 2153. https://scholarlycommons.law.case.edu/faculty_publications/2153.

58. UN News. 2022. "Ukraine: UN General Assembly Demands Russia Reverse Course on 'Attempted Illegal Annexation.'" *UN News.* October 12, 2022. https://news.un.org/en/story/2022/10/1129492.

59. Farge, E., and G. Tétrault-Farber. 2023. "Russia Fails to Return to UN Rights Body after Losing Vote." Reuters. October 10, 2023. https://www.reuters.com/world/russian-bid-return-un-rights-body-fails-after-vote-2023-10-10.

60. Gowan, R. 2023b. Interview by author. Zoom. May 5, 2023.

61. SABC News 2023. "Dr Phumzile Mlambo-Ngcuka at the Global Citizen Now Summit in New York." YouTube. April 29, 2023. Video. https://www.youtube.com/watch?v=MQVZ53RAdSw.

62. Global Nation. 2023. "Global Solidarity Report." https://globalnation.world/global-solidarity-report.

63. Gowan, R. 2023. "How the World Lost Faith in the UN." *Foreign Affairs.* November 9, 2023. https://www.foreignaffairs.com/israel/how-world-lost-faith-united-nations-gaza.

64. Gowan, R. 2023. Interview by author. Zoom. May 5, 2023.

65. Gowan, R. 2023. "How the World Lost Faith in the UN." *Foreign Affairs.* November 9, 2023. https://www.foreignaffairs.com/israel/how-world-lost-faith-united-nations-gaza.

66. National WWII Museum, The. 2021. "The League Is Dead. Long Live the United Nations." The National WWII Museum. April 19, 2021. https://www.nationalww2museum.org/war/articles/league-of-nations.

67. Ward, A. 2023. "Ramaswamy: U.S. Pulling Out of NATO Is 'Reasonable,' as Is 'Reevaluating' UN Membership." Politico. October 23, 2023. https://www.politico.com/news/2023/10/23/ramaswamy-nato-us-un-membership-00123119.

68. Global Nation. 2023. "Global Solidarity Report." https://globalnation.world/global-solidarity-report.

69. Ibid.

70. Open Society Foundations. 2023. "Barometer in Context: Debt, Development, and Climate." Open Society Foundations.

October 9, 2023. https://www.opensocietyfoundations. org/publications/barometer-in-context-debt-development- and-climate.

Conclusion

1. Malloch-Brown, M. September 2023. Foreword to "Open Society Barometer". Open Society Foundations.
2. Francis. 2023. "Address of His Holiness Pope Francis to the Conference of Parties to the United Nations Framework Convention on Climate Change (COP28)." Expo City, Dubai. December 2, 2023.
3. Erickson, D. J. 2023. "Before the Fed: The Historical Precedents of the Federal Reserve System." Federal Reserve History. https:// www.federalreservehistory.org/essays/before-the-fed
4. World Bank. 2023c. https://twitter.com/WorldBank/status/ 1653852062197719041.
5. Hutton, H. 2022. "New poll indicates strong business appetite for net zero regulation." *University of Cambridge Institute for Sustainability Leadership*. https://www.cisl.cam.ac.uk/news/new- poll-indicates-strong-business-appetite-net-zero-regulation
6. Nelson, G.D. 2018 "Rexford Guy Tugwell and the Case for Big Urbanism." *Places Journal*. https://placesjournal.org/article/ rexford-guy-tugwell-and-the-case-for-big-urbanism
7. Balisciano, M. 2023 chief sustainability officer, global head of ESG and corporate responsibility, RELX; founding director Benjamin Franklin House; interview by author, Zoom.
8. Krebs, A. 1979 "Rexford Tugwell, Roosevelt Aide, Dies." *The New York Times*. https://www.nytimes.com/1979/07/24/ archives/rexford-tugwell-roosevelt-aide-dies-recruited-for-inner- circle-in.html
9. Balisciano, M. 2023 chief sustainability officer, global head of ESG and corporate responsibility, RELX; founding director Benjamin Franklin House; interview by author, Zoom.

10. Ibid.

11. Ibid.

12. Tamborrino, K., and Siegel, J. 2023. "Big Winners from Biden's Climate Law: Republicans Who Voted against It." *Politico*. https://www.politico.com/news/2023/01/23/red-states-are-winning-big-from-dems-climate-law-00078420.

13. Denning, G. 2023. *Universal Food Security: How to End Hunger While Protecting the Planet*. Columbia University Press.

14. Berg, S. 2021. "Tony Blair's Irish Famine message not signed off by him, archive papers show." *BBC*.

15. Namorato, M. V. 1988. *Rexford G. Tugwell: A Biography*, 81–82. Praeger.

16. Gavi, the Vaccine Alliance. 2023. "Vaccine Alliance reaches more than one billion children." https://www.gavi.org/news/media-room/vaccine-alliance-reaches-more-one-billion-children

17. Figueres, C., T. Rivett-Carnac, and P. Dickson. 2023. "205: How to Talk About Climate Change So People Will Listen." Interview with John Marshall. Outrage + Optimism podcast (audio). June 21, 2023.

18. Bremmer, I. 2023. "What is a technopolar world?" *Gzero Media*. https://www.gzeromedia.com/ai/what-is-a-technopolar-world

19. Wheeler, T. 2023 "The Three Challenges of AI Regulation." The Brookings Institution. https://www.brookings.edu/articles/the-three-challenges-of-ai-regulation.

20. Rudd, K. 2022. *The Avoidable War: The Dangers of a Catastrophic Conflict between the US and Xi Jinping's China*. PublicAffairs.

21. White House. 2023b. "FACT SHEET: President Biden Issues Executive Order on Safe, Secure, and Trustworthy Artificial Intelligence." https://www.whitehouse.gov/briefing-room/statements-releases/2023/10/30/fact-sheet-president-biden-issues-executive-order-on-safe-secure-and-trustworthy-artificial-intelligence/

22. Tobias, A. 2023. "Exploring Cross-Border and Domestic Payment and Contracting Platforms." *IMF*.

23. White House. 2023c. "Biden-?Harris Administration Announces Broad New Actions to Protect Consumers From Billions in Junk Fees." https://www.whitehouse.gov/briefing-room/statements-releases/2023/10/11/biden-harris-administration-announces-broad-new-actions-to-protect-consumers-from-billions-in-junk-fees.

24. World Bank. 2021. Defying Predictions, Remittance Flows Remain Strong During COVID-19 Crisis." https://www.worldbank.org/en/news/press-release/2021/05/12/defying-predictions-remittance-flows-remain-strong-during-covid-19-crisis.

25. Hall, T. 2023. Head of Social Impact and Philanthropy at UBS, interview by author, Zoom.

26. Gates, B. 2020. "Introducing the Green Premiums." https://www.gatesnotes.com/Introducing-the-Green-Premiums

27. Crimmins, B. et al. 2022. "The Generosity Crisis."

28. Hall, T. 2023. Head of Social Impact and Philanthropy at UBS, interview by author, Zoom.

29. Ibid.

30. European Commission. 2023. "Opening remarks by President von der Leyen at the high-level event on carbon markets at COP28." https://ec.europa.eu/commission/presscorner/detail/en/statement_23_6222

31. FSC Indigenous Foundation. n.d. "Open Letter: Global South Voices in Support of REDD+." https://www.fscindigenousfoundation.org/global-south-voices-in-support-of-redd/

32. Giving USA. n.d. "Giving USA 2023 Report." https://store.givingusa.org/?utm_source=google&utm_medium=ad&utm_campaign=2205&gad_source=1&gclid=CjwKCAiAqNSsBhAvEiwAn_tmxfrpWyqeJfAY0PH9tVSvqo3ODxZhv40hRxyI9vuNOEZ5VmG7-u-6AxoCePMQAvD_BwE

33. Hall, T. 2023. Head of Social Impact and Philanthropy at UBS, interview by author, Zoom.

34. Ibid.

35. Ibid.

36. OPSI. n.d. "The Irish Citizens' Assembly" https://oecd-opsi.org/innovations/the-irish-citizens-assembly/.

37. The Global Town Hall. n.d. https://www.gth2023.com/

Epilogue

1. Thompson, L. 2023. Interview by author. Facetime. October 23, 2023.

2. Global Nation. 2023. "Global Solidarity Report." https://globalnation.world/global-solidarity-report.

Acknowledgments

1. Kalil, T. 2017. "Policy Entrepreneurship at the White House: Getting Things Done in Large Organizations." *Innovations: Technology, Governance, Globalization* 11, no. 3–4 (2017): 4–21.

References

Adrian, T., P. Bolton, and A. M. Kleinnijenhuis. 2022. "The Great Carbon Arbitrage." IMF Working Papers. https://www.imf.org/en/Publications/WP/Issues/2022/05/31/The-Great-Carbon-Arbitrage-518464.

Alemanno, A. 2023. "The Lobbying for Good Movement." Stanford Social Innovation Review 22, no. 1, 36–43. https://doi.org/10.48558/1AES-X733.

Ambrose, E. 2023. "China's CO_2 emissions may be falling already, in a watershed moment for the world." *The Telegraph.* November, 21, 2023. https://www.yahoo.com/news/china-co2-emissions-may-falling-171000096.html?guce_referrer=aHR0cHM6L y9sbmtkLmluLw&guce_referrer_sig=AQAAAFUkE9WnZ mjzZVGV1Bev0btN0HD4gBYOnzbVQpo8sZ8ZGpNz2R6K_ hpCNJZuFQiLd6Tguz_qiGyqg1OqEsQf_M0Bts_ ttxMqNKYKwLIICbtmFMoZ6r3-vMQef6quWQMXJGfzxT K3rG867oyeuFEaglP-SgiqsiipSoFOscoum3L&guccounter=2.

Australian Broadcasting Corporation. 2023. "System Operator Predicts Bluewaters, Australia's Newest Coal-fired Power Plant, Will Close by 2029." February 4, 2023. https://www.abc.net.au/news/2023-02-05/bluewaters-coal-fired-power-station-to-close-by-2029/101927824.

Balisciano, M. L. 1998. History of Political Economy, 30 (Supplement): 153–178.

Ban, K. 2020. Resolved: Uniting Nations in a Divided World. Columbia University Press.

Berfield, S. 2020. The Hour of Fate: Theodore Roosevelt, J.P. Morgan and the Battle to Transform American Capitalism. Bloomsbury Publishing.

Berg, S. 2021. Tony Blair's Irish Famine message not signed off by him, archive papers show. BBC.

Bhowmik, A. K., M. S. McCaffrey, A. M. Ruskey, C. Frischmann, and O. Gaffney. 2020. *Environmental Research Letters* 15, no. 9 (2020): 094011. https://doi.org/10.1088/1748-9326/ab9ed0.

Bolton, P., L. C. Buchheit, P.-O. Gourinchas, M. Gulati, C.-T. Hsieh, U. Panizza, and B. Weder di Mauro. 2020. "Born Out of Necessity: A Debt Standstill for COVID-19." Center for Economic Policy Research; Policy Insight No. 103 (2020), Duke Law School Public Law & Legal Theory Series No. 2020–23. April 27, 2020. https://ssrn.com/abstract=3586785.

Burke, A. 2022. "An architecture for a net zero world: Global climate governance beyond the epoch of failure." *Global Policy* 13 (December 11, 2022): 24–37. https://doi.org/10.1111/1758-5899.13159.

Busby, J. W. 2007. "Bono Made Jesse Helms Cry: Jubilee 2000, Debt Relief and Moral Action in International Politics." International Studies Quarterly no. 51: 247–275. https://repositories.lib.utexas.edu/bitstream/handle/2152/61793/Bono_Jesse.pdf.

Cashman, K. 2022. "Special Drawing Rights: The Right Tool to Use to Respond to the Pandemic and Other Challenges." Center for Economic and Policy Research. April 20, 2022. https://www.cepr.net/report/special-drawing-rights-the-right-tool-to-use/.

Cassidy, B. 2023. "A Tariff for the Climate." *Foreign Affairs*. October 5, 2023. https://reader.foreignaffairs.com/2023/10/05/a-tariff-for-the-climate/content.html.

Chater, N., and G. Loewenstein. 2023. "The i-Frame and the s-Frame: How Focusing on Individual-Level Solutions Has Led Behavioral

Public Policy Astray." *Behavioral and Brain Sciences* 46 (2023): e147. http://doi.org/10.1017/S0140525X22002023.

Chen, D. n.d. "Global Carbon Reward." https://globalcarbonreward .org/our-vision/team/founders-message/.

Club of Rome. 2022. "New G7 Research Shows Overwhelming Public Support for Nations to Act on and Invest in Solutions to the Climate Crisis." https://www.clubofrome.org/impact-hubs/ reframing-economics/grc-research.

Cork, T. 2018. "Taxpayers in Bristol Were Still Paying Debt to City's Slave Owners in 2015, Treasury Admits." *Bristol Post.* February 13, 2018. https://www.bristolpost.co.uk/news/bristol-news/taxpayers-bristol-were-still-paying-1205049.

Cuff, M. 2023. "The uncomfortable reality of life on Earth after we breach 1.5°C." *New Scientist.* June 7, 2023. https:// www.newscientist.com/article/mg25834420-100-the-uncomfortable-reality-of-life-on-earth-after-we-breach-1-5c/#:~:text=Heatwaves%20will%20be%20fiercer%2C%20 droughts,faster%20than%20the%20global%20average.

Delivery, The. 2023. CEPI, Gavi, UNICEF and WHO. the-delivery .org/delivery.

Department of Climate Change, Energy, the Environment and Water. n.d.-b. "Australian Energy Mix by State and Territory 2021–22." Australian Government. https://www.energy.gov.au/ data/australian-energy-mix-state-and-territory-2021-22.

Doran, G. T. 1981. "There's a S.M.A.R.T. Way to Write Management's Goals and Objectives." *Management Review* 70, no. 11 (1981): 35–36.

Equitable Earth Initiative. n.d. https://equitable-earth.org/

Figueres, C., and T. Rivett-Carnac. 2020. *The Future We Choose: Surviving the Climate Crisis.* Knopf.

Franczak, M. 2023. (Dr. Franczak is a Research Fellow in the division of Peace, Climate, and Sustainable Development at the International Peace Institute, IPI).

Georgiev, G. S. 2022. The SEC's Climate Disclosure Rule: Critiquing the Critics, 50 Rutgers L. Rec. 101. https://scholarlycommons. law.emory.edu/faculty-articles/32/

Government of Western Australia. 2023. "Government Emissions Interim Target." September 23, 2023. https://www.wa.gov .au/service/environment/business-and-community-assistance/ government-emissions-interim-target.

Harvey, F. 2023. UK would be a climate leader again under Labour, vows Starmer. https://www.theguardian.com/environment/ 2023/dec/04/keir-starmer-vows-to-make-uk-climate-leader-again-labour-cop28-rishi-sunak.

Hayhoe, K. 2020. Saving Us: A Climate Scientist's Case for Hope and Healing in a Divided World. Atria/One Signal Publishers.

Hove, A. 2023. "China's New Capacity Payment Risks Locking in Coal." China Dialogue. November, 23, 2023. https://china dialogue.net/en/energy/chinas-new-capacity-payment-risks-locking-in-coal/.

IEA. 2021. "Phasing Out Unabated Coal: Current Status and Three Case Studies." https://iea.blob.core.windows.net/assets/861dc94d-a684-4875-80fb-a1faaf914125/PhasingOutUnabated Coal-CurrentStatusandThreeCaseStudies.pdf.

IEA. 2023. "Global coal demand expected to decline in coming years." December 15, 2023. https://www.iea.org/news/global-coal-demand-expected-to-decline-in-coming-years.

Isaacman, J. 2023. "Partnership with Shift4 Set to Bring Even Lower Payment Processing Fees." Give Lively. https://www.givelively. org/updates/partnership-with-shift4-set-to-bring-even-lower-payment-processing-fees.

Kaplan, S., and D. Grandoni. 2020. "Stimulus Deal Includes Raft of Provisions to Fight Climate Change." The Washington Post. December 21, 2020. https://www.washingtonpost.com/climate-solutions/2020/12/21/congress-climate-spending.

Käppeli, A., A. Jennison, and D. Fattibene. 2022. "Italy's Move to the Right and the Implications for Global Development." Center for Global Development. October 4, 2022. https://www.cgdev.org/ blog/italys-move-right-and-implications-global-development.

Knaus, C. 2021. "'Don't Muzzle Them': Charities Should Be Allowed to Lobby for Political Change, Tribunal Finds." The Guardian.

September 17, 2021. https://www.theguardian.com/society/2021/sep/17/australian-regulator-wrong-to-deny-charity-status-to-anti-poverty-group-global-citizen-tribunal-finds.

Kyte, R. "Comment: Paris summit needs to heed Mia Mottley's call for shake-up of global climate finance." Reuters. June 21, 2023. https://www.reuters.com/default/comment-paris-summit-needs-heed-mia-mottleys-call-shake-up-global-climate-2023-06-21/.

Maslin, M. 2021. *Climate Change: A Very Short Introduction.* Oxford University Press.

O'Neill, T. P. 1952. "Food Problems during the Great Irish Famine." Journal of the Royal Society of Antiquaries of Ireland 82, no. 2: 99–108. http://www.jstor.org/stable/25510822.

Open Society Foundations. 2023. *Open Society Barometer.*

Patterson, K. P., Y. Jameel, M. Mehra, and C. Patrone. 2021. "Girls' Education and Family Planning: Essential Components of Climate Adaptation and Resilience." Project Drawdown. October 2021. https://drawdown.org/sites/default/files/Drawdown_Lift_Policy_Brief_Girls_Education_122121.pdf.

Polio Global Eradication Initiative. n.d. *Global Polio Eradication Initiative.* Polioeradication.org. https://polioeradication.org/

Plichta, M., and L. Poole. 2023. "The State of Prearranged Financing for Disasters 2023." Centre for Disaster Protection, London.

Pope, C. 2023. Interview by author. Zoom. March 13, 2023.

PwC. n.d. "Global Citizen's commitment to transparency." https://www.pwc.com/us/en/library/case-studies/global-citizen-sustainability-transformation.html.

Reilly, K. 2018. "'Fight Our Tribal Mindset.' Read Justin Trudeau's Commencement Address to NYU Graduates." *Time.* May 16, 2018. https://time.com/5280153/justin-trudeau-nyu-commencement-2018-transcript.

Ronald Reagan Presidential Library and Museum. n.d. "President's Private Sector Survey on Cost Control (Grace Commission)." https://www.reaganlibrary.gov/archives/topic-guide/presidents-private-sector-survey-cost-control-grace-commission.

Sheldrick, M. 2022. "Mia Mottley, The Leader Disrupting Global Financial Institutions in the Name of People and the Planet." *Forbes*. June 7, 2022. https://www.forbes.com/sites/globalcitizen/2022/06/07/mia-mottley-the-leader-disrupting-global-financial-institutions-in-the-name-of-people-and-planet/?sh=6d7e30b86d31.

Stamp, J. 2014. "Pioneering Social Reformer Jacob Riis Revealed "How The Other Half Lives" in America." *The Smithsonian Magazine*. https://www.smithsonianmag.com/history/pioneering-social-reformer-jacob-riis-revealed-how-other-half-lives-america-180951546/

Stocker, J. 2022. "Russia Can't—and Shouldn't Be Kicked Off the United Nations Security Council." March 7, 2022. https://www.chicagotribune.com/opinion/commentary/ct-opinion-russia-ukraine-united-nations-security-council-denounce-20220307-4rebrv7w4vcazan6iy6favtgwm-story.html.

The ONE Campaign. 2023. *Climate Finance Files.* https://datacommons.one.org/climate-finance-files.

UN. 2022. "Suspension of the rights of membership of the Russian Federation in the Human Rights Council." General Assembly Resolution ES-11/3. Apr. 7, 2022.

UNCTAD. 2023. *UNCTAD Counts the Costs of Achieving Sustainable Development Goals.* https://unctad.org/news/unctad-counts-costs-achieving-sustainable-development-goals

UN Office of Partnerships. 2023. "The Agreement: how the world adopted the Sustainable Development Goals." September 16, 2023. https://unpartnerships.un.org/news/2023/agreement-how-world-adopted-sustainable.

US Forest Service. 2023. "Announcing Urban and Community Forestry Funding." April 12, 2023. https://www.fs.usda.gov/inside-fs/leadership/announcing-urban-and-community-forestry-funding.

What Is the Tampon Tax? n.d. Alliance for Period Supplies. https://allianceforperiodsupplies.org/tampon-tax.

Zacks, R. 2012. "Island of Vice: Theodore Roosevelt's Quest to Clean Up Sin-Loving New York." *Anchor.*

Zipp, S. 2020. "The Idealist: Wendell Willkie's Wartime Quest to Build One World". *Harvard University Press*. https://www.hup.harvard.edu/books/9780674737518.

Zitner, A. 2023. "America Pulls Back from Values That Once Defined It, WSJ-NORC Poll Finds." *The Wall Street Journal*. March 27, 2023. https://www.wsj.com/articles/americans-pull-back-from-values-that-once-defined-u-s-wsj-norc-poll-finds-df8534cd.

Index